OLIVER'S
TWIST

OLIVER'S TWIST

*The
Life and Times
of an
Unapologetic
Newshound*

CRAIG OLIVER

VIKING
CANADA

VIKING CANADA

Published by the Penguin Group

Penguin Group (Canada), 90 Eglinton Avenue East, Suite 700, Toronto, Ontario, Canada M4P 2Y3
(a division of Pearson Canada Inc.)

Penguin Group (USA) Inc., 375 Hudson Street, New York, New York 10014, U.S.A.
Penguin Books Ltd, 80 Strand, London WC2R 0RL, England
Penguin Ireland, 25 St Stephen's Green, Dublin 2, Ireland (a division of Penguin Books Ltd)
Penguin Group (Australia), 250 Camberwell Road, Camberwell, Victoria 3124, Australia
(a division of Pearson Australia Group Pty Ltd)
Penguin Books India Pvt Ltd, 11 Community Centre, Panchsheel Park, New Delhi – 110 017, India
Penguin Group (NZ), 67 Apollo Drive, Rosedale, Auckland 0632, New Zealand
(a division of Pearson New Zealand Ltd)
Penguin Books (South Africa) (Pty) Ltd, 24 Sturdee Avenue, Rosebank,
Johannesburg 2196, South Africa

Penguin Books Ltd, Registered Offices: 80 Strand, London WC2R 0RL, England

First published 2011

1 2 3 4 5 6 7 8 9 10   (RRD)

Author representation: Westwood Creative Artists
94 Harbord Street, Toronto, Ontario M5S 1G6

Manufactured in the U.S.A.

LIBRARY AND ARCHIVES CANADA CATALOGUING IN PUBLICATION

Oliver, Craig, 1938–
Oliver's twist : the life and times of an unapologetic newshound / Craig Oliver.

Includes index.
ISBN 978-0-670-06522-6

1. Oliver, Craig, 1938–. 2. Journalists—Canada—Biography. I. Title.

PN4913.O45A3 2011   070.92   C2011-904684-9

Visit the Penguin Group (Canada) website at **www.penguin.ca**

Special and corporate bulk purchase rates available; please see
www.penguin.ca/corporatesales or call 1-800-810-3104, ext. 2477 or 2474

For my mother

CONTENTS

1

A CHILD
OF PRINCE RUPERT

My father was a bootlegger and, for a short time, a jailbird. My mother ran a successful taxi business, also for a short time. Both were alcoholics.

Their only child was born in Vancouver on November 8, 1938. When war was declared less than a year later, my father took his small family up the coast to Prince Rupert, where he found work in the suddenly busy shipyards. That job ended when a steel crate fell on his foot, severing two toes. There was no such thing as workers' compensation in those years, but the accident bestowed an unexpected benefit: His disability gave him an automatic deferment from military service.

My father soon launched himself into the more lucrative career of bootlegging. As a schoolboy, I boosted my popularity by supplying friends with premium Crown Royal bags—dark-purple velvet pouches with gold braided drawstrings—to carry their marble collections. No cheap whisky for my dad. Unfortunately, like many a good salesman, he was too fond of his own product; otherwise, we might have followed the example of the Bronfmans, who grew rich in the same trade.

Dad was smart enough; he and his buddies just drank the profits.

Murray Oliver was a handsome, good-natured man who impressed others with an easy charm and a sharp intelligence. An old beach photo shows him to be short and muscular, built like an athlete and with wavy dark hair. In his own world he was respected, and other men would approach him for advice or ask him to mediate disputes. He was twenty-five years older than my mother, Elizabeth Easton. Nevertheless they moved in together.

My mother was a lively brunette, short and slim but busty. She was one of four sisters, none of whom could be described as a great beauty, but she possessed a biting wit that did not spare those she regarded as fools, alongside an abiding empathy for those worse off than herself. Certainly, she was up for adventure. It's likely my father took us to Rupert not only for work but also to elude the law. He and an accomplice had been charged and convicted of fraud after trying to use counterfeit liquor rationing cards. There was no jail sentence, but the authorities were aware of his habits.

My grandparents are largely a mystery to me, all dead before I was born and rarely spoken of except in cryptic tones. Both families had emigrated from Scotland, the Olivers to Ontario, where my grandfather, Thomas, established a hardware store in Coppercliff, now a suburb of Sudbury, and the Eastons to Winnipeg, the birthplace of my mother. Her father, William Easton, eked out a living as a bill collector during the Depression. Trying to extract money from people who had none was no doubt soul wrenching. One day in Saskatoon, William walked into the path of an oncoming freight train. The family was scandalized when the local paper called it suicide.

Letters from William Easton to his four daughters survived him, poignant and loving messages mailed from small Prairie towns across his collection territory. Scribbled in dusty rail cars or crummy hotel rooms, they offer thoughtful moral advice on marriage and behaviour, yet they also carry a whiff of gathering gloom, a hint of chronic depression. Like thousands of impoverished Prairie women, his widow, Isabel, moved to the West Coast. There she opened a small bookstore in North Vancouver, but the family survived on the meagre earnings of her oldest son, David. All of the Eastons seemed to have a touch of melancholy. Dog-eared photos portray Isabel as a hard-faced woman gazing sternly at the photographer, the very picture of Scottish Presbyterian rigidity. Still, she wrote hopeful poetry despite a life of disappointment and privation.

The Ontario Olivers likewise went bust in the Depression and migrated to the West Coast. How my parents met or courted was never revealed to me. Whenever I asked my mother for details later on, she would feign memory loss or develop the vapours, and I could never raise the topic with my father.

Prince Rupert was still a frontier town when we landed there, originally the western terminus of the Grand Trunk Pacific Railway and the end of the line for Chinese rail workers whose children grew up to own the city's laundries, grocery stores, and popular eateries. Rupert boasts one of the world's best natural harbours, and the nineteenth-century rail baron and financier Charles M. Hayes intended that it should become the pre-eminent seaport on the West Coast. That dream died when Hayes went down with the *Titanic*, although Prince Rupert eventually came into its own as a port and staging centre.

As in many small northern communities of that era, classes and neighbourhoods were sharply divided. From their homes on Upper Third Avenue, a white-skinned elite controlled the town. They operated the law offices and banking institutions, the jewellery and ladies' wear stores, the movie theatres and car dealerships. Together, they attended meetings of the Chamber of Commerce, the Odd Fellows, and the Loyal Order of the Moose. Occasionally there were scandals, such as when a respected doctor ran off with a teenaged patient, or two Third Avenue merchants swapped wives and offspring. The gentry inhabited a separate world and did not mix much with the denizens of Lower Third Avenue—working white families, the Chinese, and the natives—except to sell them things and profit from their sweat.

The majority of Rupert's citizens lived by their own rules and worked at jobs full of risk to life and limb. Fishing and logging claimed victims every season, but bar fights and street brawls were equally lethal. A house without a gun was a rarity.

Natives occupied the lowest ranks in Rupert's caste system. At the Capital Theatre movie house and at most churches, natives were permitted to sit only in specially designated seats, the worst in the house at the Capital. That no one recognized this practice as blatant segregation did not make it excusable, even though many of the natives felt ownership in having their own seating and did not want to sit with white people anyway.

My family's own lot was humble. We lived on the second floor of a seedy apartment building, above a strip of Italian grocery stores and a dry cleaning establishment. A long staircase with a skylight at the top led to our one-room apartment. I played on the landing under the skylight until the day I accidentally tumbled down the stairs and out onto the sidewalk. The bruises don't linger in memory, but my mother's cry of anguish has stayed with me. The apartment came with an icebox and wood stove, and my parents soon bought a gramophone.

Rain was the background music of my childhood. Situated on the edge of lush Pacific rainforest with mountains at its back, Prince Rupert endured what seemed a continuous downpour, lifting occasionally to a drizzle. We wore gumboots year-round and joked of being born with webbed feet. Our famous high school basketball team was named "the Rainmakers." The rainfall could last for months on end, provoking depression and even suicide, not to mention natural disaster. I recall being woken one morning by a great roar. The rain had lashed down in such torrents that a whole section of mountainside above the town gave way, burying half a dozen citizens in a tomb of mud and splintered timber.

By 1944, our town of nine thousand souls had become a colony of America, transformed by the presence of some fifteen thousand American troops stationed in our midst. Most were with the U.S. Army Corps of Engineers, working on the construction of the Alaska Highway; others were infantrymen on their way to combat in the Pacific. The war was never far from our minds, and there were moments of genuine fright. House lights had to be turned off and blackout curtains drawn during periodic air raid warnings. No sliver of illumination was allowed while civilian monitors checked the residential streets, banging on the doors if the blackout order was violated. After Pearl Harbor, a Japanese invasion of the West Coast was expected at any time.

In this hothouse environment, everyone lived for the

moment. If life might be short, it had better be fast, and few relationships survived the ride. My earliest memories are of drunken verbal bouts between my parents, shouts of "chippy" and "whore," followed by the sounds of shattering glass, physical struggles, and cries of pain. The hostilities ceased when I called out, begging my parents to stop, but the battle resumed the moment they thought I was asleep again. I remember countless late-night parties, punctuated with the high-pitched laughter of women and the roars of inebriated men. In my sleeping place in an alcove off the living room, I played with stacks of American military caps tossed carelessly on my bed.

Then, the year I started elementary school, my mother vanished from my life as if in a puff of smoke. A photo dated 1945 shows her embracing a square-jawed man named Cliff Dahl. The courts gave custody to my father, a ruling that was almost unprecedented in those days. Either the judge concluded Mom was an unfit parent for reasons I can only guess at, or my father cruelly deceived her. One of their friends later told me that my father had lied about the date of the custody hearing. The loss of her only child—temporarily, as it turned out—plunged my mother into a prolonged depression, the first of many that would plague her as she grew older.

My father had won sole responsibility for my care, but it proved to be a burden that was far beyond him. His "work" kept him out nights or on the road, and however well-meaning, he was not temperamentally suited to child rearing. He solved the problem by shopping me around as a boarder to various households, all strangers in need of extra dollars. Before being paraded in front of these prospective foster parents, I was dressed up in a blue double-breasted jacket and lectured sternly about making a favourable impression. Some families rejected me with a sweep of the hand, even while I sat there trying to be as appealing as possible. *Nope, not our type.* Or, *he talks a lot, doesn't he?* At other addresses we made the decision ourselves, Dad marching me out while whispering that the people were assholes.

On some level these painful rebukes and the implicit rejection by my father must have registered. They added to the sting of my mother's unexplained departure, instilling a profound insecurity that would surface eventually. Until a refuge could be found for me, I was without any semblance of a normal home life. No hovering grandparents, no close connections with aunts, uncles, or cousins, no siblings for companionship or comfort. At the time, however, these experiences seemed perfectly normal to me, hardly damaging to my psyche or self-esteem. I felt no loneliness and in fact revelled in the novelty of my circumstances.

I knew kids from large close-knit families but I considered their well-disciplined lives a predictable bore. Rupert's Lower Third was my playground, and in times of my father's absence, I lived more like a child of the streets than a middle-class schoolboy. On one occasion, I lost the quarter Dad had given me for a school lunch. I had no qualms about begging from a passing tourist rather than go hungry. I was left to look after myself, at least until Dad came home well after midnight.

Evenings were spent walking a familiar circuit, often in casual search of my father, which meant traipsing up and down Third Avenue and into its seedy beer joints. I had to jump up to catch a glimpse through the oval-shaped windows of the swinging doors and into the smoky haze. The pungent odour of stale beer and wet cigarette butts tossed outside still lingers in my nostrils. My habit was to ask an entering patron to call out for Murray Oliver. If Murray did not emerge, it was on to the next watering hole until I tracked him down. He wasn't always pleased to be so summoned.

When the war ended in 1945, all the soldiers left and the town's kids played in empty barracks and gun emplacements until the government demolished them. We collected army badges and parts of uniforms—hats were big trade items. I found a small pistol that I happily assumed some other boy had lost. It had reddish grips and made a satisfying click when I pulled the trigger. Why it would not ignite the paper caps we bought for our other toy guns, I could never figure out, but I was crushed when some alert adult took it away, recognizing it for the real thing.

The war was over, but hard drinking and hard living still characterized the community. Rupert thrived in the postwar boom, providing every resource an expanding nation required. As well as benefiting from the fish and lumber harvest, the city was at the centre of recently discovered gold, silver, and copper deposits and could ship all these riches to market by sea or rail. The population swelled to twice its wartime number as fast-buck artists, speculators, and job seekers poured in. They contributed to a volatile mix of hardrock miners and fishermen, steel-handed loggers, cannery workers, and sailors on shore leave. White skins barely outnumbered a population of Tsimshian Indians and Canadian-born Chinese and Japanese.

This made for a colourful streetscape, especially on Saturday nights. Hundreds of people elbowed one another along the four blocks of Lower Third Avenue as they walked past dingy saloons, greasy-spoon restaurants, illicit gambling joints, and private "clubs" like the Moose Lodge and the Freemasons'. The narrow main drag was bordered by dozens of such enterprises, all housed in tight-fitting wood-frame buildings.

As a crowded seaport, Rupert was a smaller and more northerly version of Marseilles and attracted equally eccentric characters. There was one-legged Dominic, owner of the steam bath. He never wore anything but a black suit, the right leg pinned up at the hip. Every Christmas for High Mass, he bought a new black suit, along with a fresh pair of long underwear. Having one leg, he pointed out, saved in shoe leather. The Italian shoe repairman made and maintained Dominic's single custom boot.

Ricardo the Hook had lost a hand in the war. I was an appreciative audience for the repertoire of tricks he performed with a mean-looking, curved steel appendage, always sporting a speared cigarette. Twenty-Dollar Dolly White had launched her business during the war years. She bought a dilapidated row house and imported a collection of young ladies from Vancouver. Nearby, in the short alley that became famous locally as "The Line," Dolly's own refurbished establishment was known as the "White House," an elegant stopping place for American officers. A model of the stereotypical hooker with a heart of gold, she took an interest in my welfare and was always a reassuring presence.

Then there was Eric, the railway conductor, who for years juggled two fiancées living at opposite ends of his run from Rupert to Prince George. The arrangement fell apart when fate brought the two women together in a coach car. Comparing notes on the men they expected to marry, they discovered they were betrothed to the same fellow. Eric was horrified to see the two women step off the train together and, in unison, throw their engagement rings at him. Eric spent hours on his knees trying to retrieve the diamonds from a snowdrift.

My habitual route took me through an underpass below street level where a dank cellar housed the "Dungeon," a pool hall where men played for money and the local sharks emptied the pockets of out-of-towners. Popeye, who ran the nearby cigar store, always welcomed me with a free soft drink.

There really is no such thing as the "common people," but I suppose that is how these uncommon individuals could be described. They were the companions of my daily life in those years, and I was treated like one of them—always with kindness and never abuse. Strangers could be generous and caring, it seemed, while those closer to home couldn't always be trusted.

A dog bite eventually brought about another sharp detour in my life. At the age of eight, I was attacked while playing with a group of chums. Nearly sixty years later I still have the scars on my arm. The family who owned the dog was very concerned, and probably fearful that my father might bring a lawsuit. Evidently some kind of a deal was struck, because soon after I found myself moving in with the dog's owners, "Brick" and Mabel Skinner. I stayed with them for four years, the dog and I maintaining an uneasy truce.

The Skinners lived in a one-bedroom house on Borden Street, perched at the end of a long steep pathway on the side of the mountain. Here was family life at last, but theirs was a loveless house without much happiness. It was understood that my place in it was temporary.

Brick was a fire plug of a man and, fittingly, the fire chief down at the government docks. He was gruff and sometimes short-tempered, but not mean-spirited. His wife, Mabel, who was rigid, unyielding, and without a trace of compassion, became my tormentor. They had an adopted son my age, Jimmy, a cheerful kid who squinted badly through wire-rimmed glasses. It angered Mabel that Jimmy always seemed to be led by me, and she never stopped reminding me that Jimmy would one day be a success while I would never amount to anything. I recall one hurtful rebuff at bedtime when I forgot myself and called her "Mommy." For that slip I was sharply reprimanded. I had a real mother, Mabel told me, but she was an immoral woman who had left me behind.

Life with the Skinners was not all bad. Jimmy and I shared the makeshift attic bedroom with a boarder, an elderly man whom I knew as Frank Redman. While puffing on a long pipe that was never out of his mouth except for its ritual daily cleaning, Frank held me spellbound with romantic stories of life in the Old West. All his tales, he assured me, were based on personal experience of the lawless frontier. He claimed to have been a Montana cowboy during the 1880s, forced to flee across the border after shooting someone in a fight over a horse. His accounts of cattle drives, cowboys and Indians, and the rugged independence of the lone man on horseback—possibly lifted from Zane Grey dime novels—enthralled me and set my imagination free amidst clouds of Ogden's Fine Cut Tobacco. After the guilty excitement of women's lingerie, my favourite pages in the Eaton's catalogue were those devoted to saddles, chaps, and firearms.

I fantasized about being anyone else, anywhere else: a secret agent, a benevolent dictator, a gun-toting frontiersman living the free life on the plains with a faithful horse my only companion. It was lights out at seven o'clock, but in that attic and under the covers by flashlight, I read any book I could find or borrow.

Later, lying in the dark at my end of the attic beside the lone window, I always looked for the North Star, comforted by its constancy in a life that so far had been quite unpredictable.

Books and reading were welcome escapes, although an astute teacher had discerned a vision problem. I confessed to her that I could not read the blackboard, and glasses were prescribed. When the optician diagnosed crossed eyes, Mabel took me to Vancouver for the necessary surgery. The day after, Dad surprised me in the hospital room with my first pair of cowboy boots.

Brick had a cousin named Bill Bickle who owned a cattle ranch at a place called Grassy Plains near Burns Lake, British Columbia, a spot long since drowned by a hydro project. I spent glorious summers there with the welcoming Bickle family, who kindly assigned me my own horse, Lazy Dick. I rode the dusty country roads into town to pick up goods at the general store and was thrilled one day to be photographed by an American tourist who mistook me for a genuine ranch hand.

Ranch life held a few rude surprises, though. One morning I watched Bickle shoot a steer, then cut a hole in its side with a knife to bleed it. The steer fell on its front knees while yelping dogs lapped up the blood. This was my first experience of violent death and the episode became the stuff of nightmares for weeks afterwards. Surely this was nothing Gene Autry or Roy Rogers would ever be part of.

Growing up under the roofs of strangers imparted some inescapable lessons. Too soon perhaps, I learned to judge people with cold logic, by their actions rather than their words. I guarded my own emotions carefully, even while drawing out the feelings and motives of others. Engaging with those who controlled my fate, carefully fitting in with a minimum of fuss, became a survival technique. At the same time, I formed a conviction that every person must look out for himself before all else.

Despite a growing independent streak, I longed for my father's occasional visits. These were increasingly rare as Dad looked to expand his booze trade into new markets, but they were frequently memorable. Thanks to liquor rationing in Canada during the war, I spent many an hour standing in line at the government outlet, holding a place for Dad. In Alaska, however, booze was unlimited. Ketchican, the nearest Alaskan port to Rupert, was a wide-open town in what was then wilderness territory. It had its own red light district of tiny shacks, bars, and bordellos built on jetties out over the harbour. And its resources were only a few hours away from Rupert in the beefed-up fishing boat Murray had purchased. He made the dash across treacherous and unpredictable waters at night to load up with American spirits, then returned to Rupert where he sold the booze at a markup of 100 percent.

The risk was worth it and business was good. Murray bought one of the first and most expensive cars to come off the assembly lines after the war, a black Ford Monarch. He turned the four-door limo into a rolling liquor store, delivering the boat's haul in style and acquiring a taxi licence for cover. It was illegal to sell liquor anywhere but out of a government store and seriously illegal to do so after the government store had closed. But this only made Murray more inventive; occasionally, I was pressed into service as his accomplice. If he was on a run to sell a few bottles and spotted a police car, I hid the goods in my sweater or up the legs of my pants. If we had a passenger, the instructions were to pass the bottles to the kid when the bulls pulled us over.

Murray was popular with the natives because he offered them the chance to take booze home like everyone else. He also charged them a lower markup, rather than gouge them after hours. His largesse inevitably cut into the profits of local bar owners and the liquor tax revenues of the government. While Dad had no doubt paid off most of the local officials, the heat became too much and they reluctantly charged him with bootlegging. He served six months at Okalla Penitentiary in New Westminster, and as the son of a con, I suffered the merciless taunts of my classmates.

The first visit after his release, he was more sharply dressed than I had ever seen him, looking handsome in a double-breasted grey pinstripe suit made to measure in the prison tailor shop. Dad wasted not a minute in establishing a new business, a crap and poker game that operated out of the bridal suite, such as it was, in the St. Elmo Hotel. He was a lifelong gambler whose advice to me about the sport was a familiar saw: There is a sucker in every game and if you can't see who it is, get up and leave.

Though boarding with others, I was allowed to spend the night with Dad from time to time, closeted in the hotel suite's bedroom but listening to the action. Amid the fragrance of cigar smoke and beer was the vague thrill that something illicit, possibly even a little dangerous, was going on. The players were seated at a circular table covered in green cloth, tall stacks of bills and poker chips resting neatly by their hands. But it was the revolver beside the dealer that mesmerized me. Designed to protect the house and discourage local toughs who might be tempted to knock over the bank, it had a large steel-blue frame with the brand name "Colt" emblazoned on the pistol grip.

There was a lanyard ring on the butt and a flap-top holster with sheepskin lining, which I was allowed to wear during visits. The gun was always loaded except when I was given it to handle. The shiny bullets slid smoothly out of the six chambers. I felt utterly privileged.

The day a boy got his first gun was the bush country's equivalent of a bar mitzvah. My eleven-year-old's pride was immense when Dad took me to Joe Scott's hardware store to buy a Cooey single-shot .22 rifle. I hardly took a breath as I lifted it out of its shipping carton. The opportunities for father-and-son bonding were few in Prince Rupert and tended to centre on fishing or hunting. We had the accoutrements of neither, but we intended to share the experience. In the wilds of the city dump, Dad with his Colt .45 and I with my new rifle used the rats for target practice.

After these all-too-fleeting outings, I was returned to the Skinners. Early on, I was aware of Mabel's penchant for physical punishment. This included bare bottom spanking with one of those thick straps men used to sharpen their straight razors. For whatever reasons, I became her frequent target.

One day some infraction led to a strapping that left my buttocks and the backs of my legs covered in large red welts. By this time, I was allowed to see my mother on rare occasions, and one of her visits came shortly after the beating at Mabel's hands. Mom was horrified at the sight of broken skin and raised welts. There was a great uproar when she came to the Skinners' house a few days later and physically pulled me out of there for good. She did not have custodial rights, but she no doubt used the episode to leverage a concession from my father. I found myself moved into the basement apartment she shared in town with

Cliff Dahl. For the first time, I experienced a relatively peaceful and even loving environment.

Mom and Cliff made a good team; she was a naturally savvy entrepreneur and he was a local sports hero. They started their own taxi business and made a great success of it, being the first in the north to install portable radios in their cars. These technological miracles were almost as amazing as the X-ray fluoroscope machines used in shoe stores to ensure a perfect fit. People summoned the cabs just to hear the driver talking to his dispatcher or to another cabbie—right there in the car while it was moving, by God! The radio also saved gas, since drivers did not have to return to the taxi stand for the details of their next fare.

In addition to being the business manager, Mom herself was a driver and worked a full eight-hour shift, six days a week. Sitting in the front seat beside her at all times was her beloved dog, Winger, an imposing Chesapeake Bay retriever. He was big and powerful, weighed as much as a small man, and was fiercely protective of Mom. Winger would have taken the arm off anyone who tried to manhandle his mistress. It never happened.

Still, the long hours and constant fatigue took a toll on Mom's health. A year or so after I moved in, whispers in the dark told me something was wrong. Mom had contracted tuberculosis, a disease that haunted that era and caused the deaths of millions. She had to go away to one of the many sanatoriums in the B.C. interior for a year or more of convalescence. Cliff had no interest in single parenting, so I was on my own again. Mom never spoke of this to me, but her anguish must have been extreme. Back I went into the homes of strangers, with my largely absent father sending monthly cheques to cover my room and board. I would live with five different families between the ages of seven and fourteen.

For a time I stayed with a newly married Jewish couple in their one-bedroom apartment. I slept on the living room couch. They were a cheerful twosome and I was learning to adapt to almost any arrangement, but three was a crowd, especially at night. Many times I tried not to listen to their intimate conversation and lovemaking, but adolescent curiosity made it impossible not to. I could hardly blame them when, with great sensitivity, they told me I would have to leave.

After another round of interviews, I landed in the home of Ken and Dorothy Laird. Theirs was a simple, uncomplicated household with lots of laughter, and I was treated with the same kindness as the two children of the house. I shared a room with their son, Alan, who was my age and became my close companion.

The Lairds were a deeply religious couple who lived their Christian faith. Twice a week they attended an evangelical church and, though never pressured, I usually went with them. The services were exuberant affairs, full of gospel singing, shouted prayers, and exhortations from the preacher. This was much more entertaining than those Salvation Army gatherings favoured by the Skinners, where the congregation seemed to carry the weight of suffering mankind on their shoulders. The Lairds were true believers who badly wanted me to share their religious rapture, but I could not do it. To me and, I suspect, to their obedient son, Alan, it was just great theatre.

One notable night a famous saver of souls visited as guest preacher. I studied his performance with genuine attention and admiration. He had perfect timing, hitting the congregation for cash precisely when the sermon reached its emotional peak. The greater was the spiritual ecstasy, the larger the pile in the collection plate. Another would-be Billy Graham was a faith healer. The Lairds brought me to the altar, hoping to secure a cure for my poor eyesight. The spirit did not enter, unfortunately, despite healing hands on my eyes and fervent shouts from the crowd. I felt obliged to feign better vision so the Lairds would not feel they had failed me. The family did their best to rescue me from a sinful life generally, but I was not persuaded. Too much untried temptation lay ahead, and I was willing also to give the devil a chance to convert me.

My chief joy on Sundays were the evenings, when we were allowed to gather around the radio, Coca-Cola bottles in hand, and listen to the golden age of pre-television radio. We heard shows from the CBC and the American networks, with all the big stars of the day in comedy, drama, and music. I could not get enough of Red Skelton, Jack Benny, the Gang Busters serial, Wayne and Shuster, or the great CBC radio dramas. The earnings from a paper route bought me an ancient crystal set that gave me private and exclusive access to the radio waves. Often I fell asleep with the earphones in place.

I memorized the scripts of the famous announcers, studied their phrasing and delivery, and imitated their voices. My mirror was the audience to which I delivered my lines, my microphone a banana. Once again, I fantasized about a life and an identity far from reality, whether at the radio mike, before the movie camera, or behind the reporter's typewriter. The ability to create a world with words and pictures and to tell whatever story I wanted was something I knew I had to learn.

Mom eventually returned from the "san" and we were

together again. The taxi business had faltered without Mom's management skills, but she soon had the enterprise back on its feet, with a brand new fleet of cars. She and Cliff bought their first home together up on Summit Avenue, a nice part of town. They were now able to live Rupert's version of the high life: baseball games, curling bonspiels, frequent parties, and hard drinking. Apart from receiving occasional support cheques, Mom had no contact with my father.

My high school years are a blur, a jumble of memories of oddball teachers and cruel student pranks, a few of which almost certainly contributed to the suicide of one hapless instructor. A recent immigrant unfamiliar with North American products, he was the victim of chocolate-flavoured Ex-Lax disguised as candy and the target of waterguns filled with indelible ink. These stunts could not have helped him cope with the depression from which he clearly suffered.

Although I was academically undistinguished, an English teacher nonetheless encouraged me to write, and the study of history seemed to come naturally. I found myself penning a column for the school paper and gravitating to student politics.

My closest school chum was Art Helin, the son of a hereditary chief of the Tsimshian people, one of the largest Aboriginal nations on the north B.C. coast. That lineage made Art a prince of the tribe and he looked the part. Tall and athletic, he had the striking good looks that lead anthropologists to make a connection between the Aboriginals of the B.C. coast and those of Hawaii and the Polynesian islands. He could perform great feats of strength and was an outstanding star of the Rainmakers the year they won a provincial championship.

I was a skinny kid with too quick a tongue for my own good,

always in trouble for taking verbal shots at individuals I did not like, among them a notorious town bully. He waited for me in an alley after a movie one night, but he did not spot Art trailing behind. Art brought him down with a punch that was pure poetry in motion.

Art may have saved my life on that occasion; certainly he saved my career in television on another. At a drunken house party one evening, a guest told me I should send my "dirty Indian friend" home. I punched him in the nose hard enough to cause some bleeding, then headed for the door at a run. He brought me down about a block from the house. I was on my back staring up at a huge fist cocked and ready to rearrange my facial bones when Art caught my assailant with a flying tackle just as the hammer was about to descend.

Art was no dumb jock; he had a quick, intelligent wit that made him a favourite of my mother. Mom had a generous nature, but in the case of Art, she did an extraordinary thing for those times of casual racism. When Art was left homeless for a period after his parents moved to a reserve with no school, Mom insisted he move in with us. He stayed for a year.

While still in high school, I joined the Canadian navy reserve, hoping to train as a gunner. My vision tested too poor and they made me a cook instead. I served my years before the mast washing dishes, and one summer I was assigned to a rustbucket Department of Transport lighthouse tender. The *Alexander Mackenzie* was the last of the government's coal-fired ships. The men who worked the furnaces looked as if they were playing blackface roles in vaudeville. Even after they had washed up for meals, they wore on their faces a permanent mask of coal dust embedded in their pores.

The crew represented the bottom of the quasi-military maritime barrel. Our job was the maintenance of navigation aids, buoys, and bells, as well as re-supply and repair of lighthouses along the rugged north coast. On more than one occasion, our captain had to go ashore on some godforsaken island to mediate disputes between the families living there, resorting to the ultimate threat of no more cigarette or booze deliveries unless matters were resolved.

Captain Androsov seemed an escapee from the pages of a novel by Joseph Conrad. A Bulgarian who had served as an officer in the Russian navy of the czar, he had fought against the Bolsheviks in the 1917 revolution. There could be no doubt of his worthiness as a ship's commander, but he was a forbidding character and completely paranoid. The Cold War was in full force, and he believed his fierce opposition to the Communists made him a target of Soviet spies. They might assassinate him, if only they could discover where Prince Rupert was.

With the rank of third cook, my domain was the ship's galley. I reported to the genial and massive chief cook, Mr. Green. He took great pleasure in exploiting my inexperience. When I swabbed the officers' mess, I discovered he had given me salt water, which dried the next day into a dirty brown scum. When I delivered boiled breakfast eggs to the captain's cabin, they proved to be thoroughly rotten. The smell hung in the air for days, but an investigation of the incident was inconclusive.

The rest of the ship's crew could have served central casting as cutthroat pirates. Some were barely reformed criminals, none had finished high school, and a few were illiterate. We slept in open crew quarters in the ship's forecastle. My second night at sea, I awoke to a hand creeping through the bunk toward my genitals. Still half asleep, I came out of the narrow bed swinging and was never bothered again.

It seemed to me most of the ship's company were destined for wasted, hopeless lives. Yet no one had to tell them they would go nowhere without an education. They wanted to learn, but either they were too proud to admit it or had no idea where to start. Seeing stacks of reading material in my bunk, they dubbed me "the Professor." I spent long nights answering questions about literature and history, subjects I knew little of, although more than they.

Strangely enough, I loved the sea time and had no doubt I could rise to the officer ranks one day. I was making almost two hundred dollars a month, more than I had ever possessed in my life. This certainly beat going back to school for grade twelve, so at the end of the season I lied about my age and signed on for a full year. I had not figured on my mother's views on this idea. When the school principal called to report my failure to appear in class, Mom's reaction was swift and decisive. She hopped in her taxi, tore down to the *Alexander Mackenzie*, and made straight for the captain's quarters. The poor skipper was cornered by a harridan accusing him of everything from kidnapping to the exploitation of child labour. He invited me to ship out. It was back to high school and Mom's apartment for me.

There were compensations. Cliff, though somewhat distant, became an important and positive influence on my life. He was a skilled hunter and shooter, a physically imposing man and a superb athlete, tough but not mean. His quiet-spoken manner was reassuring, never threatening, and he personified the art of power in reserve—whether physical or intellectual.

Dad, meanwhile, had returned to Vancouver. Although our exchange of letters was sporadic, the move was apparently a good one for him. In the spring of my final year of high school, he wrote that I should expect a graduation present. Soon after, a CPR shipping agent called to tell me they were unloading an item for me. It was a 1954 Ford Meteor, used but a beauty. I was class president that year, and although a complete lack of interest in maths and science cost me my high school matriculation, the car was not reclaimed.

Those few years spent with me at home, with her business prospering and her relationship with Cliff apparently solid, were the happiest of Mom's life. She and I almost believed the worst was behind us.

2

HUNDRED-WATT WONDERS

I may owe my broadcasting career to William Shakespeare. At a party I hosted while Mom and Cliff were out of town one weekend, a guest spotted my well-thumbed Kittredge collection of Shakespeare plays and sonnets. The bard's tragedies had been a particular passion of mine in high school dramatics. The surprised visitor was an Englishman and an out-of-work actor who longed to return to the stage. While awaiting a summons from the Old Vic, he was serving as a CBC radio announcer in our obscure Pacific outpost. In his view, anyone who appreciated Shakespeare was ideally suited to employment with the public broadcasting corporation. Nothing would do but that I must come and audition for the summer relief announcer position at the local radio station, CFPR.

In Rupert, musical tastes ran to Hank Snow or the Rhythm Pals, but among those who aspired to higher art, the CBC was a beacon. The smallest CBC station in the country and the only radio station based in town, it owed its existence to the war and the U.S. army's concern for the contentment of its troops. During the war years, the Americans not only arranged for what amounted to legalized prostitution in Prince Rupert, but they also built their own broadcasting facility, stocking it with a priceless collection of the most popular records of the day. There were original label seventy-eights of the jazz and classical greats, from Fats Waller and Nat King Cole, to Frank Sinatra and Enrico Caruso. Sadly, all were thrown out during postwar renovations by an engineer who saw no value in them.

After the war, the ramshackle studio building and its equipment were handed over to the Canadian government, which in turn gave them to the CBC. The fledgling CFPR served as little more than a glorified repeater station for the national broadcaster, part of a chain of drone transmitters across British Columbia. Normally such stations were unmanned, but along with the physical assets, the station had inherited a small staff, and since no one was ever fired from Mother Corp—not then and rarely now—the tiny enterprise became a full-fledged station in the CBC kingdom with all the attendant accoutrements. Its mission was to educate and enlighten citizens in the backwoods of Canada by exposing them to a larger culture—that is, the culture of Toronto, where 90 percent of CFPR's programming originated.

Most of the ten or so employees held titles that were grandiose and inflated: executive producer, technical supervisor, station manager, and assistant manager. The rest were secretaries. But there was not a great deal to do. Between programming that came direct from Toronto via transmission cables, staff were permitted only a few slots in the off-hours for local content. The result was that seemingly endless string quartets jostled on air with hometown introductions to hits by Johnny Cash and Hank Williams. The walls of the studio building were so thin that taping had to stop when a heavy truck passed by. The control room also housed the transmitter—all 250 watts' worth and about as powerful as three lightbulbs.

I presented myself for the audition with genuine excitement and not the slightest mike fright, thanks to prior experience with the high school PA system and as a fill-in dispatcher at Mom's taxi company. To get the job I had to pass the CBC's standard announcer's test: a competent reading of an old classical music program script, complete with correct pronunciation of all proper names. "Good evening from Massey Hall," I intoned, not knowing what or where Massey Hall might be. There followed introductions to works by eighteenth- and nineteenth-century masters, some of whose unfamiliar names I had practised with a friend. Although the senior producer judged my presentation below par, he liked my "modulation," and I was hired as a summer relief announcer. No one else had applied and the station was seriously short-staffed thanks to the absence of a veteran announcer who had gone off on a binge. The fellow phoned in daily, promising to return, but he never did.

At eighteen, I was the youngest CBC staff announcer in the country, but management seemed reluctant to give an inexperienced youngster full professional acknowledgment. While the other announcers added a folksy "Uncle" to their names, the better to foster a warm connection with the audience, I was to call myself "Cousin Craig." But I did not complain. I was intrigued by radio as a listener and enthralled by it as a broadcaster. In those early days before unions, the announcer's job included news gathering and reporting. This perfectly suited my inherent curiosity about other people's business; finally, a legitimate reason to ask otherwise rude questions of important people. The element of public performance was also irresistible to someone who had enjoyed high school dramatics and public speaking. I was about to become a local celebrity and felt utterly in my element.

My tenure was to begin on July 1, a national holiday celebrated in those days as Dominion Day. Naturally, I stayed home. The station manager called with my first lesson about the radio business: News does not take a holiday, nor do news announcers. If I did not accept that, then I had better try a different line of work.

Yet my first assignment had nothing to do with news. I was put on a shift as a disk jockey, after which promotion came fast. With but a single day's training, I was thrust into the chair of the morning host, Uncle Fred, who had arrived too drunk to perform. The morning wake-up program enjoyed the station's biggest audience. For the first and only time in my life, I was hit with debilitating jitters. This was not tape, this was live radio, and that realization left me so rattled, I could barely read the control room clock. The two-line switchboard almost overheated with complaints about my incorrect time checks. Buses were missed, kids were late for school, appointments were hopelessly confused.

On the quieter afternoon shift the next day, I was given a copy of the CBC program schedule and told to deliver on-air promotions for upcoming shows. Many spots were designated "TBA," an acronym foreign to me, but judging by the schedule a program so frequently aired that I concluded it must be immensely popular. I exhorted listeners not to miss it.

Unlike other CBC stations, CFPR carried advertising spots. Within a week, sponsors were demanding my head, especially the upscale beauty salon whose establishment I repeatedly called

a "saloon." Nor was the Chevy dealer amused when I kept referring to his car as the *Chev-roo-lay* instead of the more refined
Chev-vra-lay. One morning on the 6 A.M. sign-on shift, I found
that a fellow announcer had hidden the officially approved CBC
recording of "God Save the Queen" as a prank. In desperation,
I sang it in full voice. This was an insult to the sovereign and
a firing offence in the mind of the program director, but the
encyclopedic handbook of CBC regulations saved me. While
it decreed that every programming day must begin with the
national anthem and the tribute to Her Majesty, it did not rule
out alternative renderings, as long as they were respectful. I
argued necessity and ingenuity. Still, I received the first of many
written reprimands. The program director described my trans-
gression as the worst he had witnessed in his entire broadcasting
career. Not long after, his career was cut short when he fell in love
with a local nurse and followed her east. My career continued.

I was an old pro in the eyes of the new program director,
a man who had recently left a full-time position as an RCMP
corporal. For a while, all available local airtime was filled with
music by the RCMP band. And, for a brief period, the noble
redcoat did double duty, hanging his uniform in the station closet
and donning civvies for radio work. One day I was fooling with
the revolver he'd left hanging there when, to my astonishment, it
went off, missing an individual in the toilet next door by inches.
Since the program boss had broken all the rules by leaving his
weapon loaded and unlocked, the incident was quickly covered
up and the sound of a reported gunshot dismissed as an auto-
mobile backfire.

Another time I was lucky to avoid dismissal for an escapade
that clearly violated CBC regulations. One Saturday night, after

signing off at midnight as expected, I joined some friends at a late-night party. Few other radio signals managed to pierce the mountains that ringed Rupert, and we couldn't find any music we liked. I returned to the station and put CFPR back on the air at 3 A.M. For three hours, we enjoyed our own private broadcast, with musical selections on demand and tender messages from me to my girlfriend at the time. On Monday morning, Will Hankinson, the station manager, remarked that he had awoken in the night and thought he had heard my voice sending personal greetings to all my pals. Must have been a dream, he concluded. If I had actually done such a thing, he explained pointedly, he would have had to sack me.

I was returned to nighttime assignments when Uncle Fred righted himself in the morning slot. The evening shift was usually undemanding and consisted mainly of "riding the board," which meant sitting at the control console with all its dials, knobs, and meters and making sure that network programs from Toronto were rebroadcast without too much static. Between network offerings, we cleared our throats, summoned our best deep-chest voices, and announced the station breaks: "CFPR Prince Rupert." Then we sank into boredom for another hour or more, until the next call to radio stardom.

We often wondered whether anyone in Rupert was listening to our highbrow CBC fare. To settle the matter, we decided on a test. One night, all four staff announcers gathered round the microphone during a two-hour concert by a Montreal chamber orchestra, the Montreal Baroque Trio. On cue, we opened the mike with the strings still resonating in the background and shouted in unison, "Fuck off!" No one called or ever remarked on the incident.

Frequently the network lines, which snaked their way over the coastal mountains from Vancouver, broke down—always a welcome event. Rupert was then allowed to fill the time with its own music, including a Top Ten Hits show. I was introduced, complete with echo-chamber sound effects and theme music, as "your host with the most on the coast." Elvis, the Big Bopper, Jim Reeves, Johnny Mathis, Little Richard, and Jerry Lee Lewis were given free rein.

The handling of news was equally amateurish. We had no dedicated reporters to cover local happenings, nor did we have access to wire services such as Canadian Press for world events. Our source was the local rag, the *Prince Rupert Daily News*, an operation widely acknowledged to be in the pockets of the town's leading industrialists at the pulp mill and the fish plant. We clipped the top local news and sports stories out of the paper, pasted them to a blank sheet, and read them on air, unchanged and unedited but for the correction of the odd obvious error. Weather reports were gleaned from a study of the skies through the station window. A natural curiosity led me to pursue interviews with local worthies, thus providing some homegrown public affairs content.

Station manager "Hank" Hankinson was a brilliant but eccentric former producer with the CBC International Service in Montreal, banished to the far reaches of the empire for some obscure offence. The station was his personal fiefdom. He appointed his secretary, with whom he had been having an affair for many years, to the post of assistant station manager. At the same time, lowlier staff members were made to clean the toilets twice a week and take out the garbage. During my first turn on the garbage detail, the senior announcer, Uncle

Merlin Gutensohn, offered a comforting insight. While flies buzzed around us, he explained that this was actually part of our training, ensuring that "our powerful and important positions will not make us too proud."

Hankinson was rightly regarded as one of Rupert's few intellectuals. In my first week at the station, he invited me to enrol in the weekly adult French classes he gave at the local school. He also suggested I join the Canadian Institute of Speech, an institution of his own creation with only one instructor. It specialized in public speaking and vocabulary classes, in person or by correspondence, and offered various levels of graduate and undergraduate diplomas. I declined both. Months passed before I realized why I wasn't being moved off late-night and weekend shifts. I signed up for French lessons and joined the august ranks of the institute. When the next shift schedule was posted, I found myself on days.

Both of these enterprises, especially the speaking and vocabulary training, involved serious study, and Hank had the university degrees to prove his qualifications as an instructor. Despite my resentment at the time, he gave me my first exposure to the serious discipline of effective writing and speaking. Content and style were equally emphasized and tested. Hank drove into us the idea that every word is a building block of thought, a "crystallized idea," as he put it. A few years later, when we were unionized, the bosses in Vancouver learned of Hank's management practices and invited him to resign. He was a mean old cuss but the first person of real learning I had ever encountered, and I owed him a great deal. I will never forget his delight when I phoned him in Rupert from my Washington, D.C., office on the thirtieth anniversary of the day he hired me. We laughed over those days and lamented they were no more.

My position at CFPR was intended to be a summer job only but, as so often happened in my life, an intervention by my mother played a hand in my professional fate. Mom was cruising for taxi fares down at the docks one day when a yacht anchored out in the harbour. A small tender made for shore and delivered Bing Crosby and his inseparable buddy, Phil Harris, to the wharf. Crosby was perhaps the biggest music celebrity in the world at that time, with record sales, movies, and an unprecedented multi-million-dollar television contract making him the very definition of a star. His congenial public persona aside, Crosby guarded his privacy and was an elusive character who kept the media at a distance.

That day, he and Harris were sailing up the coast on a salmon-fishing trip. They needed to make an urgent call to Hollywood, but the radio phone on the yacht was broken. My mother coolly offered to contact an acquaintance at the local telephone company, and in no time she had the two men fixed up. An appreciative Crosby asked if there was anything he could do for her. Mom informed him that her son was a local disk jockey. Would the famous crooner give her boy an interview? This struck Crosby as a hilarious idea. Perhaps he enjoyed the thought of being quoted on the wires by a virtual unknown when he consistently refused interview requests from the leading entertainment journalists.

The staff at the studio was astounded when Crosby and Harris strolled through the door—and open-mouthed when Crosby said he was looking for Craig. Sadly, my big chance was not to be: I was enjoying a day off, far from the station. Told this,

Crosby did not miss a beat. "Tell Craig his old pal Bing dropped by to say hello." In their astonishment, none of the staff thought to ask for an interview or a photograph. The incident bolstered my reputation as someone who knew a few things about the music business, or at least as someone to whom the unexpected and interesting might happen. I credit it with securing me a permanent position not long after.

For all its quirkiness, CFPR set me on my professional path and fostered my ambitions beyond Prince Rupert. It was natural to look for wider horizons, but there was too the insistent inner voice of my eight-year-old self, the child who had been taught to be wary of depending on others, who resisted any ties that might bind. *We have to escape this town*, he told me; *we'll be trapped if we stay. Let's move on and re-create ourselves.*

Ironically, he had an unintended ally in the first woman with whom I fell seriously in love, Evelyn Carpenter. She was regarded as the most beautiful girl in Rupert and, like all the women I would become deeply involved with thereafter, she possessed a reticent and reserved nature that disguised a keen intelligence. Although we shared intimacies, Evelyn held out on me sexually, not wanting to make the mistake that unhinged the lives of so many young women and their boyfriends in small towns. In those days, marriage was the only possible outcome of an unwanted pregnancy, and I could never have left Evelyn or Rupert in those circumstances. For all the trouble sex would get me into in the future, its absence at that crucial moment proved to be enormously important.

After two years I had almost worn out the office copying machine, producing resumés and application forms that I sent to radio stations all over North America. No station was too rinky-dink to hear from me, yet there was nary a bite. The CFPR crowd was not encouraging and predicted only disappointment and frustration.

Then one day in the early spring of 1959, I was summoned to Hankinson's office. I feared that my efforts to abandon him had tried his patience, and he intended to sentence me to the night shift forever. Instead he told me that the CBC radio station in Regina liked my audition tape and was prepared to offer me a job. Was I interested in a transfer to Saskatchewan? Apparently there was no resistance on his part: No one in living memory had been promoted out of Rupert to another position in the Corp. Regina, a provincial capital of ninety thousand people, represented the big leagues to me. There I might have a chance to be heard network wide, and making it to the network was what career advancement at the CBC was all about. I responded to Hankinson's question with an unequivocal yes and literally danced out of his office.

Within a few weeks, my mother was standing at her front door, fighting tears as I threw my suitcase into the trunk of the Meteor. She knew better than I that I'd never be back. The dirt road out of town followed the Skeena River, its current flowing swiftly past me as the river made its way to the Pacific. We were hurrying in the opposite direction, my alter ego and I, exulting in a new beginning. I turned east at Prince George and headed at last into the Prairies, the mountains fading from view, perhaps for a lifetime. I felt prepared for whatever lay ahead. Rupert had given me a graduate degree in the vagaries of life.

Early spring on the West Coast was late winter in Saskatchewan, and I was completely unprepared for the cold. Real winter was so beyond my experience that I fell for an old trick often played on innocents from British Columbia. After any lengthy exposure to temperatures well below freezing at an outdoor parking lot, my car would refuse to start. I could not help but notice that those cars plugged in to the lot's accessible electrical outlets had no such difficulties. Making inquiries, I was told that it was necessary to buy a car with an electric engine. I went from one smiling car salesman to the next, each directing me to another dealer who might have an electric car in stock, before I finally got the joke.

I could take no offence. Regina was the first city I had lived in, and its sophisticated bars and restaurants, its colleges and arts institutions, and its vigorous political life were rife with opportunities for learning and advancement. Plus it had television, a transfixing medium that had not arrived in Rupert before my departure. I watched so much of it in Regina that the family with whom I boarded called me the "test pattern kid."

CBK Saskatchewan was radio only, the CBC network not yet having granted television broadcasting to the province. Its offices and studios occupied two storeys of a downtown building and accommodated a youthful staff of twenty, including announcers, producers, engineers, a sportscaster, a farm commentator, and a record librarian, plus a bevy of young female secretaries. It was, in sum, nirvana.

Regina, while far from the centre of power in Toronto, was an important regional station and the only one in the province. For that reason, there was much more airtime for original local programming, especially in the afternoons and early evenings. I had been at the station a year when the network created a new position in the department known as "Outside Broadcasts." Its elite group of producer/commentators was responsible for just about everything that was broadcast outside the studio, except entertainment programming. Famous CBC names like Byng Whittaker, Frank Willis, and Thom Benson were among its members. I applied for the job and joined them, still based in Regina.

It was the closest thing to a news department that CBK could boast, since it offered no local newscasts. But clearly there was a hunger among listeners. Next to the Saskatchewan Roughriders, the province's favourite obsession was politics. The average citizen was ready at the drop of a Wheat Pool hat to debate national or international affairs. Farmers read *Hansard* for entertainment. Decades of identifying themselves as the hapless victims of forces beyond their control no doubt contributed to the locals' strongly held opinions. The weather, the railways, those eastern bankers, and the devils in Ottawa were easy targets.

Although I had no formal journalistic training or experience, I persuaded the program director that our audience needed to hear a summary, once or twice a day, of happenings at the provincial legislature. I told him it was a service no different from the weather or the daily farm broadcast, and just as essential. The technicians put a broadcast line into the legislature's press gallery and I set up the first bureau there. Before long I was spending as much time at the bureau during sittings of the legislature as I was in the office. So much of life is watching for chances and being prepared for them when they appear. More than any other opportunity, the decision to cover politics in that fervid political climate set me on a lifetime course.

The Regina station was run by one of the originals of Canadian broadcasting, R.H. "Herb" Roberts. He had been an announcer with Canadian National Railways Radio Department, the first national radio network in North America. In the 1920s, the CNR set up small transmitters along the rail line so that first-class passengers could listen on earphones to one of the wonders of the age. Anyone within range of the station transmitters could listen to broadcasts, making the network truly a national one. The CNR system became the forerunner of the CBC.

Born in Liverpool, England, Roberts managed his station after the fashion of a British colonial administrator. Head office regulations were followed to the letter, discipline was strict, and exemplary behaviour was expected. There was no written order to this effect, but all male staffers knew they should present their prospective brides for inspection and approval. An obviously poor choice might lead to a gentle father-and-son chat. Roberts once called me into his office for a reprimand after I'd played a number from a new Fred Astaire musical: "How Could You Believe Me When I Said I Loved You, When You Know I've Been a Liar All My Life?" Such a sentiment was suggestively immoral in Roberts's opinion, and he ordered the record destroyed.

If he was narrow in his personal views, Roberts made up for it with a generous heart. There was no end to his helpfulness (and therefore that of the corporation) when an employee was dealing with illness or personal problems. That was the upside of the paternalism that reigned at most CBC stations. In my case, Roberts arranged a shift schedule that allowed me to take university courses while working. I was chosen for a fast-track training program that the Outside Broadcasts Department offered in those days, and by 1961 I was preparing items for national network radio shows.

Anyone who covered Saskatchewan in those days was privileged to see nation building up close. In the fifties and sixties, the provincial legislature was both laboratory and battleground for the issues and ideologies that were debated nationally for the balance of the century and beyond. Yet history was not forgotten. In their early fervour, the farmers, preachers, and social reformers who founded the Co-operative Commonwealth Federation in 1932 had pledged to "eradicate the last vestiges of capitalism." When they came to power in the province in 1944 under T.C. Douglas, they were determined, as Marx had advised, to control the means of production, and they set up government-run shoe and blanket factories. The poor should never again be taken advantage of by those capitalist exploiters who were responsible, the CCF believed, for the Depression and the suffering of millions. Of course, the most impractical state-owned enterprises failed, but other experiments with public power companies, pensions, job-security legislation, and health insurance broke new ground. The provincial opposition parties, and the Liberals in particular, bitterly opposed every one of those programs.

Many of the early organizers of the CCF were still alive and as committed as ever in the late 1950s. I developed an enormous admiration for men like J.H. Brocklebank, a terrific orator who had spent many Saskatchewan winters travelling from one isolated farm to another carrying the message that democratic reform was possible through united interests. "Brock" travelled by horse-drawn sleigh and carried a tiny stove; many nights he had to huddle beside it in a makeshift shelter to wait out a blizzard. He and others like him were principled and earnest, but they were never doctrinaire. They were ahead of their time in believing that government spending was necessary to achieve their aims, but not to the point of burdening taxpayers with onerous deficits. The CCF founders were not profligate spenders; they feared debt would make them the slaves of the big banks.

When I arrived in Saskatchewan, Tommy Douglas had been the highly successful CCF premier of the province for fifteen years. His governments had pioneered the social safety net that became one of the defining features of Canadian nationhood. His impact on the nature of Canadian society was immense, not only through his social policies but also through the brilliant men whom he influenced. Among the gifted civil servants in the Saskatchewan government were Al Johnson and Tom Shoyama, both of whom went on to become senior mandarins in Ottawa. Under Lester B. Pearson and Pierre Elliott Trudeau, they adapted the Douglas doctrine to national policy. In 1961, when Douglas moved to Ottawa as leader of the CCF's successor, the New Democratic Party, he made that doctrine more politically palatable on the hustings. It was Tommy Douglas, not Pearson, who created the modern welfare state that Canadians cherish. Pearson was only a willing instrument.

Tommy was never a firebrand or socialist hard-liner. Many times he had to oppose the far-left wing of his own party. At one provincial convention, he fought hard against a faction that was demanding Canada pull out of NATO. There is a lesson in his political success for a modern generation of New Democrats, and that is to broaden the base of support and never allow the party to become captive to special interests, whatever the cause.

Douglas was the most stirring public speaker I have ever heard. Trained as a Baptist minister, he used his rhetoric to inspire trust and confidence in his listeners. He had a rare ability to arouse emotions while at the same time conveying the intellectual and practical merits of his argument. Invariably, his remarks were leavened with a charming self-deprecating humour.

None of us ever called him anything but Tommy, and he always enjoyed good relations with reporters. It helped that he had an irresistible personality, a warm Scottish burr, and considerable media smarts. In the days before digital video was even dreamed of, the reels of film in our bulky cameras often ran out at inopportune moments. When we were to film one of his speeches, Douglas instructed us to signal him when we had to change film magazines. At that point, he lapsed into an anecdote until, at a wave from a reporter, he knew we were rolling again. He did this so seamlessly the audience did not notice and no important part of the message was lost to the camera.

As everyone knows, Douglas championed the greatest social policy reform in the nation's history. His campaigning for government-sponsored universal health care coverage in the 1960 provincial election pitted his party and his administration against most members of the medical profession in the province, the right-wing establishment across the country, and the formidable health industry of the United States whose proprietors knew very well what was at stake.

By 1962 the CCF government had introduced the necessary legislation, but before it had passed the doctors withdrew their services and the hospitals shut down. With the public in a near panic and tensions high, the government sought to break the strike by bringing in sympathetic physicians from elsewhere in Canada and from the British National Health Service. The College of Physicians and Surgeons responded with fear tactics, questioning the competency of the imports and threatening that doctors would flee the province if the act went ahead.

Douglas could be passionate too, but he tried to defuse the general atmosphere of anger and hysteria. On one occasion he stood before an enormous outdoor crowd of pro-government supporters. Before the speech, a group of doctors had packed the front rows. They tried to blend in with the CCF crowd, but their well-pressed work shirts and new jeans were a dead giveaway. Just as Douglas began to speak, they let out an ear-splitting roar, followed by shouts, taunts, and booing. Douglas let the waves of protest flow over him. With perfect timing, he waited until they paused for breath, and then asked, "Is there a doctor in the house?"

The crisis attracted all the CBC News heavies from the East, even for a time the corporation's Washington correspondent, James M. Minifie, a famous internationalist who had lost an eye in the London Blitz. I was designated as an aide and temporary travel agent, getting the new arrivals around and helping with local connections. My youthful sensibilities were somewhat shaken when a Toronto television crew invited me to join a production meeting at their hotel. I found it hard to concentrate while the producer chaired the meeting from his place under the sheets, an apparently unclothed female script assistant asleep beside him. Everyone else carried on as if all were normal.

However vicious the health insurance fight, Douglas's proposed legislation was widely supported by the people. Saskatchewan's hardbitten grain farmers and their families believed in the value of co-operative action and government intervention, designed as they saw it to protect the vulnerable and powerless. The doctors and the government eventually struck a compromise, and within a decade every Canadian citizen was protected by a national health insurance program, the scheme we cherish as medicare.

Those Saskatchewan years shaped my own world view and political philosophy. I saw that government can be a force for good, that the state must intervene to ensure economic fairness, and I learned from the example of Tommy Douglas that generosity and warmth trumps cold calculation and hard-heartedness every time. The experience led me to believe that state power exercised with restraint and judgment was preferable to rampant individualism.

No one fought universal health care more fiercely than Ross Thatcher, ironically a former CCFer who had become provincial Liberal leader just in time to contest the 1960 election campaign against Douglas. I came to believe that Thatcher was at times unbalanced. When he went into the out-of-session legislature one day at the height of the medicare crisis and tried to kick in the door of the chamber (repeated a few times for the cameras and shown around the world), I thought I was watching a man out of control.

After he became premier in 1964, local reporters, often under pressure from editors loyal to the Liberal Party, gave Thatcher a free ride. Tape recorders were not widely used then, and politicians could later deny their dumb remarks, leaving the reporter vulnerable. Journalists felt obliged to translate or at least soften some of Thatcher's more incendiary comments. Speaking to one group of reporters, he allowed that the trouble with natives was they were "breeding like fucking rabbits." In newspaper accounts, this became a sympathetic reflection on action to deal with an exploding Aboriginal population. More famously, he declared during a dispute with francophones in the province, "I am not going to let those goddamn frogs blackmail me." Translation: The premier indicated the government was anticipating difficult negotiations. We all knew that if we quoted Thatcher directly, he would simply issue a denial. If it was the word of a reporter against that of the premier, the friendly provincial press barons knew where their interests lay.

Thatcher was ahead of his time in one regard: inventing the enemies' list long before Richard Nixon. Shortly after Thatcher had moved into the premier's office, he called me in for a chat. Out of his desk he pulled a sheet of paper and waved it in the air. "Here," he said, handing it to me, "are names of all those goddamn socialists I intend to fire." There were dozens of civil servants, including a number of the most capable deputy ministers of the day.

Covering the Saskatchewan legislature in those days had its share of drama, but also plenty of mischief. A fair number of socialist politicians, whose wives would never allow them to drink, regarded the illicit press gallery bar as a home away from home. Reporters played low-stakes poker every second Friday and were regularly cleaned out by a young Cabinet minister named Allan Blakeney, later to become an outstanding provincial premier. Whenever it became necessary to throw caution to the winds and ante up another nickel for the pot, Al discouraged timid gamblers by ordering, "all ribbon clerks out of the game."

The parties that marked the end of the legislative sessions were always riotous—and usually all-male—affairs. The Douglas government had developed a well-oiled propaganda machine that churned out copious press announcements. To demonstrate our independence, we journalists piled a stack of press releases on the marble gallery floor and set them on fire. The blaze was then extinguished through the simple expedient of reporters urinating on it.

Saskatchewan had curious news priorities all its own, as I learned one quiet lunch hour at the office in November 1963. I received a call from an obviously distraught woman. Was it true, she wanted to know, that President John F. Kennedy had been shot? I assured her this was not the case and she was immensely relieved. I pointed out that had anything of such earth-shaking import occurred, I, the local representative of the vast CBC News organization, would know about it. Having satisfied her, I decided to check the wires anyway. In the teletype room, the bells were ringing wildly. There it was in one terse line: "Dallas ... the President has been shot."

I rushed to the control room and told the producer we must interrupt the daily farm broadcast with a bulletin. I admit I was eager to read it. He looked at me like I was mad. "Not a chance," he declared. "Farmers need to know stock and grain quotes and nothing can stop the daily agricultural market reports." In the studio, the farm reporter continued his tedious recitation of the prices of common-to-medium cows on the Winnipeg Exchange until finally the network broke in from Toronto with a special on the Kennedy assassination.

The shift to the Outside Broadcasts Department opened the door to occasional television opportunities. Whenever an eastern-based unit came to town, they did not miss the chance to exploit my contacts, and occasionally I was asked to do interviews with the individuals selected to appear on-camera. After a time, I was teased for having the most recognizable back of the head on the Prairies. No matter, I was working with top writers, directors, and crews and learning the ropes.

The country had a chance to see my better side during federal election night in 1962, when the television news department pulled me in to cover Tommy Douglas. As leader of the NDP, he was seeking election to Parliament in a Regina constituency, and his supporters were so certain of the outcome, they had mounted a huge sign at the Saskatchewan Hotel identifying his headquarters there as the Victory Ballroom. The news department thinkers in Toronto were likewise confident of a Douglas win and assigned an inexperienced kid to report the predictable outcome.

I had never worked so hard to prepare as I did that night. As I came to know the players and the constituency, I began to sniff out evidence of a massive campaign against Tommy by an alliance of business figures and medical professionals. They could not defeat medicare, but they could defeat the man who fathered it. The nation was stunned when the capital city of Saskatchewan rejected its popular former premier, but I was ready with the backstory and delivered it to a national television audience.

In 1965, the network brass singled me out again to appear on the network's national election night broadcast covering John Diefenbaker. Dief had set himself up in his private railway car, parked in the station siding in Prince Albert. By then I knew the Chief pretty well and accepted that he had little use for the national press, much preferring the local media, which in his mind included me. I had interviewed him many times. On the first occasion I recall asking him nervously for his opinion on how the Liberals were running the country. "Young man," he scolded me with mock impatience, "you must learn to spell. The Liberals are *ruining* the country, not *running* it."

The election was on my birthday, November 8, which one of Dief's aides drew to his attention. I was outside on the station platform with the television crew when Dief invited me in for a drink. He was famous for such small courtesies toward his staff and others he liked. As any reporter would, I inquired how he thought the night would go. To my astonishment he replied, "I think we may lose the night." This was news, but I was sure he believed the conversation was off the record. To assuage my conscience on the matter, I went on television and announced that senior aides to the Opposition leader believed they were about to lose the election to the Liberals. That sent reporters on the train scurrying down to his car, demanding the names of the loose-lipped aides. Dief killed the story, stating that no staff member of his had ever said such a thing, which was literally true. Nonetheless, Dief was correct and his party was defeated that night.

Diefenbaker was a wonderful storyteller, with a laugh that dissolved into a maniacal cackle, but he was also a puzzle to his contemporaries. I discovered one clue to his nature when I interviewed the man who was his first law partner in the village of Wakaw, Saskatchewan. The fellow described Dief as "an old bullshitter," a successful defence lawyer who owed his triumphs to an ability to act. I came to believe that was both his strength and his weakness as a politician. In Opposition, where he could thunder in the Commons and on the stump against the sins of the Liberals, he was unsurpassed. But as a prime minister, confronted with the challenge of holding a caucus and a country together while implementing policies and solving problems, he found that acting was not enough.

Though some are better than others at hiding the fact, all politicians are vain and possessed of oversized egos. Dief's was larger than most, and he became paranoid and vindictive to those he considered his enemies, a group that grew as he aged. Dief was such an instinctive partisan politician that after a while he became a one-man party, estranged from many fellow Tories.

Surprisingly, Pierre Trudeau always enjoyed and respected John Diefenbaker. When Dief became seriously ill on a vacation to Ireland in his later years, then Prime Minister Trudeau sent a government jet to bring him home. On his first day back in the Commons after his recovery, Dief rose to attack the Liberal government for its excessive use of government aircraft. Trudeau doubled over with laughter at his desk across the aisle.

Dief stayed on in Parliament after the Conservative Party ousted him as leader in 1967 and spent much of his time undermining his successors, Robert Stanfield and Joe Clark. He was particularly spiteful to Clark, often referring to him in conversations with me as the "so-called leader." Since he could bring himself to trust only the most supine loyalists, he had few real friends toward the end of his life. He came to national politics as a Conservative but, more than that, as a genuine Prairie populist. He could have achieved so much with the gifts he undoubtedly possessed if not for his inability to rise above the flaws in his character.

～

Increasingly I found myself working less for the Outside Broadcasts Department and more for various national news programs, in those days small operations with few resources of their own outside of Montreal and Toronto. I was also starting to have qualms about the soft and fluffy nature of the OB stories I was assigned. Our Toronto bosses were largely veterans of wartime radio, a league of gentlemen who did not approach their jobs as journalists or even as serious news executives. Their preferred story was the uplifting, positive event; their ideal correspondent, the man who reported it in a way that reflected the best interests of the country. The folly of this old guard philosophy was fully revealed during coverage of the one event that delighted them above all others, a royal tour.

In 1964 the Queen visited Atlantic Canada to celebrate the one hundredth anniversary of the series of conferences that had led to Confederation. From Atlantic Canada she would travel to Quebec, and I was given a plum assignment as commentator for her arrival in Quebec City. Premier Jean Lesage had launched Quebec's Quiet Revolution, but the separatist movement he had unwittingly unleashed was anything but subdued. The arrival of a British monarch at the Anse au Foulon and thence to the Plains of Abraham was to the separatists a red flag. The Queen's route followed the footsteps of General James Wolfe, a humiliation intolerable to Quebec nationalists, who announced that if the monarch went ahead with this plan, they would stage a massive protest. British security meanwhile demanded reassurances from the RCMP regarding the Queen's safety.

In advance of the tour, at least a hundred CBC personnel were brought to Ottawa for a week of special training in the art of covering royalty. We joked about classes in Hushed Voices 101. We were told never to refer to "the Queen," only to "Her Majesty." We were instructed in the differences between half-mast and half-staff, as well as how to recognize military rank insignia and the varieties of horse-drawn carriages. Bill Herbert, the executive producer, took aside those of us who were to do live commentary and gave us a stern and unequivocal order. If the Queen was attacked or, even worse, injured, we were not to mention it and our camera crews were under similar orders to cut away from such a shot. No royal blood would ever appear on the CBC. Moreover, we were not to give exposure to the separatist protesters.

On the day of the Queen's Quebec City appearance, the crowds were huge, noisy, and emotional. They were kept under tight control until the Queen alighted from her carriage for a walk across the lawn and into the National Assembly. Hundreds of demonstrators rushed police lines, and just as many Quebec provincial police stormed into the crowds with truncheons swinging. The scene was a full-blown riot, but television viewers saw only a tight close-up of Her Majesty making her way serenely along the roped-off walkway, gracious and unperturbed. In my earphones the director was shouting instructions to stay with the shot. The sound engineers did their best to muffle the tumult, though some ugly noise surely leaked through. Just out of camera range, a furious melee was threatening to spread, but I followed the prescribed script.

The true nature of the event could not be suppressed, of course, and Canadians soon knew the essential dishonesty of the CBC's coverage. My own role in the mess convinced me it was time to make a change to the news side.

⁓

Mom had not been out of Rupert for years, so in 1962 I invited her for a prairie visit. From the moment she arrived, she was uncomfortable and so insecure she needed to telephone friends back home every day. She did not want to go anywhere or see anything and insisted on staying in a hotel. A dinner that I arranged to introduce a girlfriend of the time deteriorated into a tension-filled standoff between the two women, which I could neither ease nor end. Mom could not operate out of her comfort zone, it seemed, and while I had suspicions about the extent of her drinking and worries about her emotional state, I chose to believe that she could pull herself together once home.

My father died later the same year. Our time together after I'd moved in with Mom and Cliff could be measured in hours rather than months or years. Even before he died, then, my father was no more than a ghostly presence in my life, a character from an old home movie. I felt no deep sense of loss upon his passing, only regret at never finding the opportunity to untangle our family history. I did not have the courage to call Mom; no doubt she learned of his death from his sister, as I did. She never mentioned him or their marriage again.

My father died alone, just as he had lived in his final years. After a lifetime of heavy smoking and drinking, he was felled by a stroke and found slumped over a writing desk in a rented basement room. According to my aunt, in front of my father was a half-finished letter to me, though I never saw it. I was the sole beneficiary of his will, and it astonished me that he had actually had a lawyer draw up a proper document. There was money, quite a bit of it, left over from his bootlegging years. Although I never remember him saying so, he obviously loved me. That, at least, was no mystery.

During much of my Saskatchewan sojourn, I was a loner. I worked irregular hours and filled any leisure time with university classes and lessons in voice and drama. There was little opportunity for close relationships, a condition that suited the child within me, always warning against commitments that would slow me down. My usual pattern was to jump ship as soon as things got serious, leaving a string of women to wonder what had gone wrong.

But meeting them in the first place was not difficult for a bachelor in the broadcasting business, and in 1964 I met Linda, a winsome blonde whose supple figure rendered even the alter ego temporarily speechless. She exhibited a quiet character that only enhanced her appeal, and soon we were involved. A wedding date was set for August 1965, but the night before the nuptials I panicked. While the bride-to-be and her mother and sisters fussed over arrangements, I bolted from the house into the dark. The next day I fought the eight-year-old through the ceremony and the reception afterwards, attempting to drown out his protests that this was a huge mistake, that I was incapable of enduring the intimacy of marriage.

I took it as a good sign that Linda was one of the few women in my life that my mother truly liked. No matter how bad Mom's behaviour, Linda was non-judgmental and forgiving. She had to be when Mom failed to show for our wedding with no explanation. Still, we had her blessing from afar and that, I hoped, would be enough.

Shortly before my marriage and despite the debacle in Quebec City, the head of Outside Broadcasts in Toronto offered me a promotion to Winnipeg and another dramatic change in my working environment. The CBC's home on Portage Avenue, where some five hundred employees served the corporation's needs, rivalled the nearby Eaton's store in size. For all that, this headquarters of the CBC's operation in the Prairie provinces did not produce out of its numerous television studios a single national show on a regular schedule. But it did produce segments for shows originating in Toronto and lots of local programming, alongside a strong radio operation. I was lucky to be in the rare position of working for both services and, better still, I was expected to contribute to their respective news departments when required. I intended to ensure that I would be required, and often.

Making television programs in those years felt very like showbiz, and we imagined ourselves as a snowbound Hollywood North. Certainly, many did their best to imitate the frenetic lifestyle, with booze, sex, and, infrequently, drugs. Producers were kings, constantly orbited by talented writers, editors, technicians, make-up artists, and an endless stream of female script assistants. The bar next door was named the "Riviera" and anxious callers were told their spouses were in Studio R, unable to return calls. The city's print and broadcast journalists imbibed daily at the Winnipeg Press Club, conveniently located in the basement of a comfortable hotel. It was not a milieu to sustain marriages, and mine was no exception. My son, Murray, was born in November 1967, but I almost missed the event, caught running between the hospital and live coverage of the Conservative convention that elected the hapless Walter Weir premier of Manitoba.

Linda deserved better than the short marriage we had, which ended amicably after five years. It is a tribute to her kind nature that she allowed me unlimited access to my son, and I worked hard to have time with him. Mercifully, we have built a close and enduring friendship.

Almost as soon as I had joined the three-person OB staff, it became clear that the airtime assigned to it by the network was being squeezed. We still had jobs and salaries, but we were broadcast orphans. Fortunately, one of the greatest of the CBC's broadcasters, Harry Boyle, had come up with an idea for a daily half-hour news and public affairs show he called *Across Canada*. Each region of the country produced one show a week, and every show had its own anchor. The young Lloyd Robertson, like me a refugee from the OB Department, fronted the Toronto version.

One of my first items for the show caused something of a furor. I learned that German troops and tanks would soon be training in Canada for the first time since the end of the war. They would be rehearsing mock battles at the vast military training ground at Shilo near Winnipeg. When I relayed this information to Winnipeg's feisty Jewish community, seeking comment, they organized a protest rally at the site. Germany was our NATO ally, but many members of the city's large Jewish community were either Holocaust survivors or the children of survivors. Almost everyone had lost someone and the Canadian government had not considered the affront that this represented.

The story broadcast that week on *Across Canada* highlighted the striking similarities between the uniforms worn by present-day Wehrmacht soldiers and those of the Nazis. Perhaps unwisely, I interlaced pictures of their training routines with archival World War II footage. Only the swastika was missing. I was accused of provoking an incident, a charge I could not deny, and the corporation's bosses felt it necessary to issue an apology. I was given a verbal dressing-down, but the producer who worked with me was demoted. He was assigned to the religious program that opened the station each morning and, ever after, when I ran into him in the hallway, he greeted me with hands clasped in prayer.

I spent most of the following year writing and producing programs around the country's centennial celebrations. If there was a small town on the Prairies I did not visit, I would like to know its name. I will never know who recommended me for it, but at year's end I was presented with a Centennial Medal by the federal government. I was so chuffed that I wore it on my pyjamas for a week.

Set against the pure pride and joy of that memorable year was the reality that these were tumultuous times. Both the war in Vietnam and the U.S. civil rights struggle had radicalized the left, and the effects were felt around the world. Closer to home, Quebec's Quiet Revolution was percolating, Canada finally adopted its own flag, and Prairie grain farmers faced an income crisis. The CBC News department was overwhelmed by demands for coverage at home and abroad.

The head of the news department in Toronto was Joe Schlesinger, later to become one of the nation's most-admired foreign correspondents. He came to Winnipeg for a meeting that ended with an offer to make me the first national television reporter in Saskatchewan. I had to agree to go on the cheap: There would be no crew of my own, just local hires. I was also expected to report for national radio. But what an opportunity! Still in my twenties, I was working full-time for the nation's largest and most influential news operation. Mom would be able to see me in Rupert, where TV had finally come to town. It was back to Saskatchewan and my old nemesis, Premier Ross Thatcher.

Perhaps because I was always inclined to play a story for all it was worth, maybe even to overplay it, I seemed to attract trouble to myself and to Mother Corp. At a massive anti–Vietnam War demonstration in Saskatoon, a group of protesters asked me for a match. To my surprise, they used it to set fire to a large American flag. The footage made great viewing on that night's television news, but the Mounties had seen me hand over the match and accused me of staging the event. More criticism from CBC executives followed, and Thatcher sent a letter of regret to the U.S. ambassador.

I came to grief on another occasion when Otto Lang, minister for the Canadian Wheat Board, was to make a major grain sales announcement. I planned to film a group of farmers as they watched the announcement and then reacted to it. A few members of the Farmers' Union were duly invited to gather in a spacious beer parlour at Indian Head, Saskatchewan. They were willing but insisted that, as non-drinkers, they did not want to be associated in the item with the demon rum. I agreed without hesitation. It was a hectic night of editing, and I did not have time to screen the whole piece before it was fed to Toronto and played to a national audience of millions. Unfortunately, the editor needed "cutaways" to cover so-called "jump-cuts" between comments by various farmers. As a result, the item was full of close-up shots of well-filled beer glasses being hoisted from the tables.

The Farmers' Union organized a protest in front of the CBC building, complete with placards bearing my picture. I was attacked for distorting reality, for making teetotalling farmers look like beer-swilling boozers. Poor Knowlton Nash, then the head of CBC News, spent weeks fending off complaints from outraged farm organizations and Members of Parliament. I had unwittingly broken my word.

I was on the road a lot and became friendly with a circuit judge. He phoned me one night with the details of a horrendous murder-suicide involving six people in the tiny native community of Buffalo Narrows, Saskatchewan. This honest man wanted Canadians to know the terrible conditions in which natives were living. He told me where and when the bodies would arrive. When the RCMP pulled in to the dark garage of the funeral home in Prince Albert, they were blinded by an explosion of television lights. The lights exposed the bodies stacked in the back of a truck like so much cordwood. This time the new CBC News boss, Joe Schlesinger, had to come to my defence. He did so, citing the value in exposing viewers first-hand to the failure of federal Indian policy and the disregard for Aboriginal lives.

I wish I had been as daring when covering the next royal tour, the 1970 visit to the Arctic by four members of the royal family. The Americans were challenging Canadian sovereignty in the Arctic, so the Trudeau government decided to use the high profile of the royals to remind the world that the Royal Navy had mapped the Arctic and claimed it for Britain. It was part of Canada's heritage as a former colony.

I doubt that there has been another occasion when those of us in the media have had such close access to the Queen, Prince Philip, Charles, and Anne. I related well to Charles, about nine years my junior, and found him engaging and witty. In those days before Diana and his misadventures with the British newspapers, Charles was also disarmingly frank. Over informal cocktails, I told Charles we had met when I did the live broadcast of his investiture as Prince of Wales at Carnaervon Castle, an encounter he pretended to remember. He perked up when I recalled the troubles witnessed by his mother six years before at Quebec City. I suggested to Charles that these did not represent the true sentiments of Quebecers and told him he should make a trip of his own. "No thanks," he said. "I am afraid the separatists might plant a bomb and blow my ass off."

Charles's father went on to lecture me about the fact that Canada was not a colony anymore and if we did not want to have the Queen as our head of state we could simply say so, "and put an end to the thing. We don't have to be here if we are not wanted." Both Charles and his father were admirably candid and I wanted to report the exchange, but I was told such chats were considered off the record.

None of us, however, could refrain from using a later comment by Philip to the effect that the Canadian Arctic was "a garbage dump." He was referring to the thousands of empty oil barrels that littered the landscape. His bluntness upset his Canadian hosts and somewhat embarrassed the Queen, but there was no apology and everyone recognized he was right. Later, the federal government ordered companies operating in the North to take their fuel barrels out with them.

I was just settling in back in Saskatchewan when the ripples of a management shakeup in Toronto hit my shores. Joe Schlesinger had appointed himself CBC's correspondent in Paris. His replacement, the thoughtful and decent Peter Trueman, asked me to join the national newsroom in a management position. If I could take the heat for two years, he promised me the top reporting job in London would follow. Peter did not last in his own post for those two years and, of course, his replacement claimed never to have heard of our understanding. But I knew none of that when I packed my bag once again and headed for Toronto and the worst two years of my life.

3

DRAWN TO POWER

I had joined the CBC in the final years of its most glorious era. There was very little competition from private broadcasters and the corporation enjoyed a huge share of the radio audience. It was headed by distinguished visionaries like Charles Jennings, the father of future ABC news anchor Peter Jennings, and Alphonse Ouimet, the man credited with creating national television broadcasting in two languages. Its leading broadcasters—reporters like Frank Willis and Norman DePoe, and actors like John Drainie—were admired role models. Many of its producers, such as Lister Sinclair and Harry Boyle, were legends in the News and Public Affairs departments. Boyle and Bill Herbert mentored a younger generation that included Lloyd Robertson and me. But our pride in the CBC as an institution and our respect for its burgeoning upper management began to wobble after the radio era gave way, almost overnight, to television.

In the late 1950s, there was a sudden expansion of the corporation and not enough talent, especially in the management ranks, to fill the need. Many of the old guard from radio couldn't make the transition to the new medium, and parts of the CBC came under the control of men who did not know their business, administratively or technically. While in Winnipeg, I was called to a meeting at which a senior executive complained that we were shooting too much expensive film stock. He proposed we all be given still cameras. With these we would snap sequential photos, place them on a cartwheel, and spin it, thus creating the effect of film. At first everyone giggled, thinking this adaptation of flip-book art was a joke. When it became clear that the man was serious, we all fell into an embarrassed silence.

Like it or not, however, Toronto was the centre of the country's broadcasting industry, the centre of the known universe to those of us striving to get there. I believed it was where I belonged. On my first day at CBC Television, I made my way to the Corp's national newsroom, located in a rundown wreck of a building on Jarvis Street in a neighbourhood that had seen better times. The day before, following a fatal accident, police had disabled the only elevator in the building. I walked up the five floors to my new office.

Stepping into the reception area of the open working space, I was greeted by a tiny figure who sat not behind a desk, but on it. He was a sadly deformed character known as "Snarley," because of his raspy voice. When I introduced myself, he burst into laughter and announced to the room that the "fucking hayseed" had arrived. Almost as one, the staff stood and walked out as if taking a group coffee break. I understood this to be a gesture by members of the union. I had made the switch to management, and that made me their natural enemy.

My professional home for the next two years was known as the "Boneyard." It was, like the newsroom in Evelyn Waugh's satiric novel *Scoop*, a graveyard of broken dreams. Up until then I had imagined that such a collection of eccentric, self-destructive, and absurd characters could exist only in a work of pulp fiction. Never before or since have I experienced such a poisoned workplace. Years of incompetent bosses and bull-headed unionists had undermined any sense of common purpose. The mandate handed to me was to clean out the Augean stables. I would be joined in the effort by another newcomer, Tim Kotcheff, who had been brought over from the Public Affairs Department, where he had produced numerous award-winning shows. Together we would act as producer-managers of the news department.

The unit employed roughly a hundred individuals, mostly men, as reporters, editors, writers, and assorted hangers-on, all of whom wallowed in rumour, complaint, and power struggles. A few were known for treachery and corruption, and some were on the take from organizations and private companies, accepting favours in exchange for positive coverage. Drugs of all kinds were consumed, and fights were not uncommon. I learned that many staffers routinely padded their time cards, adding thousands to their paycheques. One reporter often claimed more than twenty-four hours a day and got away with it. When I refused to sign off on fraudulent cards, one of the news editors took me aside and warned me that I might soon find myself in a dark alley with a knife in my ribs.

Down at one end of the large floor were the offices of my predecessors, men cast aside but not let go in past reorganizations. They came and went silently, morning and night, waiting resolutely, if bitterly, for their pensions. The walking dead cast me a piteous glance as they shuffled by my desk. One advised me to choose my cabal carefully lest I be caught on the losing side in the next management shakeup. Another had been officially dismissed but was so distraught that he refused to leave his office. The old friends who had engineered his demise felt too guilty to have him forcibly removed, so for a time he lived in his office, cooking on a hot plate. When I passed him in a hallway late one evening, he told me with a lopsided grin that he was going to change the sheets on his desk.

A few individuals in the newsroom had been my colleagues as reporters and I thought of them as friends. One in particular sought me out socially, and for a time we seemed on close terms. Then I learned that everything I told him was being passed to the news guild that had assigned him to spy on me. Such duplicity and contempt for the corporation that gave these individuals a good living infuriated me. If employees felt they owed the CBC nothing, not even an honest day's labour, I had no compunction about firing them—and I did.

In a courtyard next to our building sat a four-storey brick structure known as the "Kremlin." It housed the offices of more than a dozen Corp vice-presidents, every one of them despised by the lower ranks. One day I sought out the revered Harry Boyle, then chief of national Radio Public Affairs. He stood with his back to me, staring silently out his window overlooking the Kremlin. Long minutes passed. Abruptly, he pulled up the window sash, stuck out his head, and shouted in the direction of his bosses, "Assholes! Frauds!" He closed the window and turned to me as if it had never happened. Harry was known to take a drink or two in those days, but no doubt he had cause.

Perversely, in this environment the inner eight-year-old thrived. He was perfectly at home with the idea that life was a battle, that it took all our strength and wiles to prevail against our enemies, that there was no room for charity or compromise or unguarded vigilance. His delight in our circumstances told me something.

～

Whatever her frailties, I always respected my mother's instincts. Her judgments could be swift, yet almost without exception they proved correct, so I didn't hesitate to seek her counsel on career decisions. Mom had listened for years to my complaints about the CBC's vast bureaucracy, its management incompetence, and, more recently, its truculent staff. As usual, her advice was blunt and clear: "Get out of that place," she told me. "They're all jerks."

The career-saving rescue she recommended that I accept came at the hands of Don Cameron, a renowned and much-admired news producer, with an assist from Pierre Juneau, then chairman of the Canadian Radio-television and Telecommunications Commission, the regulatory body of Canadian broadcasting.

Juneau had turned his eye on the nation's private broadcasters and in particular CTV, the commercial television network that was at its most profitable in the sixties and seventies. Although CTV called itself a network, it was in reality a disparate collection of independently owned local television stations that came together to buy American sitcoms and dramas en bloc. These shows were purchased cheaply, and then peddled to Canadian sponsors at exorbitant prices. Since most Canadian viewers had a choice of only two or three stations in those days, CTV's market share was impressive and its annual profits typically in the 25 percent range.

The paltry amount spent on Canadian programming at
CTV was a fig leaf to keep the regulators at bay: The network
did not even have a national newscast worthy of the name.
Most news broadcasting and what passed for public affairs was
done by the local stations. The network's idea of national news
programming was to fly local film footage to a central studio,
first in Ottawa, later at CFTO in Toronto, and hire an anchor
to front it on air. There were few national correspondents even
in Ottawa. A *Globe and Mail* columnist of the time branded the
private owners as "pirates and buccaneers" for their plunder of
the airwaves.

Then in 1970, Juneau announced stringent Canadian
content regulations for private broadcasters and attached tight
deadlines for implementation. With their federal broadcast
licences on the line, the board members at CTV moved quickly
to assemble a serious national and international news service.
The only place to find people with the necessary expertise was
the CBC, and CTV promptly sent out its raiding party. Their
first steal was one of the corporation's outstanding correspondents, Tom Gould, who then brought aboard Don Cameron,
my boss at CBC News and a man known in the Corp's corridors
as "Craze" Cameron.

Flamboyant, self-indulgent, and the architect of countless
madcap and risky adventures, Cameron was one of the last of
the swashbuckling, hard-drinking, womanizing newsmen, a
club that included his friends Norman DePoe and Peter Reilly.
Shooting wars were his great passion, and he had made his
reputation for bravery, if not foolhardiness, in his coverage of
the Vietnam War for the CBC. Once in the producer's chair, he
couldn't resist following his correspondents into the field, just to

check on how things were going. He would insist on dragging everyone as close to the action as the local military would allow, then insist equally on their accompanying him on drinking binges at the local bars and whorehouses.

In 1983, one of Cameron's CTV reporters, Clark Todd, was killed in the civil war in Lebanon. Todd's crew were forced to flee without him to save their own lives. Don and a colleague left the executive offices in Toronto, flew to Lebanon, and risked their skins going into the war zone to find Todd's remains. They drove up into the Chouf Mountains in the midst of an artillery barrage of the kind that had killed Todd, found his putrefying body, and brought it home.

My first meeting with Don Cameron—or rather the first time I shook his hand—was a classic "Craze" story. In 1962 a crew from his groundbreaking CBC program *Newsmagazine* was in Regina covering the medicare fight. They invited me to join them for a drink. While we chatted, the conversation kept being interrupted by remarks that seemed to come from under the large table where we sat. A disembodied voice insisted that we tell him the name of the most beautiful woman we had ever seen him with. Finally, one of the group explained that the voice belonged to their boss, Don Cameron, and he introduced me by name. A hand emerged from beneath the table in a friendly greeting. I clasped it, uttering the usual pleasantries, but I never did see the man's face.

On my first day at the Corp's Jarvis Street premises, I had hoped to find Cameron in his office where I would impress him with my readiness for action. His door was closed tight and when I knocked there was no answer, though I could hear murmured exclamations from inside. I banged on the door more insistently and, after a moment, Cameron and his secretary emerged, rearranging their clothing. He gave no sign of discomfort, but welcomed me with a compliment on my "edgy" reporting style and reassurances that we would get along just fine; after all, his son and I shared the same name.

Cameron was a completely undisciplined and self-interested human being. Though he possessed a fierce intelligence, he was ruled by instinct and whim. Yet he had two saving graces: He was capable of enormous and sudden kindness and sensitivity, and he possessed the ability to recognize talent in others, gifts they were often unaware of themselves. Of course he exploited that talent for his own purposes, but in the process he crafted careers for two generations of broadcasting luminaries at CBC and CTV, among them Knowlton Nash, Pamela Wallin, Sandie Rinaldo, Michael Maclear, Bill Cunningham, and Lloyd Robertson.

Once at CTV, Cameron had the answer to its problem of how to meet the CRTC's content rules without undermining the lucrative evening schedule. He would create the country's first early morning news and current affairs show, aiming to repatriate the substantial Canadian audience for the American *Today* show on NBC. Armed with CTV's fat wallet, he hired many of his former CBC co-workers as cameramen, film editors, and reporters. He offered me the job of producer. Since I was already producing a news-hour program at the CBC—also a Cameron creation—the position seemed ideal.

The alter ego had no trouble with the idea of fleeing the Corp. *Keep moving,* was his mantra, *stay ahead of enemies and critics.* And Mom had caught my mood at that moment: While there were many individuals I appreciated and admired as professionals at the CBC, there were others I could not abide. It was time to take my leave. It helped too that Cameron was one of Mom's favourites, a man she recognized on first meeting as a boozer and manic-depressive like herself.

Before giving formal notice, I went to see my immediate boss, Knowlton Nash. It took me two days to get an appointment, and when we met, he was pleasant but rather indifferent. His parting words were that CTV's commitment to a breakfast talk show would not last more than six months and that I would soon be back, looking for work. I submitted my resignation without regret.

Cameron assembled a small team of seven or eight for the new morning show. We occupied three dingy offices in the windowless basement of CFTO, the network's flagship station in the suburb of Agincourt, well north of downtown Toronto. The lack of daylight and circulating air soon produced sallow complexions and constant colds, but we were eager. Early on we brainstormed possible names: *Canada in the Morning* was too long; *AM Canada* might be confusing; *Canada AM* put the country first and felt just right.

My editorial staff of four chase producers pulled together seven and a half hours of interviews a week. The working day started at four in the morning, and the show went on air at seven. In the first year, it was a ninety-minute production, ending at eight-thirty; in the second, it went to two full hours. Since we could not start lining up the next day's guests at such early hours, it was a long shift for everyone on the editorial side. Not everyone had the constitution to endure such a schedule, and staff turnover was brutal. One producer was so miserable and cranky at the prospect of arriving in what seemed the middle of the night that Cameron banished him to days. The subterranean quarters did not help, but comfortable in management's carpet city a few floors above, Executive Producer Cameron was oblivious.

We needed stars to attract an audience, and Cameron hired two high-profile co-hosts. Popular weatherman Percy Saltzman was lured away from CBC Toronto, and Carole Taylor, a local personality and show host, was called up from CFTO. Both were expected to draw viewers in the critical Toronto market.

To the public, Percy was an easygoing yet polished performer in front of a chalkboard weather map, beloved for his signature toss of the chalk at the end of every meteorological report. But Percy was far more than that. He was a serious man, an intellectual in the European Jewish tradition, and as with many of his generation, the injustices of the Depression and the horrors of the Holocaust had deeply affected his outlook. He possessed a deep ethical sensibility combined, at that stage in his life, with a lot of anger. The world was a tussle between good and evil for Percy, and he believed that television could be an instrument for overdue change. At our story meetings he was full of ideas, most of them heavy with social relevance.

Carole, on the other hand, had an engaging interviewing style that was perfectly matched to the largely female audiences for morning television in those days. Though her entree into television had been the crown in a Miss Toronto beauty pageant, she was nobody's fool. In her early twenties, she had a sharp, incisive mind, as well as high standards and unvarnished honesty. She also had a perfect understanding of where she wanted to go and what she needed to learn to get there, an attitude that would eventually take her to a highly successful career in British Columbia politics.

The show was launched on September 11, 1972, and in the early weeks our strategy was to position the much-older Percy as the lead personality and father figure, with Carole acting as his attractive assistant. That script did not last long. The story editors who produced and researched the segments wanted Carole to interview their guests. When these guests began to include political figures and other prominent individuals, Percy rebelled. We had a heated exchange in which I had to remind him that our show was primarily an entertainment vehicle with hard news on the side. He was not anchoring a documentary unit intent on exposing the corruption of government or the crimes of industry, even if that would have suited him better. I tried to persuade him to relax and enjoy himself.

But to Percy, lightening up meant selling out. One morning he interviewed actor Michael Caine about his role in a just-released war movie. Percy accused Caine of being a fake: What did a fancy-pants British actor know about war? In fact, Caine had fought in Korea as an infantryman in a London regiment, once engaging in hand-to-hand combat against Chinese mass attacks. He told viewers of being in the skirmish line the day the armistice was signed in Panmunjeom, afraid he might be the last man to die. It was riveting television but showed the risks of Percy's style.

During a week the crew spent in Ottawa, Percy also came off second-best in an interview with Pierre Trudeau. He told the prime minister that he was sick of Ottawa politicians fighting like children in a sandbox and suggested they should simply get together and agree to solve the problems of the country. Trudeau countered that, unfortunately, democracy was messy. If Percy could arrange for all those irritating and argumentative people to join one big political party in which everyone agreed on all policies, Trudeau said he would be happy to lead it.

It became apparent that viewers were tuning in because of Percy but staying because of Carole. The tension between the two grew so great that we had to hold separate story meetings every morning. Decisions over who would handle which guests became a negotiation to test the wisdom of a Solomon. Percy's irritability was compounded by the fact that he was not an early morning person; as the weeks passed, he arrived at the studio at 4 A.M. looking increasingly haggard and worn. Plus he was carrying a heavy workload, more than a dozen interviews every week. Don Cameron had made the mistake of telling him that he was to make guests earn their airtime—a hard news concept not appropriate for what was essentially a talk show. But Percy took it seriously. He researched every interview meticulously, and then felt deeply frustrated when the time given to his segments was, in his view, too short to develop his subject.

His wife monitored the show at home with a stopwatch. Every "intro" and "extro," and every segment, whether Carole's or Percy's, was timed to the second. At the end of the show, Percy received a full report and then confronted me. If Carole had been given even a minute or two more camera time, then I was failing to provide them equal exposure. He accused story editors of showing favouritism, steering their interview subjects away from him.

After a time, he was right to complain. The audiences were responding strongly and positively to Carole, and we decided to shift the weight of hosting duties in her favour. Until then, very few women had been on camera in public affairs programming; they were largely confined to the petticoat ghettos of the traditional "women's page." We believed we had a potential new star and wanted to make the most of her.

Though the tensions were kept from the audience, the show blew up in our faces one day only a few months after it began. Percy burst into the cafeteria where Carole was having coffee and, totally without cause, unleashed a verbal tirade at her. Carole's cool self-composure seemed to upset him all the more. Pale and shaking, he went home, never to return. A doctor later told us he was suffering from exhaustion.

I blamed Don Cameron and myself for Percy's failure. We learned what many networks have discovered over the years— that compatibility is everything where co-hosts are involved, and doubly so on morning programs. Workdays that start before dawn are enough to unhinge even seasoned performers. We should have known too that Percy was not flexible enough to share the limelight with someone whose skills he could not learn to respect.

Canada AM was soon off and running again under Carole and a string of other co-hosts. After a year, she left for *W-5*, the network's weekly prime-time news and public affairs show. Norm Perry, another CBC alumnus who had most recently been an investigative reporter and program host at CFTO, eventually became *Canada AM*'s long-running host, alongside Helen Hutchinson and others, most notably Pamela Wallin and Valerie Pringle. In my three years as producer and later as deputy director of news, I had to fire only two hosts, both hired on a whim by Cameron. One, a stunning former model, asked on air where Saskatchewan was and referred to London, Ontario's Stratford Festival. The other was an eccentric Quebecer whose thick accent lost us our audience in the West and whose insistence on a silk shirt open to the navel and gold chain necklace cost us credibility in all parts of the country.

As Don Cameron and Tom Gould, by then CTV's vice-president of news, expanded the fledgling news service, I was promoted to assistant director of the unit. The producers of the national news, news specials, *Canada AM*, and *W-5* reported to me. This allowed Cameron to hit the road whenever boredom overcame him, as it frequently did, and also relieved him of the blame whenever things went awry, which often happened.

The news department—the backbone of any broadcasting company—had not yet jelled. The staff of mainly print-based news editors resented the recent CBC arrivals; worse, they knew little about electronic news-gathering techniques or sophisticated production technology, and resisted any attempts at change. We ex-CBC types were sure of ourselves in this arena and more than a little arrogant.

That confidence did not survive the night of the federal election in October 1972. Once every four or five years, election night broadcasts offer news departments the opportunity to show their stuff. It is the only time a network's entire news team is pulled together for a single broadcast, a test of on-air talent as well as production and technical skills. The competition between the networks is fierce. That year we were determined to top the CBC in the ratings. Lloyd Robertson was the Corp's anchor, and we relished the idea of beating our old friend, not to mention challenging the CBC's standing as the accepted broadcaster of record for major national events like elections.

CTV invested a small fortune in a massive set at CFTO, then one of the largest television studios in the world. For this high-profile event—the second electoral test of the Trudeau government—Tom Gould hired a computer company to create a state-of-the-art election returns reporting system capable of sifting through millions of pieces of information quickly and accurately. No more waiting for dry returns from Elections Canada. We would have the fastest riding-by-riding results, earlier computer-generated projections of winners and losers, stunning on-air graphics, and even instantaneous candidate profiles. Computer programming was still in its infancy then, and words like *gigabyte* and *download* were hardly part of our vocabulary, but the new computer experts assured us the machinery would work.

Come election night the results poured in smoothly from polling stations in Newfoundland, and we were confidently declaring winners well before the competition. If this kept up, the CBC would be humiliated. But when heavier returns from the Atlantic provinces were received, the system began to falter. The combined returns from Quebec and Ontario swamped it completely and the apparatus crashed before our eyes.

It was still early in the evening; more than a million people were watching. Even though the early results and projections on the big boards behind the anchor desk had frozen with the computer's demise, signing off was out of the question. We fell back on the official results from the returning officers, but they dribbled in slowly. What to do? Expediency being the mother of invention, our only recourse was to steal results in the crucial races from the other guys. With CBC Radio coming through my headphones, I crawled under the set's central desk. From this position out of camera range, I scribbled "elected" and "defeated" results on slips of paper and handed them up to our unflappable anchor, Harvey Kirck. He read the bulletins with great authority, all the while quite aware of the comic scene we made. We became giddy and soon began declaring winners and losers on educated guesswork, though the election itself was no easily predicted romp. Robert Stanfield's Conservatives succeeded in reducing Trudeau's Liberals to a minority government. In the contest of the networks, we beat the CBC with the speed of our results at least, but we did it with their own returns.

There was a more visible public relations disaster not long after. The *Toronto Star* decided to profile both national newscasts by putting a reporter in each newsroom on the same evening to compare broadcasts. As luck would have it, the night they chose was a big one for political news out of Ottawa, with several stories slated for coverage. At the top of our newscast, the CTV video link out of the capital broke down just as the first item was introduced. It came back only sporadically and at the wrong moments. Each time Harvey introduced an Ottawa item, it failed to materialize. That night he signed off with a deep sigh, "My name is Harvey Kirck. I think."

These were pivotal years in the history of the country, and we struggled to build a modern news operation capable of keeping up. The charismatic René Lévesque and the Parti Québécois brought the possibility of Quebec's separation to the forefront of the national agenda. Trudeau and the Liberals were returned with a majority in 1974, the better to confront Lévesque, but the PQ nonetheless took power in Quebec in 1976. The economy was threatened by rampant inflation, leading to the imposition of wage-and-price controls, and by an OPEC-led hike in oil prices that saw shortages at the gas pumps. At home we deepened our coverage by establishing a large bureau in Montreal and adding reporters in Toronto, Vancouver, and Ottawa. We opened foreign bureaus in London and Washington and, most far-reaching of all, in Beijing and later the Middle East.

Meantime, the CBC news department was finally turning itself around. The year after I left, they hired a hard-driving no-nonsense newspaperman, Denis Harvey, as chief news editor. He shook up the ranks and succeeded in restoring the Corp to its accustomed place at the top of the nightly TV news ratings. Although we had made significant progress on the editorial side of the ledger, we needed some bold initiative to keep us in the game in the eyes of viewers. Once again Don Cameron had the answer.

In 1976, Cameron called me in the middle of the night to announce that he had decided to pluck the top news anchor in the country, Lloyd Robertson, out from under the complacent CBC brass. I told him he had been drinking too much, advised him to go back to bed, and hung up to do the same myself.

Little did I know how unhappy Robertson was at the CBC, chafing under the restrictions imposed on him by myriad union contracts, especially those that governed on-air news readers. There is a famous, probably apocryphal, story that captures the situation. One writer on the news desk was a terrible typist, constantly hitting the wrong keys. He handed a script to a staff announcer in which the words *Soviet Union* were typed as *Soviet Onion*. The announcer went on the air and dutifully reported the actions of a Communist vegetable. Viewers complained and the supervisor accosted the reader, incredulous that he should flub the name of a country that was in the news every day. The announcer replied that his job description required him to read the copy exactly as written. The rest was a problem for someone else.

Not only did the contracts prevent Robertson from writing a word of his own copy, he was not allowed to suggest items for coverage or change the lineup of the stories he presented. Although he knew the country and its leaders better than any of the editors he worked with, his views were not solicited or seriously regarded. Cameron shrewdly offered a deal that would give Robertson a free hand in editorial matters.

Nonetheless, Robertson was reluctant to walk away from his career at the CBC. It was, he said, like a nun forsaking the convent. He pleaded with his bosses and finally delivered an ultimatum: Change the contracts so journalists and announcers could write as well as read the news, or he would leave. The feckless managers who were then in charge at the corporation made desultory efforts, but the unions were unwilling to relinquish an inch of their jurisdiction. In the face of union resistance, management threw up its hands. No other broadcasting organization would have allowed its top personality to jump ship for an increase in salary that amounted to peanuts in network budget terms.

The axis of Canadian television tilted with Robertson's defection from what was then the pre-eminent national news organization to its upstart rival. Robertson brought instant credibility and gravitas to CTV News and everything it produced, enhancing the work of other CBC heavyweights already hired by Cameron, such as senior correspondents Bill Cunningham and Michael Maclear. The editorial product had been greatly improved, but it took Lloyd Robertson's arrival to draw public attention to our television news service. For the first time, Canadians had a serious alternative to the old grey mare on Jarvis Street.

Robertson shared the anchoring duties with Harvey Kirck, the face of CTV's late-night news since 1963. Harvey was a strong anchor with a great gift for copywriting, and a gentle giant who graciously accepted his new sidekick, even though he must have understood that Robertson was destined to replace him as chief network anchor. To Robertson's credit, he insisted that Kirck be given a pay raise to his own level. The two worked together in an atmosphere of mutual admiration.

The duo's popularity was such that audience share began to slip away from CBC News, a trend that continued for the next thirty-five years. It happened in spite of the fact that CTV often did not have the resources to compete with the CBC's news service. Then as now, CTV was a commercial broadcaster obliged to show a profit and could not hope to match the publicly funded CBC in the number of its editorial staff or crews. Whereas we typically covered important events with a crew of three, the CBC sent more than a dozen from various branches of their English and French news services.

Yet we could compete in the personalities we chose to put on-camera. The CBC was notoriously uncomfortable with reporters who might appear to have strong opinions or even forceful personalities of their own. Against their competent but somewhat grey reporters, we put up a cast of interesting and colourful correspondents. One of the best for editorial skill and on-air presence was Henry Champ. He was CTV's first reporter in Quebec in the mid-sixties and later its bureau chief in Washington and London. Champ spent fifteen years with CTV before moving to NBC News in the United States; most recently, he was Washington correspondent for CBC Newsworld.

A talented and gutsy reporter, Champ had the good looks of an Errol Flynn with the larger-than-life panache to match. Once, after a northern canoe trip, I was returning home aboard a cruise ship sailing south from Alaska. Out on deck one night I saw a lovely young woman alone at the railing, blonde hair blowing in the breeze. I hastened to introduce myself to the lady, who was an American. When I told her I was a Canadian, she had only one question: "Do you know Henry Champ?"

In 1972, when the Soviets and the West were still in the grip of the Cold War, we sent Champ to Moscow for the famous Canada-Russia hockey series. After his return, I received a call from a member of the RCMP security service who was eager to interrogate Champ about a relationship he had struck up with a Russian woman. It seemed his companion was a KGB spy. Using such agents to compromise and later blackmail unwary Western men was a common KGB trick. "Hell," Champ declared, "I was just screwing her—not revealing any of the nation's secrets."

Champ was a famously hard worker, but he had a habit of disappearing on assignments, which always worried the news management. After one AWOL episode, Cameron ordered me to fire Champ. Reluctant to do so, I summoned him to a meeting with Cameron and me, at which Champ offered an unexpected alibi: He had never left the office. He was at the table of a week-long poker game in the cavernous basement of the CTV headquarters at CFTO and had been available to the assignment desk at a moment's notice. Cameron docked Champ a week's pay and told him he did not want to see him in his office again. "At these prices, I can't afford to be here," Champ declared, sweeping out the door.

We were far more seriously concerned, however, when we lost touch with Champ in the chaos surrounding the fall of Saigon in April 1975. Until a few days before North Vietnamese forces had overrun the city, Champ was filing regularly. His sudden silence was ominous; we knew many had died in the final American retreat. There was relief when Associated Press sent out a wire photo of a desperate crowd of Vietnamese trying to board a U.S. embassy bus to the airport. At the door of the bus, struggling to keep the mob at bay, were Henry Champ and a U.S. marine. Champ was fending off a crush of people attempting to climb aboard and likely topple the overloaded vehicle; the scene was frenzied and no doubt dangerous. We had every expectation that Champ had made it.

The critics of commercial television always fear that sponsors will interfere with news coverage or attempt to influence it in some way. In all my years at the private network, I experienced only one attempt to do so, and it happened early in my tenure as assistant director of the news service.

One of my responsibilities was the public affairs show *W-5*. In mid-1973, OPEC imposed an international oil embargo and energy prices escalated alarmingly. North American oil suppliers were accused of taking advantage of the shortages by jacking up prices more than necessary. To improve their image with a skeptical public, the oil companies launched a multi-million-dollar advertising campaign of which CTV was a major benefactor. The Big Oil ads presented a series of so-called facts in defence of their pricing practices. At the same time, *W-5* produced a carefully researched documentary laying bare the many falsehoods at the core of the slick campaign.

Before the item could be broadcast, management, in the person of Tom Gould, killed it on the grounds that it was libellous. I protested, going so far as to obtain a written opinion from the network's own lawyers that the story was acceptable for broadcast. No dice; again, a few senior executives refused to let the item run while the *W-5* writers cried foul. I found myself caught between intransigent management and a staff in revolt. I had either to lead or to step aside—the latter course ensuring that I'd be forever branded an ethical coward. I refused to axe the piece and asked for a meeting with Murray Chercover, the network president. My immediate boss, Cameron, was off on a binge and not to be found.

By now the Toronto newspapers were picking up rumours, and management likely considered firing me for insubordination. But that was not an option after a number of high-profile colleagues lined up behind the cause of editorial freedom. To my surprise, senior correspondent Jack McGaw, host Carole Taylor, and producer Mike Maclear all threatened to quit if I was thrown overboard.

Both sides faced off at an uncomfortable meeting in Chercover's office. Chercover was nervous, as he always was when confronting a tough decision. He loved the glamour of the television business, but he hated having to deal with intractable issues, including squabbles among his employees. I made my case, but failed to consider the matter strategically. In my inexperience, I had left no room for compromise or a face-saving escape route for either party.

Chercover came down on the side of the *W-5* documentary,

which ran unedited the next Sunday. He had done the right thing, backing his editorial staff over his advertising sales department, and the ads never reappeared. But I knew there would be fallout from our stand on principle, and it was not long coming. A reorganization of the news department was announced soon after: Don Cameron, who had surfaced in time for the session in Chercover's office, was demoted a notch. I was banished to the snows of faraway Ottawa. My superiors decided Ottawa bureau chief Bruce Phillips needed support in managing his three-person operation on Parliament Hill. Apparently, I was expected to resign after the humiliation of being busted to what was in essence a bookkeeping job. Cameron reminded me that pride cometh before a fall, and we decided to hang in together and scheme for his return to power rather than quit the field.

In fact, the timing was propitious. Being a department manager had lost its appeal and I saw in Ottawa a chance to return to my first love, political reporting. On the personal front, it was likewise time for a change. The woman I had been living with in Toronto took her leave while I was on a northern canoe trip, cleaning out the apartment but forgetting her guitar. When I returned, I put the instrument in the fireplace, finished the last of the rum in my backpack, and fell asleep in my Arctic bedroll to the sounds of snapping guitar strings.

In the winter of 1974, I pointed my rusting Volkswagen Beetle in the direction of Ottawa, where I was not wanted nor much needed. Bruce Phillips certainly felt that way. For years, he had been one of the country's outstanding print reporters and television commentators. He had a well-tuned critical mind and ample credibility with viewers. But organizational skills and respect for deadlines were not in his makeup. He was not lazy; he simply believed there were better things to do with his life—playing golf, for instance—than work fourteen hours a day.

His three Ottawa reporters—Gail Scott, Mike McCourt, and Eric Malling—were experienced pros. During my stint in CTV management, I had hired the tenacious Malling from the *Toronto Star*. Scott, to the network's credit, was the first female network correspondent on Parliament Hill. McCourt's skills eventually took him to ABC as a foreign correspondent. All three were frustrated by the daily uncertainty of not knowing who would be covering what story or when. The assignment desk in Toronto was similarly exasperated by the bureau's unpredictability and disarray. So I seized the opportunity to take charge or at least bring some order to the chaos. I also broadened the loose mandate I had been granted to get myself back into political reporting and connect with the men and women who made things happen in those exciting years. The Liberals had regained their majority the previous June and appeared to have the momentum and talent to accomplish great things.

Bruce Phillips and I soon came into conflict over who should have final say on what we would file for the evening's national news broadcast. Phillips's friends and contacts were largely drawn from the business community and the Conservative Party. I felt the focus should be on the Liberals who were, after all, the folks in power. One of our disputes concerning coverage became so heated that he invited me to the parking lot to settle the matter. He was the bigger man, but I had been competing in marathons and believed that if all else failed, I could outrun him. Usually we managed to compromise, mediated by a Scotch or two.

As the months passed, a factor in my favour was Phillips's frequent absence; he had almost a second career as a board member and then president of the prestigious Royal Ottawa Golf Club. When at the club, he left instructions with his secretary for any callers from the Toronto office to be told he was in a meeting and would call back. He often did so from the fairway. Increasingly I made the decisions about what stories would be covered and by whom (including a few I snagged for myself), and when it became clear that head office was satisfied with the on-air results, Phillips was content to enjoy the credit as bureau chief.

In those days, before press gallery members had offices off Parliament Hill, everyone worked together in a crowded, smoky room on the third floor of the Centre Block. It had been the "hot room" for generations of parliamentary reporters whose photos, dating back to the nineteenth century, adorned the walls. Since we worked cheek by jowl, everyone knew what everyone else was saying, rendering the media's coverage of the Hill even more uniform than today. Reporters who had not bothered to cover certain events often borrowed others' "dupes," carbon copies of filed stories. Sometimes they stole them out of the trash if colleagues wouldn't hand them over.

We had a blind pig, an illegal bar, and when the filing was done for the day, the cry went out for Scotch and beer, which gallery staffers hurried to us at twenty-five cents a pop. It was a zoo of a place. Here the rise and fall of politicians was decided and agreed upon, or so we believed. There were critical opinions freely exchanged, occasional trysts in the backroom, and now and then fistfights between competing newspapermen. The *Toronto Star* was an influential voice during this time, with John Honderich serving as its Ottawa bureau chief, and Richard Gwyn's column attracting an avid readership among those seeking a glimpse into the latest thinking of Liberal power players.

Members of the Cabinet, and even the prime minister, sometimes visited the hot room. Plenty of Opposition members wandered up from the Commons chamber just below, joining reporters for drinks and the indiscreet trading of rumours and secrets about friends and enemies. There was a famous incident involving one of Diefenbaker's ministers, an over-the-hill ladies' man who had been denying for weeks that he had had an affair with Gerda Munsinger, the German-born prostitute and suspected East German spy. One of the reporters showed another minister, George Hees, a picture of the woman naked and asked if he thought it had been doctored. "The eyes are wrong," he said, "but everything else is right." What was said and done in the hot room was off the record, reflecting a cozy relationship between reporters and those they covered. Today such camaraderie is no more than a distant memory, which is just as well in many respects, but it was the norm when I arrived.

One of my first calls was to a lifelong friend from British Columbia, Iona Campagnolo. We had grown up together in Prince Rupert and at one time I had dated her sister. Iona had worked her way up the political hierarchy from school board to city hall to national politics, winning a federal seat in our hometown riding of Skeena. By the time I landed in Ottawa, she was an admired member of the Trudeau Cabinet and a rising star in the Liberal Party. Trudeau took advantage of her popularity by making her a Cabinet minister shortly after the 1974 victory.

Being a woman in politics is difficult at the best of times, but Iona was also strikingly beautiful and unmarried, which caused no end of gossip and speculation. Trudeau could do all the dating he wanted as a single man, but in those days the same standard did not apply to female public figures. Iona needed a tame and easily explained escort for various social events, and I was pleased to fill the role. We were never romantically involved; then as now, we enjoyed a friendship grounded in mutual trust and loyalty.

Our relationship gave me an entree into the political and bureaucratic corridors of power that I could never have achieved on my own. I was introduced to Cabinet ministers, made personal friends among senior mandarins, and above all, enjoyed frequent contact with Pierre Trudeau. We discovered a mutual passion for paddling and the North, and he later included me among his guests at official and unofficial functions.

The city's social scene was energized by any event Trudeau attended, although the most coveted invitation, with or without him present, was dinner at Allan Gotlieb's. A deputy minister and later undersecretary at External Affairs, Gotlieb and his wife, Sondra, had made of their home a sort of intellectual salon, and the city's political and bureaucratic elite routinely gathered there. My life in those days was a blur of cocktail parties hosted by the Gotliebs and others, dates with women who worked for Cabinet ministers, and endless hours at the office.

In the process of becoming an Ottawa insider, I inevitably compromised myself. It was a delicate balancing act to broadcast a hard-hitting story on the government's failures one evening and then face the principals at a cozy dinner party the next. In time, I reached a stage where I knew too many things that could not

be reported because I had learned them in confidential circumstances. This made me increasingly uncomfortable, especially in
the company of two or three Cabinet members who chatted freely
about Cabinet affairs, heedless of my presence. More than once
a minister who was having difficulty getting Trudeau's attention
asked me to intervene with "the boss." I attempted it only once.
Trudeau himself was discretion personified and never divulged
a crumb of newsworthy material, even as we shared canoeing
adventures on some of the country's more treacherous rivers.
Perhaps that too was compromising, though I have no regrets
about time spent in that extraordinary man's presence.

In half a century of covering national politics, I have often
speculated about the nature of charisma. Politicians either have
it or they do not. It cannot be learned but it can be burnished.
It is the flame that draws us to individuals whose causes may be
good or evil.

Charisma is not defined by gender. Margaret Thatcher,
Indira Gandhi, Eva Perón, even Golda Meir, had it; so too do
Kim Campbell, Belinda Stronach, and Iona Campagnolo. Nor
is it necessarily connected to physical appearance. Think of
the wizened Albert Schweitzer; Charles de Gaulle, with a nose
that earned him the nickname "Cyrano"; Winston Churchill,
a dumpy gnome; or Franklin Delano Roosevelt, helpless in a
wheelchair. Charisma asks for discernible intelligence and a
generous spirit, both traits exhibited by Bill Clinton, Tony Blair,
and Barack Obama. Though sometimes attached to high office,
that pedestal alone does not confer it. Joe Clark, Jean Chrétien,

and Preston Manning missed out. Brian Mulroney possessed it briefly; Stephen Harper remains a charismatic in waiting.

In my experience, charisma comprises an absolute certainty about oneself and an aura of power held in reserve. It is as old as the mysticism of the medieval sorcerer and as alluring as any siren. Pierre Elliott Trudeau was Canada's only truly charismatic leader. He never understood why he was so blessed and once told me he never so much as wanted to lead a Boy Scout troop. But he knew he had charisma and he used it.

Trudeau was not one to allow close relationships with men or women, and his own sons often found him distant. He kept himself aloof and did not show his cards until others had revealed themselves and their intentions. Above all, he valued his privacy and believed others must feel the same. When one of his most admired Cabinet ministers, Don Macdonald, was in emotional pain over his wife's cancer, Trudeau said nothing. Macdonald feared that his circumstances might affect his work and wanted Trudeau to understand. A colleague asked if I would raise the issue with the PM and solicit a few words of support for Macdonald. Trudeau declined to offer them, regarding any gesture as a gross interference in the man's most personal affairs.

He expressed similar sentiments to me after the death of Terry Fox, a national hero who attempted to run coast-to-coast in aid of cancer research. Although Trudeau greatly admired Fox's bravery and determination, he was reluctant to participate in a special CTV fundraising broadcast. I encouraged him to recognize how Fox's odyssey had captured the nation's heart. He protested that he would simply appear insincere, as if pandering to public opinion and exploiting a young man's tragic demise. I argued that if he expressed his genuine feelings, he would give voice to

the nation's sentiments and be appreciated, not condemned, for
doing so. In the end he relented, but not happily.

Trudeau's discomfort with open displays of emotion was well-
known and perhaps he most feared any spill of personal feeling.
There was a revealing moment during one election campaign
stop in Newfoundland. The advance man took Trudeau on
an unscheduled visit to a community centre for children with
mental and physical handicaps. The prime minister was visibly
moved, even close to tears, as he circulated among the stricken
but cheerful kids. He made a graceful-enough tour and exit, but
in the parking lot afterwards, he turned on the aide in a fury,
"Don't ever do that to me again."

A complex childhood, caught between a flamboyant, risk-
taking father and a stern, somewhat disapproving mother, plus
a Jesuit education, no doubt formed his essential character.
An amateur psychologist might see Trudeau's life as a struggle
between two contradictory natures battling to dominate his
psyche. As a young man, Trudeau had been hopelessly smitten
with a Montreal woman who was his intellectual equal, but
the relationship foundered. Later, his romancing of actress and
singer Barbra Streisand gave the sheen of Hollywood stardom
to Trudeau's early years as prime minister. Few knew that the
Streisand affair became a serious attachment. Friends who spent
time with the couple were struck by their mutual admiration
and obvious enjoyment of each other's company. But Streisand
knew better than Trudeau that their lives were incompatible,
and it was she who ended the romance.

Many of the same friends were stunned at Trudeau's surprise
marriage in 1971 to Margaret Sinclair, the daughter of James
Sinclair, a former Cabinet minister in the governments of Louis

St. Laurent and Lester Pearson. In fact, she and Trudeau had been dating in secret for some time. In her, Trudeau found the kind of woman his mother most likely would have warned him against but who no doubt would have fascinated his father.

Although Margaret was anything but an old-fashioned girl, Trudeau decided to observe an old-fashioned custom. Before the marriage, the prime minister sought parental consent from the father of the bride. According to a Trudeau intimate, he and James Sinclair met alone in the den of Sinclair's Vancouver home. Sinclair had no idea what Trudeau wanted, but expected the prime minister to ask his advice on some government matter. Trudeau caught him unawares by announcing his desire to marry one of his daughters. Which one? Sinclair inquired. When Trudeau replied that his choice was Margaret, Jimmy was not encouraging and suggested instead that another daughter would be much more suitable as a prime minister's wife.

Trudeau's marriage seemed to fly in the face of his upbringing and a lifelong dedication to asceticism, discipline, and reason before passion. On this occasion he opted for self-indulgence and pure physicality; in doing so, he rejected his own intellectualism and also a number of other women, accomplished and intelligent, who regarded his choice with silent chagrin, if not bitterness. Margaret, thirty years his junior, was a self-described nature child who had lived a free-spirited life of casual sex and drugs. She was catapulted unprepared into the serious business of being the chatelaine of 24 Sussex Drive, a challenge even for a mature political wife. She bore three sons in quick succession and finally broke under the strain.

Most Canadians admired the dignity with which Trudeau endured the pain and embarrassment of their terribly public breakup. Some closer to the marriage were critical of Trudeau: Rather than try to help Margaret, they felt, he closed down and in effect cut her loose. Her revenge was instinctive and unbridled, as witnessed by her behaviour at one of the annual parliamentary press gallery dinners of the time. Trudeau dreaded these much-anticipated events, at which reporters and politicians made speeches poking fun at one another and sometimes themselves. He was not at home telling funny stories and he detested having to feign friendship with people for whom he often had little respect.

In the fall of 1976, however, Trudeau was at one such dinner, and Margaret was at her most outrageous. During the pre-dinner reception in the Centre Block's Hall of Honour, Margaret blew marijuana smoke in the face of the RCMP commissioner, who had to pretend not to know what it was. Later, she would not leave the all-night party at the press club on the other side of Wellington Street from the Parliament buildings. A Cabinet minister, Bryce Mackasey, was sent to fetch her, but she dismissed him with the accusation that he was a "little ass kisser." Finally, Trudeau himself showed up to take his wife home over her loud objections. This was about as humiliating as it could get for a man as proud and private as Trudeau.

A few months later, I broke the story of the couple's plan to sign a separation agreement. For a full day after the item was broadcast on the CTV national newscast, I fielded calls from newspapers and radio and TV stations around the world, but I declined to elaborate. A close prime ministerial aide had tipped me off about the couple's intentions. I always believed that Trudeau wanted to end the swirl of rumour and get the facts out without doing so through the usual method of a government press release.

After his separation and divorce three years later, there were many women in his life. (Of all the gossip about him, the rumour that he was gay was the most outlandish.) Late one evening I answered a knock at my door to find a romantic interest of my own on the front step with tears streaming down her cheeks. She told me that Trudeau had dropped her because she was becoming too serious. Another time, I took a particularly interesting young woman to a dinner with Trudeau. She had just returned from the Middle East, where she had narrowly missed being forced into sexual servitude by a member of the local ruling family. The next day, Trudeau tracked down her phone number and invited her over to 24 Sussex for an evening swim. I was not mentioned.

Yet another time, when an attractive female TV personality and I interviewed Trudeau at the CTV studios, the lights on the set had barely dimmed before Trudeau whisked his new acquaintance away for dinner, leaving me eating his dust. Never did I hear any of these women speak disparagingly of him, nor did any of them try to exploit their affairs for momentary fame. Their discretion was amazing, though not all were left enchanted by the experience. On a hiking trip with Trudeau into Banff National Park in 1978, I witnessed a mix-up that caught him out in a genuine faux pas.

The night before the climb, we had met in Trudeau's suite at the Chateau Lake Louise for pre-dinner drinks. As usual, he had an attractive young woman with him whom he had invited to join us for the next day's hike. While a small group of us were chatting, a member of Trudeau's security entourage came over and whispered something in his ear. He reacted by slapping his forehead in a gesture that said *Oh, my God*. I assumed that he must have received distressing news of serious national import and my reporter's ears perked up. Moments later, another stunning young woman joined us, and it soon became apparent that the prime minister of Canada had unwittingly double-booked himself. Needless to say, neither of the ladies was happy with the situation.

Trudeau tried gently to push one of the women in my direction, and since I was unaccompanied, nothing would have pleased me more. But she was having none of it. In a manner that would have made any good feminist despair, the two women began to fling catty remarks at each other, deepening Trudeau's embarrassment. Finally, when it came time for dinner, no further prevarication was possible. He had to decide which woman would sit next to him. After a brief flurry of musical chairs, the woman less favoured made her unhappiness known. She told everyone at the table how she had met a member of the prime minister's RCMP security detail while on a trip to Hawaii. He told her, she claimed, that so many women were coming and going from 24 Sussex they could not keep track of them all for security purposes. Trudeau replied: "Would you be able to recall that Mountie's name? I would like to arrange for him to spend the rest of his career mushing huskies in Tuktoyaktuk."

Trudeau's third term began with the heady victory of a majority government in 1974, but the mood soon soured. By the next year, the oil crisis was upon us, the economy sank and inflation soared, and Finance Minister John Turner resigned in open defiance of Trudeau's leadership. Two months later, the government introduced wage-and-price controls to widespread public protest. At the same time, Trudeau was badly distracted by the collapse of his marriage and deeply concerned about the welfare of his sons. Senior aides were instructed that nothing short of a national emergency could be permitted to interfere with his time with the boys. His attention to the job was not what it had been, and his government began to drift.

Despite or perhaps because of the malaise, those were hedonistic times for many in the Liberal government. Trudeau himself never tolerated the use of drugs and drank hardly at all, but among his aides, a few ministers, and the occasional high-ranking bureaucrat, such recreational consumables were part of the lifestyle. The parties were raunchier, the sex easy, and the pot ubiquitous. It was one protracted end-of-an-era blowout before the 1979 collapse.

Watching Trudeau from the press gallery or from the bow of a canoe was to see a contradiction personified, a man caught between idealism and realism. In his early political days, he sought a dialogue with Canadians based on reason and rationality. Instead, the masses were ready to follow him blindly, without question—the opposite of what he professed to want. The idealism was quickly set aside in 1972, when it looked as if Trudeau might lose his second election campaign. He turned himself over to the party's backroom boys and submitted to a campaign of endless photo ops in which even his flower-child wife was exploited.

Some denounced Trudeau's reluctance to get down and dirty in politics, and did their best to help him do it. Such a moment came early in the 1974 election campaign when the campaign managers decided to send Trudeau on a photogenic and seemingly up-close-and-personal train trip. In his private car one morning, Trudeau sat down for coffee with one of his political gurus. The fellow had worked long and hard to keep Trudeau in office and he was blunt. "I would like you to put me in the Senate," he said. "Absolutely not," Trudeau replied, and left the room. The individual never did get the reward many thought automatic. Referring to Trudeau's indignant reaction to this frank appeal for an appointment, one of the campaign staff murmured, "What the hell does he think it's all about, anyway?"

But by the spring of 1979, Canadians were fed up with the Liberals and with a prime minister who seemed increasingly remote, arrogant, and unconcerned. A fatalistic gloom took hold of the government benches and one senior member of the Cabinet told me frankly that his own government had become "an essentially corrupt operation." Within weeks of the 1979 election campaign launch, Trudeau and his aides knew they would lose, yet according to one of them, Colin Kenny, the prime minister never became angry or irritable even as he endured the rigours of cross-country travel and the animosity of hostile crowds.

Kenny recalls that one wet night during a long car ride to some town or other, Trudeau reminisced about another rainy night, this one from his childhood, when he was invited to join his father and his friends at the family kitchen table while they drank, gambled, and told stories. His father made a ten-thousand-dollar wager with one of his drinking buddies that depended on which line of raindrops would win the race to the bottom of the windowpane. On another occasion, Trudeau watched while his father and another man stepped outside to settle a fifteen-thousand-dollar bet on who could piss the farthest.

According to Kenny, Trudeau was serene and graceful in defeat, telling his devastated staff that the sun would rise the next day and "we will enjoy our lives." After handing in his resignation to the Governor General a few days later, he hopped into his open 190 SL Mercedes convertible, threw his arms up, and shouted, "Free at last, free at last," stealing a line from Martin

Luther King. In private, however, he seemed lost and even lonely. He buoyed himself by maintaining the conviction that he would be back in office. To most observers, this seemed a delusion. In a capital obsessed with power, the conventional wisdom was that his time was over.

Many Liberals who once would have begged to touch the hem of Trudeau's coat now were writing him off. Some felt safe in letting old complaints and grievances about him surface. No doubt he felt the hurt of the long fall from power, but he tried not to show it. When I had dinner with him after he'd moved into Stornoway, the Opposition leader's residence, I found the tables stocked with the house matchboxes from 24 Sussex Drive. He said he had brought them with him to save the Treasury money when he moved back. It was clear to me that he was uncomfortable, however, and I felt sure he would step down as Liberal leader.

Not long after, I got a call from Trudeau asking if I could come over to his office and bring a cameraman. I found him in a rare emotional state. He had decided to quit, he informed me, because he wanted to spend as much time as possible with his sons. He would give me the only television interview on the matter, an extraordinary coup. Shortly after the camera started to roll, I heard a dreaded click from the film magazine. The cameraman had forgotten to reload; we were out of film. Would Trudeau do it all over again, please? No, he would not, and moreover the confessional moment when he was prepared to talk about the overwhelming demands of political leadership had passed. He knew he had revealed his vulnerability and was not about to make the same mistake again. Trudeau's official announcement of his intention to step down as Liberal leader came in June. Most Canadians believed they had seen the last of him and turned their attention to the newly elected Tories.

It has always been my motto to "stay in with the outs" because the outs have a way of coming back. A crop of younger Conservatives—Don Mazankowski, Ray Hnatyshyn, and John Crosbie—refused to wallow in self-pity and recrimination after their defeat back in 1974, and I was glad to give them airtime while they warmed the Opposition benches. They were a canny lot who knew how to get under the skin of the Liberals, and they made for good television in the process. Like unindicted co-conspirators, reporters cultivate and befriend politicians who are out of power in a way that is impossible with those in the ruling party. I cannot say, though, that Joe Clark was on my radar.

One day in February 1976, I was working in the hot room at the House of Commons when I received a phone call from the office of a Member of Parliament I had never heard of. The Conservative Party national convention had just convened in Ottawa and my caller was a flack from the office of Joe Clark. Clark was a little-known MP from Alberta whose bid for the leadership the press corps regarded as a joke. Did anyone want to do a one-on-one interview with Mr. Clark, was the offer. I covered the mouthpiece and shouted out the question to the room. Laughs and jeers. "Too busy," I said—a telling tribute to my prescience and that of my colleagues.

The main contenders were Brian Mulroney and Claude Wagner, two Quebecers who despised each other. Wagner was a former Liberal who had run for the leadership of the provincial party, losing to Robert Bourassa. The Conservatives recruited Wagner and he accepted monies from a secret slush fund to make the move, a fact he denied to Mulroney. Wagner was stiff and formal in contrast to Mulroney's garrulous Irish personality. At the convention, they became locked in a balloting impasse, their respective supporters refusing to change their votes. This allowed Joe Clark to come up the middle and pull off one of the most stunning leadership upsets in history.

A few days later, Clark visited his new office in the Opposition leader's suite in the East Block and I stood beside him while one of my colleagues tossed on his desk the *Toronto Star* with the headline "JOE WHO?" across the front. Joe laughed, but it would be years before he could live down that nickname. His receding chin became a symbol of his supposed timidity as a leader, and he was taunted for his physical awkwardness, his wife's refusal to take his name, and the fact that he had never held a permanent job outside of politics and had no real interests other than a devotion to public policy.

I soon discovered Clark to be better than his critical press: always a thoroughly decent, thoughtful person without an ounce of mean-spiritedness. Yet many looked upon even these admirable qualities as evidence of a weak character. He couldn't win.

Shortly after he took the Tory leadership, Clark decided to do a tour of British Columbia, perhaps the most disastrous ever seen in Canadian political circles. The party organization failed him completely. En route up the coast, in one small town after another, scheduled events never happened. On more than one occasion, when our Otter float plane pulled up at the local docks, not a soul would be there to greet the new leader. Reporters called taxis for the whole group to get us into one town or another, where more often than not Clark would go unrecognized at public events. When he met with the media, Clark initially insisted that the local press be allowed the first questions. At one stop, the town's reporter savaged him with charges that he was a loser who wouldn't survive in the job. Clark, smiling, turned to the national press, and pleaded for some actual questions.

It was in northern British Columbia, where the reception was no better, that Clark locked horns with Mom. I had chronicled this rolling debacle night after night on the national news. Finally and mercifully, we neared the end of the trip, which by sheer coincidence was to wrap up in Prince Rupert. Clark hoped to rescue himself with a final news conference at the Rupert airport. Mom, of course, was there to see me off and sat with me in the press section.

When I stood to ask a question, Maureen McTeer cut me off with an ill-tempered declaration: "There goes Craig Oliver already, crapping on my husband again." I sat down speechless, but not Mom, who had probably had more than a few drinks by this time. She warned McTeer to shut up and leave her little boy alone, or she would come over and do her serious harm. Clark intervened to cool his wife and I did the same with Mom.

The Vancouver media loved it, presenting the confrontation between a reporter's mother and the Opposition leader's wife as a front-page story. Joe Clark made it worse for himself when he denied that Maureen would ever use the word *crapping*, as the journalists had reported. Their audiotapes proved otherwise and kept the story going for another day. Always the first to do the decent thing, Clark sought me out to apologize, but the incident had made the national news. When I got back to Ottawa, I ran into Trudeau in a Commons corridor. "You have never scared me for a minute," he said, "but I sure don't want to run up against your mother!"

In 1979, the prime minister's mantle came too soon for Joe Clark. Being a political leader is like being the lead canine in a dogsled team. You have to be tougher and smarter than all the other dogs and fight to keep your position every day. It was an open secret in Ottawa that there were two hard-core Conservatives whose mission it was to bring Clark down: MP Bob Coates and Coates's chief of staff, Rick Logan. A third individual, Pat McAdam, who worked for Conservative MP Gordon Taylor, was also put on salary at Iron Ore of Canada where Mulroney was president, though his main occupation was to organize against Clark on Mulroney's behalf. These genial assassins regularly graced the press club or the press gallery hot room, leaking the latest plot against Clark to the eager scribes. It was not in Clark's character to become as mean, cunning, or duplicitous as some of those who opposed him.

Clark had savoured his election victory for barely twenty-four hours before he undermined his own credibility. During the election campaign, he had promised unwisely to move the Canadian embassy in Israel from Tel Aviv to Jerusalem. All of us knew such a move was impossible; it was an affront to the Arab world that would have cost Canada dearly, and a serious reversal of Canada's long-running policy on the issue. Of course, the move was bitterly opposed by our own Department of External Affairs, whose mandarins made no secret of their view. We all assumed Clark would drop the campaign rhetoric and gradually let the idea die.

At his first news conference as prime minister, Clark had the opportunity to backtrack. I raised the issue in the opening question. But he insisted on his determination to follow through, adding for good measure that it was time the bureaucrats at

External got the message and understood who was in charge. The neophyte was displaying a touch of arrogance. A wiser and more confident leader would have nuanced the issue. Clark felt the need to prove his toughness, but he had stumbled right out of the gate. Eventually former PC leader Robert Stanfield was appointed to make recommendations—"Stanfield of Arabia," we called him—and of course he told Clark to forget it.

Clark's able Cabinet soon settled into middle-of-the-road progressive administration, six seats short of a majority but governing well. Sadly, Clark himself was running far behind his party in popularity and respect. The Tories had inherited a large deficit from the free-spending Trudeauites, and a critical policy objective was to bring the budget and the economy back on track.

Then came December 13, 1979. That day I had lunch in the parliamentary restaurant with Don Mazankowski, then minister of Transport and a man widely respected for his unshakeable good nature and personal integrity. Mazankowski told me the government was heading for a vote that night on Finance Minister John Crosbie's budget. This short-lived document was an early effort at deficit-reduction and might have saved Canadians considerable misery in future years, but it was hugely unpopular. If he wanted to, Maz said, Clark could dodge the confidence vote, but the government intended to allow itself to be defeated. I was dumbfounded. The Liberals were running high in the polls in Quebec and Ontario and the Conservatives' gambit seemed suicidal. Maz appeared to doubt the wisdom of the decision, but he was nothing if not loyal. Clark's brain trust apparently judged the polls wrongly and believed they could beat the Liberals and win a solid majority.

That night they were defeated on a budget vote in a raucous

Commons session. Clark's many detractors claimed he lost because he couldn't count, but it was worse than that. Clark and his circle knew they would go down and they let it happen. Ironically, one of the least arrogant men I ever met in politics was defeated by his own hubris.

Equally ironic were the repercussions for the country, for without the Conservatives' miscalculation, Trudeau would never have had a chance to return to power. Most people forget that Trudeau had announced his resignation as leader and had no intention of returning. After the Commons defeat of the Conservatives, Keith Davey went to Trudeau on bended knee and begged him to stay on as leader for one more trip to the polls.

I spent every moment of the 1980 campaign with Clark, a heartbreaking exercise that went from bad to worse. The reporters travelling with him, including me, taunted him unmercifully. Certain of Clark's qualities had become fixations in the minds of his travelling press, and we sought out comments or situations that fitted those and made for an easily understandable story. Unfortunately, he helped us out. We all had a field day when he made a speech in Prince Edward Island—"Spud Island"— about "potato power." Small errors or gaffes that would have been ignored elsewhere were magnified and given far more space in the narrative than they deserved. Meantime, Trudeau's return to the field was warmly welcomed and on his plane a largely adoring press crowd allowed him a comparatively free ride. It didn't hurt that some of Trudeau's key aides were literally in bed with principal reporters.

As the Clark campaign gradually slid off the rails, an ugly mood took hold. Near the end, on one late-night flight from Halifax to Vancouver, the press corps bottomed out. We had loaded up with lobsters and wine before leaving, and within a few hours everyone was roaring drunk. The floor of the plane was littered with empty bottles and lobster shells crunched under foot. At one point, a reporter forced his attentions on an airline hostess in her compartment in the back. Two of us had to drag him off the distraught woman. She was allowed to leave the campaign plane crew, but no one ever disciplined the journalist.

In an all-too-familiar example of Tory infighting, even Clark's allies in the provinces turned against him. On a visit to the Ontario premier, Bill Davis, Clark's aides tried desperately to persuade us that the two leaders were equals. But one of the premier's top aides had been assigned to tell us privately in what low esteem Clark was actually held by the Conservative government of the country's largest province. They would, he indicated, even welcome a return of the Liberals to power. I spent a whole night drinking with Southam News columnist Charles Lynch and the New Brunswick premier, Dick Hatfield. Hatfield regaled us with stories of how the party intended to "put Clark on the cross and crucify him" after he lost the election.

The nadir was Clark's interview in Vancouver with the redoubtable talk-show host Jack Webster. In his rough Scottish brogue, Webster started the interview by stating flatly, "Yer finished, Joe Clark. Yer finished and ya know it." It was, in a sense, a moment of truth. Anyone on the bus who might have been uncertain about the election outcome was uncertain no longer. From then on, the accepted wisdom was that we were travelling with the loser.

On the morning of February 18, the last event of the Clark campaign took place on top of the CN Tower in Toronto. As a magnificent sun rose over Lake Ontario, a girl sang the most popular song from the musical *Annie*. The words were perfect: "Tomorrow, tomorrow, I love ya tomorrow ..." Maureen McTeer began to cry, Joe Clark's eyes were wet, and most of their hard-core supporters were choked with emotion. We flew that day to Clark's Alberta riding for the election night results. I told our viewers that Clark had been graceful in defeat. More than that, I had never seen him display bitterness or anger or self-pity throughout the whole ordeal.

I did my best to cover Joe Clark and his short-lived govern-ment carefully and fairly. But thanks to my well-known Liberal connections, it became a delicate matter for me to be critical of Joe without the appearance of bias. My canoe tripping with Trudeau the summer before had drawn attention from the press gallery and among political insiders, and even though I would have had a front-row seat with the new administration, my credibility with viewers had been compromised. Following the 1980 election, Don Cameron, who had returned as the undis-puted czar of CTV's news department, and I agreed that I should move to Washington for a period of political delousing. My exile lasted almost a decade.

Before leaving Canada, I wanted to make a trip back to Prince Rupert to see Mom. During our brief visit near the end of the 1980 election campaign, she had seemed unsettled, but there was no time to investigate. In fact, it was worse than I had imagined. Her beloved Cliff, the only man she had ever loved, had left her for a younger woman. They lived nearby, so Mom could not avoid them and every encounter broke her heart a little more.

His abandonment reinforced her already-low self-esteem, and she sought comfort in the bottle.

On the telephone, Mom's distress was clear. At times her conversation was almost incoherent or interrupted by long pauses. Sometimes I would hear a dish or a glass break. She lied about drinking, claiming only to be tired.

Cliff had sold the taxi business that Mom built up over twenty-five years, and their home as well. She received only a small share of the house proceeds and nothing from the sale of their business. I was furious and wanted her to take him to court. Even after he left town, she said she couldn't do it; she loved him still.

Mom took a job running a seedy motel on the edge of town, the Totem Lodge, where she stripped the beds, did the cleaning, and worked the front desk day and night for a rough clientele. She kept a small .22 calibre Harrington & Richardson revolver in the desk drawer. More than once when a rowdy gang of road workers was tearing a room apart, Mom found comfort in knowing the revolver was handy. She turned the motel into a money-making operation for the owners, who had the decency to give her a large cash settlement when she left the place a decade later.

Throughout these years she sank into depression more easily and drank more heavily. She had only short-lived romantic liaisons and must have suffered terrible loneliness, but she would not let on, nor would she leave Rupert. A thousand times she assured me she was okay and promised to stay on the wagon. I knew better, but it was what I wanted to believe.

4

INTO THE CANOES

In 1973, friends in the Yukon had invited me to join them in a month-long expedition along the Trail of '98 on the seventy-fifth anniversary of that famous trek. The route took us hiking across the Coast Mountains along the historic Gold Rush Trail, over the Chilkoot Pass, and then north by canoe from Lake Bennett at the headwaters of the Yukon River to Dawson, the city of gold. The paddling on this slow-moving river was relatively easy for the novices in the party, of which I was one.

At Hootalinqua, a camp spot along the river, I slept in the open under a canopy of stars so dazzling I might have been gazing through an observatory telescope. It seemed every star in the cosmos was suspended overhead, clear and distinct, a sight to send the spirit soaring. The expanding universe must be one of humankind's most profound discoveries. If the universe is not static, then how did it begin? And does not everything that is set in motion have to come to an end? As these thoughts played out in my mind, some lighting man in the sky switched on the northern lights, aurora borealis. Better than Oscar Night in Los Angeles, they were nature's searchlights, criss-crossing each other and beaming up into the infinity of the heavens.

The experience of that trip was transcendent, and so powerful that it started a network of friends and me on a lifetime of wilderness travel by canoe. I relished the escape from the weight of workday routine and was lured into unknown terrain where the outcome of the journey could never be fully predicted. Over three decades, we ventured out to some of the most remote places on the continent, paddling sections of every major watershed from the Pacific to the Atlantic. Drawn ever farther north while we grew in skill and experience, we were eventually stopped only by the end of open water at the top of the world. We made the first descents in modern times of seven Arctic rivers, including the Ruggles on Ellesmere Island, said to be the world's most northerly navigable river. In Alaska we shot down the Noatak, the last major watercourse before the continent ends. Other years we paddled through swimming herds of migrating caribou and alongside pods of whales and curious grey seals, their heads bobbing up from the waves to look us over. All this we did before the recent boom in ecotourism and before magazines like *Outside* and *Canadian Geographic* made such adventures popular and commonplace.

These journeys lay in the future when I returned to Toronto from the exhilaration of the Yukon in August 1973. I soon found a kindred spirit in CBC executive producer Tim Kotcheff. Though I had moved to CTV, making us professional competitors, we remained good friends. Tim was a fisherman and experienced camper, neither of which I could claim to be, but we had both read about the then remote and much-fabled Nahanni River and we agreed to canoe it together. We trained hard, devoting months to canoeing and map-reading courses and practising on the French and Magnetawan rivers in Ontario. We would run the rapids, then drag our canoes back upriver to run them again, dumping on purpose until we were no longer terrified of the churning currents. In 1974, we set out for the Northwest Territories and the Nahanni.

Nowadays, much of the Nahanni River is a National Park Reserve, and so heavily travelled that camp spots must be booked in advance. But when Tim and I first visited, it was the wildest of untouched rivers. The Nahanni rises in the Mackenzie Mountains near the border between the Northwest Territories and the Yukon in an area never flattened by the ancient glaciers. The river has worn into the rock for thousands of years, forming canyon walls that in places tower 1200 metres straight up and justify the reputation of that part of the river's course as the Grand Canyon of Canada. As it races southeast toward its confluence with the Laird River, the Nahanni picks up speed and volume. Just past the halfway point, it crashes over spectacular Victoria Falls, twice the height of Niagara.

Legend had rendered the Nahanni full of mystery, with tales of the notorious Headless Valley and warnings of dangerous, thick mists that shrouded its limestone canyons. We decided to paddle the lower stretch where the river was fast and cold with a few rapids that were tricky dumpers. We were frankly nervous about doing it alone. Grizzlies abounded, and the RCMP detachment in Watson Lake advised us to take a weapon when we checked in with them in advance of our expedition.

Before breaking camp one morning, Tim and I decided to see if we could actually hit anything with my old Colt .45 revolver. We blasted away for a while with practice shots, and then packed up hurriedly as a heavy rain rolled in. Rather than stow the revolver with my gear in the bottom of our canoe as usual, I shoved it into a holster under my waterproof poncho. Tim and I wasted no time in hitting the fast current.

Late that afternoon, we were surprised to see a wisp of smoke in the distance and a prospectors' tent pitched just above the river-bank. Two dishevelled and rather rough-looking figures waved to get our attention. They introduced themselves as prospectors, searching for the reputed lost gold seam that Indians claimed lay waiting up the Flat River, a tributary of the Nahanni. They were almost out of food, they told us. We had plenty; in fact, we were very clearly overloaded with supplies. I spotted a shotgun by the tent belonging to the prospectors and thought they should be able to hunt at least, but we handed over a five-pound can of chicken. The bald, talkative one gave us a wide grin that revealed a missing tooth. The other spoke little, but stared hard at our high-detail aerial survey maps. They had never seen charts like these. It occurred to me that the maps might arouse suspicion that we too were gold seekers.

Tim and I were about to take our leave when the bald fellow invited us to see the remains of a cabin built by R.M. Patterson, author of the classic work on the South Nahanni, *The Dangerous River*. They said it was only a short walk into the bush. After twenty minutes of trudging through the rain-soaked, murky forest, I began to feel uneasy. I have always had an overactive imagination, so perhaps I was mistaken that every time I tried to drop back to the end of the line, one of the men found a pretense to wait me out. Both carried large sheath knives. As the walk continued, we all fell silent, stomping through the thick bush. I put my hands under my poncho for warmth and unexpectedly found the pistol grip.

Finally the leader stopped and turned toward us. So did the one behind me. For a few seconds no one moved or spoke, yet in that moment of suspended time, I felt a frisson of genuine fear. I slipped my finger inside the trigger guard. Then the tension suddenly broke as one of the fellows pointed to a pile of logs, the remains of Patterson's cabin. I felt ridiculous about it later; as a rule, I am repelled by confrontation or violence. Yet I knew for certain I would have shot the first one who pulled a knife. Were the poor fellows showing a courtesy to unexpected visitors or did they change their murderous minds at the last minute? I'm still not sure.

Over the course of this trip and others, Tim and I learned our strengths and weaknesses as a paddling duo. Chiefly we learned that when the course of the river dropped out of sight, as if falling off the end of the earth, the rapids ahead had to be approached with respect. Some close calls brought on the slow realization that to paddle as a twosome was foolhardy: No help would be available if we capsized in those icy waters. Moreover, forced into such close company for weeks on end, we sometimes grew testy. Arguments were few but inevitable. There was no one else to mediate, no one else with whom we could blow off steam.

This was never more apparent than during a long duet down the Pelly River in the Yukon in 1975. After surviving a confusing rapid, Tim and I disagreed loudly over who was to blame for almost wrapping our canoe around a rock. Anger collapsed into sullen silence. Making camp by a desolate, muddy, and mosquito-infested riverbank, I rejected Tim's suggestion that the boat be brought up fifty yards into our campsite. I retain an image of Tim looking like Humphrey Bogart in a scene from *The African Queen* as, knee-deep in mud and with the bow rope wrapped around his shoulder, he dragged the leaden canoe up an incline into camp while I sat sipping a glass of overproof rum.

The silence continued on the river the next day and was finally broken when Tim spoke up. "You know what?"

I was glad the dispute seemed behind us and replied, "No, what?"

"You are an asshole," he announced, "and more than that, everyone in Toronto thinks so." Our work lives and the big city thousands of miles away had intruded. I was forced to consider that every time I walked down Queen Street or Jarvis, all the passersby held me in secret contempt.

All such bickering faded when Tim and I focused on the more immediate perils of our expeditions. Once we had acknowledged that travelling such remote cold-water rivers on our own was too risky, we opted for safety in numbers by founding a larger canoe group. As a nod to my new Ottawa address, we named ourselves the "Rideau Canal and Arctic Canoe Club" and began to recruit members.

In the years following, some fifteen other men joined us on one or more trips, with a hard core of eight who seldom missed a season. The job of official inviter and social convener fell to me, although the veterans had a limited right of veto over new candidates. Some who joined our little company of adventurers in spite of the objections of existing members are now the closest friends of the protesters. I will never tell.

Weaving together a team for an expedition does require serious planning. The logistics of food and transportation are critical, as is the choice of river and prior study of its hazards. We never took a guide, though I would have welcomed a Sherpa more than once. Every trip can absorb one relative beginner if the rest of the crew are seasoned wilderness paddlers. Those who savour travel by canoe are often loners by nature, but the dangers of paddling in remote places make the support of companions essential. There is always a tension between individual and group interests, and often the self has to be sublimated to the needs of the state.

Vanity and ego make unwelcome travelling companions in life and on rivers. Everyone must agree on common goals as the only way to prevent disputes and maintain even tempers when the going gets tough. (I recall one canoeist who literally foamed at the mouth, yelling at the group to end the trip rather than face what he was convinced would be certain death by drowning downriver.) After a good-natured personality, the next priority is compatibility. People who share similar interests and a like-minded view of the world are obviously the easiest to spend time with in close company. If sharp disagreements occur and tempers rise, there is nowhere to go.

I established the practice, soon an annual ritual, of polling friends and likely candidates every fall to solicit interest in an expedition for the following summer. In the early years most of us were single, with good jobs that allowed for the expense of state-of-the-art gear and the cost of commercial flights to a jumping-off point in the north, followed by private charters to some remote destination in the High Arctic.

Just as mountain climbers keep a list of iconic peaks so too did we compile a catalogue of desirable rivers. Winter evenings were spent searching maps, looking for an obscure waterway that no one else had heard of, measuring its vertical drop, judging its velocity, and discovering the waterfalls or other obstacles that would require portage. During a reunion a few weeks before spring, we chose that year's river from among the collective wish list. There was little room for debate over when to go: Depending on latitude, we had only a narrow window of decent weather between mid-July and mid-August. We then assigned or reconfirmed the logistical duties and arranged ourselves in paddling pairs.

Tim Kotcheff and I were a smooth-operating duo by the mid-seventies and naturally formed up one of the canoes. With Tim and his faulty hearing in the bow and I with my poor eyesight in the stern, we were dubbed the "Affirmative Action Canoe." I was able to hear big water ahead, and shortly after Tim would be able to see it and then direct me where to steer. Early on, Tim became our acknowledged river master, always careful and cautious but ready to take calculated risks. As his family was in the restaurant business, he also assumed the role of one of two head chefs in the party. I took on responsibility for the pre-dinner happy hour, pouring out two carefully measured rum daiquiris per man per night under watchful eyes.

Among the early joiners was Peter Stollery, then a Member of Parliament for Toronto Spadina and later a senator. Peter is the most physically brave person I have ever met, the man you want to be next to in the trench during the tumult of battle, though not necessarily afterwards. He is the guy who will win the Victoria Cross posthumously.

Ted Johnson was executive assistant to Prime Minister Trudeau when I first met him, and he soon assumed a leadership role in navigation, knowing more than any of us about compass directions, canoe repair, and the emergency radio. He and I did much of the advance work, canvassing northern outfitters for canoes to rent and booking aircraft and hotel rooms.

Ted was our official historian as well, a keeper of detailed notes, and a student of Arctic history and geography, researching the relevant explorers' journals. On the Back River, we had nightly readings about the lost Franklin expedition and ended the trip at Starvation Cove on the Arctic coast within sight of the permanent pack ice that trapped Franklin's two ships forever.

David Silcox was an author and a nationally respected arts bureaucrat. I was doubtful when his name first arose. We had never met and I had in mind the stereotype of a retiring and limp-wristed Prufrock. Instead, along came a fellow built like a truck driver and just as down to earth, resolute, and strong. While others were considering what to do, David simply did it. He shared the head-chef hat with Tim.

John Godfrey was the trip intellectual and philosopher. A university professor when I first knew him, he later became a distinguished Liberal MP from Toronto and a member of Paul Martin's Cabinet. He insisted we devote attention to our intellectual as well as physical nourishment and proposed that we plan a list of topics for campfire conversation, along with a reading program. But he was no wimp. In fact he was unflappable under the most trying circumstances.

In a serious wreck on the Korok River in 1982, John's canoe went down for good. Having managed to survive a swim down a series of cascading ledges, he came ashore on the other side of the river. We could see him yelling from the far bank but could not make out his meaning above the incessant roar of the water. Thinking he might be hurt, I waded out as far as I dared to catch his words. "Time for a group photo!" he bellowed. The resulting picture shows five men lined up in front and a tiny figure waving in the far background.

Every group has to have its contrarian and we loved ours. Bill Williams was the camp doctor, an outstanding cardiologist with Ottawa's Heart Institute. With penetrating intelligence, Bill tested our diagnoses of conditions on the rivers and often chose his own path through a rapid rather than follow the lead canoe. In medicine or in river travel, I never found cause to doubt his judgment.

Eddie Goldenberg is famous as the lifetime shadow of Jean Chrétien, serving him as friend and adviser in good times and bad. Eddie's approach to wilderness travel was simple: Go slow and above all take no unnecessary chances—the same strategic advice he gave Chrétien for years. As for his skill as a canoeist, it must be said Eddie often had more heart than talent. For keen insight and understanding of his fellow paddlers, though, he could not be matched.

Robert Fowler was a rising mandarin in the Foreign Affairs Department when he joined the group; later he would serve as foreign policy adviser to three prime ministers: Trudeau, Turner, and Mulroney. After distinguished performance in other top public service posts, he became Canada's longest-serving ambassador to the United Nations and went on to do important work for Canada and the United Nations internationally. In 2008, Bob emerged alive and feisty after five months as the hostage of al Qaeda kidnappers in Niger. His survival was no surprise to those of us who had witnessed his tenacity on so many northern forays.

Denis Harvey was a much-admired news executive, one-time editor-in-chief of the *Toronto Star,* and later the head of CBC English television, though a blunt-speaking and demanding boss. An active life as an amateur athlete had led Denis to multiple surgeries and so many artificial body parts that we called him the "Bionic Paddler," yet his steel knees did not keep him from several hardship trips.

Lawyer and later Liberal Cabinet minister Allan Rock was always a great asset with his unshakeable good humour and concern for the needs of others. There was a strict rule that, no matter how bad the weather or the circumstances, he who drew duty for the dishes did them alone, allowing others to look after their personal affairs after the evening camp. At the end of one of the worst days I can recall—a dangerous paddle in high winds across a lake so broad the shoreline could not be seen—that night's dirty dishes fell to me. It was wet and cold and the insects were merciless. Everyone disappeared into their tents, leaving me with pots, pans, plates, and utensils from what had been a greasy meal of several courses. Everyone, that is, but Allan. I warned him that when his turn came I would not return the favour. Canoe rules are a brutal business. To my great relief, Allan scrubbed away by my side and would not quit until I could fall exhausted into my sleeping bag.

Every time we had a trip where events went against us, John Macfarlane swore never to come again. But every season when the roll call was taken, he was there. In professional life, John was a magazine editor and publisher, at one time also a book publisher and broadcasting executive. On our trips, he was the camp sophisticate, assistant chef, and Tastevin, who took seriously his assignment of choosing the correct wines and providing a printed daily menu.

And what menus they were. The gorp-and-granola set in the Wilderness Canoe Association has often criticized our group for its high-living cuisine on the rivers. But there is no reason why canoeists on a long trip have to eat farty freeze-dries unless they regard privation as part of the sport. The canoe is designed to carry freight and there can never be too much good food and wine except on a portage. The idea was to plan the trip so that each day's meals were prepared and packed in advance and the heaviest food and canned goods eaten before the toughest overland treks.

We transported a reinforced cardboard box designed by chefs Kotcheff and Silcox. It contained layered compartments to provide insulation, with a block of dry ice on the lowest level. Since in the Arctic the nights were cool and the days seldom really warm, fresh meats, even ice cream, could be preserved for up to twelve days. Typical dinner fare was that of August 1, 1990, two weeks into that year's trip on Melville Peninsula: *Smoked Salmon with One Beer Each, Grilled New York Strip Steak and Mushrooms, Pan-fried New Potatoes, Caesar Salad,* and a 1985 California Central Coast Pinot Noir.

A few others joined us when they could, among them Bill Fox, the witty communications director for Brian Mulroney, and Quebec author and CBC French news executive Jean Pelletier, son of Gérard Pelletier, one of the "three wise men" brought from Quebec to Ottawa by Lester Pearson. Trudeau Cabinet ministers Judd Buchanan and Hugh Faulkner were occasional companions.

In 1975, we did the Pelly River in the Yukon; in 1976, the Missinaibi near Chapleau, Ontario. The next year we went to the Northwest Territories and the Snare River; in 1978, it was the Noatak River in Alaska. The summer of 1979 found us on the Hanbury and Thelon rivers, back in the Northwest Territories, and in 1980 we paddled the Hood.

All of us shared either politics or journalism, and lively, uninhibited debate was never lacking. Only twice did a disagreement between individuals result in a permanent fracture: One was a searing argument over the Middle East that deteriorated into personal insult, and the other erupted over the choice of a campsite after a miserable fourteen hours of paddling—a testament to the gruelling conditions that could warp otherwise reasonable minds.

Most of us were in our early thirties when we started out and of course we had long discussions about women, the focus of which shifted over the years from opportunistic sex to relationship survival to ultimate resignation or enviable contentment. We shared private thoughts and fears in a way that is possible only when a bond of absolute trust and loyalty has been tested and found firm. On the worst days, when everything that could go wrong did, John Macfarlane was fond of declaring, "the Huns may throw everything they've got at us, but we can take it!" That comment brought to mind Shakespeare's *Henry V* and his salute to his "band of brothers" before the Battle of Agincourt. A stretch, perhaps, but a sentiment that came close to my feelings for our own happy few.

On any river, a cardinal rule of survival is that every canoe is responsible for the canoe behind it. If a craft is lost from sight around a bend, one must stop paddling or even pull over until the follower reappears. The brigade moves at the speed of the slowest canoe, preventing the convoy from becoming too strung out and its members losing contact.

This practice was faithfully observed except on one occasion: on the Nahanni, which I traversed for a second time in 1978. When we reached our agreed-upon nighttime camp spot, one canoe was missing. Judd Buchanan, then the federal minister of Indian Affairs, and his canoe partner, John Gow, were nowhere to be seen. As the leader of that expedition, I felt wholly negligent, but my concern was allayed by the knowledge that Gow was the ultimate survivor.

An experienced mountaineer and former president of the Association of Canadian Mountain Guides, Gow was famous for an incident that had taken place in Alberta a few years earlier. He was a passenger in a light plane searching out a location for a new helicopter ski resort in high-mountain wilderness when the aircraft hit a treetop and crashed. The pilot and a second passenger were killed. While awaiting rescue, Gow knew he should set the plane afire to attract searchers, but he could not bring himself to immolate the bodies of two old friends.

When help failed to arrive, Gow walked in deep snow and freezing temperatures for a week until, close to death, he stumbled into a campsite. His head injuries required plastic surgery and he lost both legs below the knee. Gow later joked that he carried personal insurance against bears as a result: Should a grizzly threaten, Gow intended to throw the bear his artificial foot. That would convince the animal that he and his companions were not worth eating.

Nonetheless, standing watch on the sandbank and gazing upriver into the midnight sun for much of the night, I was gripped by a terrible foreboding. By morning, I was sick with worry and guilt. I tried to paddle upstream to look for the two men, but the powerful Nahanni current made any serious progress impossible. What to do? David Silcox and I decided to head downriver and find help while the remaining six stayed behind in case the lost men showed up.

By pure happenstance, Silcox and I came upon a powered raft, property of the Parks Department, hidden in a cove. We commandeered it and headed back upriver. We found Gow and Buchanan just breaking camp about ten miles above us, in fine form except for mild hangovers. They had made a frying pan out of green boughs, cooked up bacon and toast, and finished a forty-ouncer of Scotch. Despair vanished with the morning mist, replaced by exhilaration. I was even able to join in the laughs when Gow accused me of being the lost one for having sailed past the camp location we'd agreed upon as our destination. Lesson learned.

On these outings, encounters with our fellow men were rare but always memorable. On the Yukon River in 1975, Tim and I had pulled ashore to make necessary use of the great outdoors when we noticed a long-neglected, lopsided log cabin in the woods. Curious about its story, we toured the premises, which still held a store of pots and dishes and boasted tattered chintz curtains. Perhaps a hunter or two had used the cabin during the season, but it had obviously not been permanently occupied for many years. When I idly pulled up a loose floorboard, I found beneath it a bundle of letters—as many as a hundred.

They were a man's love letters, dating from the years following the gold rush to the First World War—nothing steamy, just simple declarations of obvious affection in a somewhat-stilted Victorian style. The notes held the details of the writer's daily life, his poor health, and his abiding regard for his female friend and former companion. They were all signed by *Herb* and addressed to the postmaster in a long-abandoned gold rush town on the river near Dawson City. However, the postmaster was clearly a postmistress. The letters referred to her work carrying the territorial mail on foot and by dogsled up and down the river. I considered taking some of the most affecting correspondence with us, but thought better of it. Too much like grave robbing.

But I did note the name of the intended recipient on the off chance she might still be alive sixty years later. I asked after her at the museum in Dawson. Sure enough, she was living at her home on the outskirts of town. When we arrived at the small, neat house, we found that a faded white cross was nailed to the door. An old gal with a sharp, lively eye opened the door a crack. We told her our story and were invited in for tea. As she made for the kitchen, she laid the old single-shot pistol she'd been carrying on the sideboard.

The cross on the door was in honour of Herb, who had been dead for years. No other man ever courted this woman. He had come up from Seattle in the years after the stampede when many people were still taking out enough gold to make a living. She and Herb had been together for a few years, but the easy hand-mining went dry and he moved south. She never saw him again, nor forgot him.

We were paddling the Snare River in the Northwest Territories in 1977 when we came upon a man in a vague brown uniform sitting on the river's edge, his back turned to us while he studied a cluster of log buildings that might have been hit by a tornado. We shouted a greeting and he swung around, startled, a semi-automatic rifle cradled in his arm.

Hungry grizzly bears whose normal seasonal diet of caribou had been affected by a recent decimation of the herds had besieged this tiny Dogrib village. The evidence of the animals' strength was astonishing. The bears had torn the roofs off sturdily built log homes. In the wrecked storehouse, five-pound cans of food were flattened and punctured clean through by the bears' teeth. The footprint of one beast, captured in spilt flour, was a foot and a half in breadth.

Something was clearly wrong with these animals, since grizzlies are usually shy creatures. The game warden was waiting to kill them if, as expected, they returned. Yet he himself was an odd character. From Florida originally, he was a naturalized Canadian who had served two tours as a Green Beret in Vietnam. No doubt he had seen a lot of death there, and now he was here, killing grizzlies alone. Clearly this was a man who had come to the end of the continent to escape something. The encounter led to later reflection that there are hungry bears inside many of us too, their savage appetites making demands that are hard to resist, regardless of the consequences.

In 1979, I invited Pierre Trudeau to join us for a three-week trip down the Hanbury and Thelon rivers in the central Barren Lands. Trudeau was smarting from the first defeat of his political career at the hands of Joe Clark, and I thought he might find solace and distraction in those lovely and remote rivers. He was an experienced paddler and we had no qualms about his abilities, though his well-known cool demeanour and recent public setback gave some of us pause as to the quality of his company.

Trudeau and I had a mutual friend in Eric Morse, a much-admired guru to generations of wilderness canoeists, whom I had met when I moved to Ottawa in 1974. Morse was in his seventies then, but still tripping with his wife, Pamela. He was a serious scholar of northern travel, paddling, researching, and

writing books on the canoe routes of Arctic explorers and fur
trade voyageurs. The son of a colonial administrator in India,
Eric had an Old World charm combined with a sharp wit. I
spent many delightful hours with him at his habitant-style
home—canoe in the front yard—in the Gatineau Hills north of
Ottawa and on a number of Ontario rivers.

For twenty years, Eric led a group of close friends, most of
them senior public servants, on Arctic canoe trips. When he
was justice minister, Trudeau joined one expedition on a voyage
down the Coppermine River. It was at a party at the Morse
home that I approached the uncharacteristically subdued former
prime minister with the suggestion that he get away from the
political scene for a time and come canoeing with us. He was
intrigued when I proposed that he team up with Jean Pelletier,
son of his oldest friend, Gérard, and he soon accepted.

Trudeau asked for no special treatment, nor did he receive
any. There was no security detail and no retinue of assistants,
and he seemed happy to be free of both. However, it was not
possible to forget whom we were travelling with. At every airport
on flights from Ottawa to Yellowknife, Trudeau was received like
a rock star.

The trip under way, it soon became apparent that
Trudeau's natural leadership ability was not confined to the
political arena, yet he never exerted an assumed authority
or displayed any arrogance. Whenever he felt we should do
something, he outlined his reasons carefully and put them to
the group with no attempt to force his view. Once a course
of action was agreed upon, however, Trudeau could be tough
and unyielding. Though light conversation was not his forte,
he enjoyed a good laugh at clever comments or casual mishaps

along the way. He was careful never to mock anyone who did not find his own situation humorous, and he was also not one to laugh at himself.

Trudeau did the dishes, went for firewood, and helped drag canoes around with everyone else. As a wilderness traveller, he was always disciplined and well prepared. Around the campfire at night, he was quiet and thoughtful, taking only one drink at our evening happy hour. He joined in our conversations, political or otherwise, but would never reveal anything of a personal nature. One of Trudeau's most admirable qualities, as a politician and a man, was a complete lack of bitter or vindictive feelings toward anyone. On that journey, he scolded a member of our group for an unflattering personal assessment of one of his political opponents. "Confine your attack to the policy, not the personality," Trudeau admonished.

We had two uneasy moments on that trip. The first came on a day almost too hot to paddle, when we were drifting lazily with the current. For a while a herd of migrating caribou joined us, hundreds of animals swimming all around us as they forded the river at different crossing points. Occasionally they bumped our canoes, but paid us no more attention than they would floating logs.

The canoes were strung out in line, Trudeau in the foremost with mine close behind. Soon we came upon a group of grizzlies sitting quietly on their haunches on the shoreline. They were obviously trailing the herd and happily digesting a meal of the last straggler they had picked off. To my astonishment, Trudeau pulled up onshore, leapt from his canoe, and trotted toward the big bears that, seeing the former prime minister descending on them, shook themselves and bolted away to a nearby ridge where they sat down again. Trudeau made to follow. I grabbed my heavy-calibre revolver from my day pack and bolted after him. By the time I reached the ridge, the bears had torn off across country, leaving their pursuer alone and apparently disappointed. I was angry and pointed out that his recklessness could have risked the lives of us all had the bears turned on him and others tried to come to his aid.

"Well," he asked, "how many bullets do you have in that gun?"

"Six," I replied.

"No problem," he said.

There had only been five grizzlies.

The other awkward exchange came a few days later. Before the invention of portable satellite positioning gear, navigating by map and compass through the Barren Lands was a chore. On lakes, in particular, where there are few major landmarks, everything looks pretty much the same at water level. We were canoeing through myriad lakes on our way toward the outlet of the Hanbury and had stopped for lunch at the intersection of two, each beckoning in a different direction. I had plotted out a course days before, and even though the compass reading can sometimes appear questionable I had learned never to override it. When lunch ended, Trudeau headed off without comment in the wrong direction. The others followed without question—that charismatic attraction still at work—as I stood sputtering on the shore, warning them of their error. Tim Kotcheff and I stayed on the shoreline while Trudeau led the group five miles down to the end of a sucker bay. Heavy winds and a sharp-edged rain blew in and hit them in the face as they began the hard paddle back to us. As Trudeau rounded the corner to turn into the correct lake, he muttered a line from a then-popular television satire, "Sorry about that, Chief." When Trudeau was out of earshot, someone remarked that as prime minister, he was always leading in the wrong direction but everyone followed him anyway.

Doubtless Trudeau's legacy as a nation builder will be long debated, but his reputation as a fireplace builder is unquestioned. On reaching any campsite, his routine was the same: After assisting his canoe partner with the setup of their tent, he devoted himself to the construction of our cook fire. These were no flimsy, thrown-together structures; Trudeau had the heart of an artist and could probably have become a successful architect. Rocks were carefully chosen, sometimes chipped, and shaped to fit. Sand was the mortar that held all the elements together. Some fireplaces were two-storey jobs with warming ovens complete with doors. Before pots and pans were allowed to rest, a glass of water was placed on the grate to be certain the cooktop was precisely level. Another curious habit of Trudeau's was his need to wash the dishes twice over when he took his turn at dish duty. Once was not enough for this most meticulous of men.

Trudeau was intolerant of the quick and shoddy work of others. I once made the mistake of doing him a favour, or what I thought to be a favour. Without his noticing, I built a perfectly serviceable fireplace while he was still setting out his personal effects under canvas. He walked down to the circle of canoes we always set up around the camp kitchen and gazed with evident contempt at my efforts. Wordlessly, Trudeau swept the whole thing aside with his boot, dropped to his knees, and began to fashion one of his own designs. At this site he discouraged all pretenders by including a chimney.

Even when he was hundreds of miles from the nearest settlement, Trudeau never let go of his sense of who he was or his position in the eyes of the country. Once, when the weather turned so ugly we considered calling in a plane and quitting the trip early, Trudeau would have none of it. Ignoring the rest of the group, his reasoning was simple: "They"—whoever "they" were—"will say I could not do it," he told us. We stayed.

As it happened, there was some criticism of the trip planning on the Hanbury adventure, criticism directed at me as the official organizer. Talk of a canoe group leadership convention arose, but Trudeau was supportive. "Pre-empt them," he advised. "Quit and no one else will want the job and they will beg you to come back."

Two days later a float plane passed low over our group. Trudeau looked up at the circling aircraft and pronounced: "The Clark government has defeated itself and they are coming for me." These were ironic and amusing comments at the time, of course. Except that six months later, the universe unfolded just as he had described.

～

For all of us, there were occasions when our relationships as summer travellers intersected helpfully with our professional lives. Only once did I ever exploit that connection shamelessly.

The year after canoeing the Hanbury I was assigned to Washington, and in the spring of 1980 I was sent to cover the simmering civil war in El Salvador at short notice. Only then did I discover that I had allowed my passport to lapse. An admirably fussy visa officer at the Canadian embassy informed me that I would need someone in a prominent position back home to vouch for my identity, since I did not even have my birth certificate.

In what I concede was an inappropriate answer, I gave her the name of the recently elected prime minister, returned to office after defeating Joe Clark in February. She scolded me for making light of a serious matter. Her tone apparently changed, however, when she heard Trudeau's familiar voice at the other end of the line in Ottawa. He was greatly amused that his fellow river runner needed a character reference.

If the Trudeau connection had been responsible for greasing the skids under my Ottawa tenure, it also opened doors at the Canadian embassy in Washington. America, I concluded, was going to be a great gig.

5

WASHINGTON ASSIGNMENT

I arrived in Washington on the eve of Ronald Reagan's inauguration in 1981, a moment when America was on its ass. The nation's economy was in a deep slump, as was its mood. Interest rates were the highest since the Civil War and inflation ran at double digits. Perhaps worse, the country's confidence had been shaken in November 1979 by the capture of sixty-six American hostages at the U.S. embassy in Iran, an ordeal that lasted well over a year for fifty-two of them. Jimmy Carter, though later regarded as the nation's best-ever past president, proved a weak and indecisive chief executive. Carter's effort to rescue the Americans held prisoner in Teheran, dubbed Operation "Eagle Claw," came apart in military incompetence and death in the desert. It seemed every tree in Washington displayed a commemorative yellow ribbon, constant reminders of a country held captive and a great power rendered impotent.

The inauguration of a first-time president is a powerful tonic for Americans, however, and hope and optimism are soon restored. The ascendancy of Ronald Reagan promised a return to a much earlier era in U.S. history. There would be no more humiliations; it was back to Theodore Roosevelt's policy of "speak softly and carry a big stick." Although in the last days of Carter's presidency his administration had been working mightily behind the scenes to secure the hostages' release, everyone in Washington wanted to believe another story, never confirmed, that shortly before Reagan took office he had sent an ultimatum to the Iranian mullahs: Release the hostages immediately or face the bombing of Teheran. Twenty minutes after Reagan was sworn in, the hostages were on their way home. The exhilaration was palpable among the throngs that lined Pennsylvania Avenue to see the new president pass by.

My own giddiness at kicking off my tenure as CTV's Washington correspondent with this historic event was tempered somewhat by a personal twinge of loss. I had left behind a serious relationship in Ottawa with a woman who did not want to uproot her son or her legal career to follow me south. The reporter I was replacing, Mike McCourt, had already left for his new job with ABC News, and I knew no one in the capital. I felt more than a little forlorn after Harvey Kirck and I finished our upbeat inauguration broadcast that night.

I had found an apartment in a restored late-nineteenth-century brick building on 16th Street, an elegant and leafy avenue that runs straight down to Lafayette Square and the White House. In the plan laid out by French architect Pierre L'Enfant, the street was intended to be a *grande allée*, lined with foreign embassies paying homage to the president. Nowadays, the embassies are scattered across the city, but the street still boasts many grand old buildings, including the famous Hay-Adams Hotel.

As my furniture was being moved in, my neighbour on the

floor—a black U.S. marine officer—asked me wryly if I minded the fact that I was stationed right next to "Indian country." The capital had been desegregated for years, but there was a clear demarcation between the black and white sections of the city, and we were the dividing line. The only other tenant on the floor was a retired U.S. Air Force bomber pilot who had experienced an epiphany during the Cuban Missile Crisis of 1962. It came while he was at the controls of his bomber on an aircraft carrier off the coast of Turkey, waiting for the coded message that would have sent him to destroy a Russian city with his nuclear payload. He passed tension-filled hours with the engine running, not knowing if he would be ordered to take off or stand down, and the experience changed him forever. He left the service after his tour was finished, and when Vietnam took American soldiers into another conflict, he was one of the leaders of the veterans group that opposed the war.

A major concern in relocating to Washington was finding proper medical care for the glaucoma that I had been diagnosed with five years before. Fortunately, one of the world's outstanding glaucoma specialists and researchers, Mansour F. Armaly, practised in Washington, and he agreed to take me on as a patient. I was in good company. His other patients included then vice-president George H.W. Bush and King Hussein of Jordan. My visits to Dr. Armaly's office were always impressive. First I was seen by an assistant or two who took various tests and measurements. Then I was ushered into a spacious consulting room to wait for the great man himself, who arrived with a retinue of attentive interns in his wake. Dr. Armaly was invariably gracious, modest, and gentle, always putting me at ease with a kindly touch on the knee. He was a Palestinian and the many hours I spent in his company over the next few years left me with a lifelong affection for his people.

In Washington's journalistic pecking order, a Canadian reporter ranks just slightly higher than Radio Zambezi. Compared with the kind of access to power we of the CTV crew had dined on at home, Washington was a starvation diet. There might be the rare moment when a Canada-U.S. issue seized the attention of the political class, but most of the time we hovered below their radar. But I had one advantage and it took no forced effort on my part to exploit it: I was a single, straight male in a typical government town full of married men and single women. These smart and ambitious women had come from all over America to be successful in politics, government, or the media, and in the competition for companions the odds were stacked in my favour. Very often the outcome was as much friendship as it was romance, but either way the women I met were far better connected with the capital's political grandees and their staffs than I could ever hope to be.

I considered myself lucky to become a friend of Margaret Carlson, deputy Washington bureau chief for *Time* magazine, and then as now a regular on the network political talk shows. I confess that when I escorted someone as influential as Margaret, I had to park my ego at the door and accept my role as part of the scenery. On one occasion, seated across from one of the nation's most celebrated television news anchors, I dared a conversational sally concerning Canadian premier Richard Hatfield and how he'd been caught carrying marijuana while on tour with the Queen. The acerbic David Brinkley replied, "Does that mean Canada has finally become interesting?"

One of my closest pals was Patricia Ellis, the foreign editor for the *McNeil/Lehrer News Hour*, the PBS program that was a standard-bearer for political reporters and a must-watch for all political junkies. I found Robert McNeil, a native Montrealer raised in the Maritimes, somewhat stiff and formal in his manner, but Jim Lehrer, an easygoing Texan, was his opposite. No doubt this formula accounted for their success as a news anchor team for twenty years.

Pat's own story was the classic American immigrant tale. Her grandfather had arrived in the United States as a penniless Jewish refugee. The immigration officer at Ellis Island gave up on his hard-to-spell Polish name and arbitrarily gave him a new one, Ellis, after the famous reception centre. Eventually he established himself as a successful businessman and formed a close friendship with Theodore Roosevelt, then New York's commissioner of police. Pat's father was a lawyer who set up his first practice with the future agent to the stars, Swifty Lazar. Pat knew everyone and her unaffected warmth and thoughtfulness gave her easy entree to the Washington whirl. I might find myself at a birthday party for the chairman of the Democratic Party one evening and at a dinner with a senior Republican senator the next.

There were other chance connections that I worked to advantage. My Washington producer had once dated Marlin Fitzwater, a press aide to Vice-President Bush and then to Reagan. Fitzwater was a farm boy from Kansas, and we found we shared a small-town-in-the-West kind of kinship. When the U.S.-Canada free trade negotiations became heated, Fitzwater was a valued source, and I suspect he also arranged more Reagan sit-downs for me than a strict rotation between networks would normally have allowed.

Many years before, I had shared the hardship of a climb over the Chilkoot Pass with a California state senator and his wife. They knew Fitzwater's predecessor, James Brady, an immensely popular press secretary to the president. Brady was not one of Nancy Reagan's favourites, arousing her ire with small jokes at her husband's expense. During a presidential campaign stop a few months previous, Reagan had made a bizarre statement about old forests and the threat to human health posed by forest fires. Later, gazing out his window as the candidate's aircraft took off over a national forest, Brady pointed out the sight below to the surrounding reporters and declared in mock horror, "Killer trees!" I connected with Brady soon after my arrival, but we never had the more leisurely get-together we'd promised ourselves.

On March 30, 1981, I was in Toronto for that day's broadcast of *Canada AM*, sitting in for an ailing regular host. After the day's early start, I returned to my hotel room for an afternoon nap, only to be awakened by a telephone call from the newsroom telling me that Reagan had been shot.

It hardly seemed credible. Reagan had been in office less than three months and it was inconceivable that the United States might once again suffer the agony of an assassinated president. The networks were already broadcasting the story that having delivered a speech at the Washington Hilton, a few blocks from the White House, Reagan was about to step into his limousine when a gunman who had inserted himself behind a line of reporters started shooting. I was supposed to be there, covering his address to the Construction Trade Unions. Soon I was on a Learjet booked by the network and headed for George Washington Hospital.

The White House line was that Reagan was fine, that his condition was not life-threatening. But the chaos and sense of crisis at the hospital, where ashen-faced staff and relatives hurried past the media scrum, belied the official assurances. Only later did we learn he had nearly died from loss of blood due to a pierced lung. But the old thespian had a memorable line ready. "I forgot to duck, honey," he reportedly told Nancy. He also told his surgeons that he hoped they were all Republicans.

I sprinted the nine or so blocks to the White House, where the press briefing room was packed. Some correspondents were in tears after hearing that Jim Brady had been shot and killed. This was untrue, though he had been critically wounded and suffered lasting brain damage. Here, too, all discipline and order seemed to have collapsed. Normally the vice-president would have taken over in such a crisis, but George Bush Sr. was in the air, flying home from a foreign tour. So who was in charge? The lack of clarity was frightening, and Secretary of State Al Haig soon made it worse. Dashing up to the microphone at the head of the small room, Haig looked frantic and sweaty, not at all the calm-under-fire commander one would expect of a former general. He spoke as if briefing the troops. "As you know," he intoned, "the president took a round in the chest. I am in control here at the White House." In fact he was far down the list of those constitutionally able to replace an incapacitated president. Haig, who later threw his helmet into the ring for the presidential nomination, seemed just a mite too eager.

After the shooting, the security surrounding the president would never be the same again. Gone were the days of simply flashing a pass and being buzzed through a White House gate. The pass now restricted reporters to the two-storey press room and the lawn in front. All other areas of the sprawling executive offices were off limits without an escort. The Secret Service used the incident to win an arrangement they'd always wanted: They closed off the streets in front of and beside the White House, distancing it from street traffic and pedestrians. Perhaps such measures were necessary to protect presidents, but they somehow diminished the lustre of this advertisement for America's open democracy and the notion of government by the people, for the people.

CTV's offices were next to ABC's quarters in the heart of the downtown. We shared the street with the Mayflower Hotel, a favourite luncheon spot for many of the city's well-known citizens. (A wall plaque noted that J. Edgar Hoover had lunched there every day for a quarter century but did not mention that his alleged lover and assistant, FBI director Clyde Tolsen, had accompanied him.) Only four of us were in the bureau: a staff cameraman, a soundman, a locally hired producer, and me. Down the street, our competition at the CBC numbered about twenty. My bureau chief counterpart there was Joe Schlesinger, for whom I had the greatest respect and affection, so ours was a friendly rivalry.

The daily routine was generally predictable. I called the Toronto assignment desk every morning to decide what story we would file that day. Usually the topic was obvious, although from time to time that decision became a protracted negotiation. Then we set to work collecting interviews and videos for the item we would assemble and edit for that evening's newscast. We had contracts with three American networks that allowed us to weave some of their material into our items. This was known as a "U.S. melt" and it is standard practice for everyone in the business. Of course, more often than not some breaking event would intervene and I would be grabbing the next flight to a destination elsewhere in the country, there to package an entirely new item.

I was settling in, but still operating without a White House pass, the high-security photo identity card that was essential for access to the precincts of official Washington. As soon as I had arrived, I underwent a detailed police check and finger-printing, but after a few months of anxious delays, the Secret Service requested that I be fingerprinted again. The agent who took my prints the first time had apparently done a poor job. A year passed while I worked without clearance. Finally an apolo-getic agent called to ask for a third fingerprinting session. This time two Secret Service experts, after a close examination of my fingers, informed me that I was a one-in-a-million curiosity. I had no latent prints: The fingertip whirls that would normally distinguish me from others did not exist. Proud as I was to be such a rare specimen, I was more concerned that the absence of prints would deny me the coveted pass. I should have chosen a life of crime, the experts told me with a laugh, but they gave me their approval since the distinct smudge I produced would just as surely identify me.

Soon thereafter, a blue-bordered envelope bearing the White House seal arrived in my mailbox. It was an invitation to a private dinner party hosted by the president and Mrs. Reagan. Naturally, I suspected a hoax by the people in my office, but just to be sure I called the presidential social secretary. I could hear the doubt in her voice as she informed me coolly that she would check and call me back. Next day, her tone had changed dramatically. "Ron and Nancy" did indeed want to have me over for dinner with a small group of friends, presumably people I would know well. They included such luminaries as Secretary of State Haig, Katherine Graham, publisher of the *Washington Post*, and the *Post's* executive editor, Ben Bradlee, of Watergate fame. Our old friend Bob Hope would be dropping by for drinks but couldn't stay for dinner.

I bought my first tuxedo and on the appointed night showed up, invitation in hand, at the security door of the White House. From there I was escorted to the Roosevelt Room with other arriving guests. When I was announced to my hosts, a startled look crossed Mrs. Reagan's face, but Ronnie welcomed me warmly. At dinner I was seated beside the somewhat subdued wife of the director of the FBI, though we eventually found a happy conversational topic in her children. (She did not mention her ill health and it was a shock when she succumbed to cancer within days of that evening.)

At one point after dinner, I went out on the Truman balcony with a glass of champagne. It had begun to snow very lightly, the marine band was playing in the background, and Reagan joined me for a breath of fresh air. Just like home, I told him, and he recalled how cold Toronto had been when he visited there during one of his past speaking engagements.

I left that evening with a feeling of euphoria, speculating on the career benefits of so dazzling a debut in Washington's power circles. I was soon disabused of that notion. A few days later, a friend from CBS called to say that "Craig Oliver is sure pissed off at you." Who? That would be the American Craig Oliver of NPR and PBS, a much-admired figure in public broad-casting—and an acquaintance of Nancy Reagan. Like me, he had a White House press pass, but it was to my address that the invitation had been sent. With the pass and the invitation, I'd had no trouble getting through the front gate security and into the president's private dining quarters. I treasure the keepsake photo in which Nancy is clearly perturbed that the Oliver she is shaking hands with is not the one she invited, yet she said nothing about it.

What I saw in Reagan that night supported the widely held observation that he didn't care and barely noticed what social set he was in. His was an anecdotal mind, more interested in people's stories than their status or rank. Reagan seemed to accept everyone as an equal and to trust what they told him. It was Nancy who had to make the tough judgments about people who might try to abuse their access to him. She spotted the phonies and hangers-on and shunted aside those who were not useful. All leaders need a spouse like that.

My next meeting with Reagan was in the Oval Office itself. In advance of the G7 economic summit in 1983, the White House agreed to a sit-down interview with the president and a group of reporters from the G7 countries, an unheard-of privilege today. As we took our places, Reagan noted that I was from Canada and asked me to remind him to tell the story of his desk, the one used by John F. Kennedy and other presidents before and after him.

The interview over, Reagan's senior staff moved in to whisk him away, but to their evident annoyance I intervened to ask about the desk. He walked over to the massive oak piece and motioned me to join him behind it. "Look here," he said, instructing me to reach under the desktop where I felt some large steel bolts. "They are shipwrights' screws," he explained; the desk was made from the timbers of the HMS *Resolute*, one of the vessels sent out on the international search for the lost Franklin expedition in the mid-nineteenth century. To my surprise, Reagan was quite familiar with the tragic mystery of the 128 British seamen who had died in the quest for the Northwest Passage, and together we bent to examine the piece more carefully.

He knew the fascinating history of the Franklin Expedition and told it well: how the *Resolute*'s British crew had abandoned the vessel in the Arctic ice in 1854, and then an American whaler found it adrift in the North Atlantic. The American government subsequently restored HMS *Resolute* and returned it to Queen Victoria in 1856. Two decades later, the *Resolute* was taken out of service, but Victoria ordered the creation of at least two desks from its timbers, one of which was presented to President Rutherford B. Hayes in 1880. It resided in the White House thereafter and was retrieved from storage by First Lady Jacqueline Kennedy for her husband's use in the Oval Office.

Exasperated aides broke in to insist that this president get on with his schedule, which was running late. I was hustled out while Reagan shrugged apologetically as if there were nothing he would rather do than spend more time chatting about Arctic history.

At another session with reporters held before the 1985 G7 summit, I asked Reagan how he felt about Canada's defence spending, at the time the lowest per capita of any NATO country except Luxembourg. Reagan launched into the answer of another question altogether, one having to do with the nation's deficit. I summoned up my courage and interrupted him to bring him back to the point. He corrected himself and the session went on smoothly. After it ended, he came up to me and apologized, pointing out that I had been seated on his left, his bad ear.

Since I briefly had Reagan's attention, I asked if he might allow his official photographer, who was in the room, to take a photo of the two of us. While the shot was set up, I knew better than to engage Reagan in small talk about matters of policy. Instead, I asked him about horseback riding and his eyes lit up. It was well-known that every Saturday morning he travelled to Camp David to ride. Striding across the White House lawn toward the waiting helicopter, clad in riding breeches and cowboy boots that flattered his powerful build, he was the very picture of all-American athleticism.

In Bonn, Reagan told me stories about the famously uncomfortable McClellan saddle, developed just prior to the Civil War by the army general of the same name. Reagan mentioned that he himself had been a second lieutenant in the U.S. Cavalry, to which I responded with a raised eyebrow. He then pointed out that horse soldiers had not been officially "dismounted" until 1941. It was great fun at Washington dinner parties, when the conversation invariably turned to Reagan, to drop the fact that the president had ridden with the cavalry. When asked where I had heard such a thing, I replied that Ron himself had told me about it. A pathetic bit of one-upmanship, I admit, but irresistible.

The photograph was later signed and framed and made its way to the wall behind the reception desk of the tourist motel Mom was now managing in Prince Rupert. Vacationing Americans en route to Alaska were delighted to see their president's likeness prominently displayed, but were not entirely convinced that the chap beside him was the desk clerk's son.

The chance to observe Reagan up close confirmed for me the judgment of one of his Cabinet secretaries, who explained that what you saw was what you got. I saw a natural performer, a Hollywood actor who understood he was playing the role of a lifetime. In the era of image management, he could be cast in any role: a believable commander-in-chief when the Libyan dictator Muammar al-Gaddafi needed to be cut down to size; a supportive padre to the nation when the crew of the space shuttle *Challenger* lost their lives before the eyes of millions; a huggable Republican to counter the mean-spirited extremists who had previously characterized the right wing of his party. He was full of contradictions, spoke a lot about God but rarely attended church; lauded the family, although he himself was divorced and estranged from some of his children. Yet he cut the kind of heroic figure that makes Americans swoon—a man possessed of strongly held beliefs and, in his public life at least, morally beyond reproach. Above all, Reagan was no phony.

There were any number of irritants in the relationship between Canada and the United States in the early years of Reagan's regime, and the hard-line anti-Communists in the president's circle ranked our prime minister high on the list. Trudeau's friendly relations with the Soviets and holiday-like visits to Cuba were anathema to them, as was his government's economic nationalism. At a Senate hearing around this time, Robert Hormats, Undersecretary of State for Economic Affairs, condemned Canada's embrace of measures like the National Energy Program as the act of a Third World country, on a par with leftist dictatorships in Latin America. The Reaganauts needed a willing partner in their anti-Communist crusade, and

Trudeau's refusal to co-operate with their economic embargo of Nicaragua in 1985 infuriated them.

The Americans were also gazing jealously at Canada's vast oil reserves and were eager to make a deal that would allow them access and a measure of protection from the uncertainty of Middle East supplies. They sought a continental energy policy, even though they believed they would not get it from Pierre Trudeau, or at least not on terms they would find acceptable.

A visit by the prime minister to Washington in 1981 did nothing to improve relations. A Trudeau aide reported to me the Canadians' frustration with Reagan's simplistic world view, while the Americans greeted Trudeau's promotion of détente with a new generation of Soviet leaders as collusion with the enemy. In his usual contorted style, Al Haig summed up the discussions as "atmospheric dissonance." A friend who was close by when Trudeau and Reagan conversed between themselves reported that they got along just fine. They simply weren't hearing each other.

The situation was no better a few years later when, just before he left office, Trudeau embarked on a much-criticized world tour to promote peace. He received a chilly reception in Washington. Undersecretary of State Lawrence Eagleburger told reporters he believed Trudeau was smoking something. On his way out of the White House, the prime minister publicly condemned what he called "Pentagon pipsqueaks" who were committed to the arms race.

In February 1984, I had a truly bizarre encounter with William J. Casey, director of the Central Intelligence Agency and a former wartime spymaster with its predecessor, the Office of Strategic Services. I was introduced to him at a dinner party where the subject of Trudeau naturally arose. In a casual, matter-of-fact way, he remarked, "I guess Trudeau is quitting in a few days." I was nonplussed and thought I had missed some breaking announcement, but when I phoned Trudeau's press secretary, Pat Gossage, in Ottawa later that night, he had no such information, nor was there any speculation. And yet less than a week later, Trudeau took his famous walk in the snow and announced his resignation from politics.

Did the CIA have 24 Sussex bugged? Were they eavesdropping on the prime minister's phone calls? I concluded the guess must have been a fortuitous one; why would someone in Casey's position give away secrets? Casey died of brain cancer in 1987, but not before his role in covert activities in Afghanistan, in various Soviet bloc countries, and in South and Central America became common knowledge. An old friend of his, columnist William Safire, wrote after Casey's death that the CIA had been concerned that the cancer might have impaired Casey's judgment before it was detected.

The administration was looking beyond Trudeau well before his formal departure, however, and they were quick to recognize a more congenial figure in Brian Mulroney when he became leader of the Progressive Conservative Party in 1983. He and his beautiful wife, Mila, attracted some attention in the local press, and I was invited to appear on the *McNeil/Lehrer News Hour* where I predicted Mulroney would win Canada's next federal election. As it turned out, Mulroney had an ally in Washington that he might never have expected.

Allan Gotlieb was the sociable Ottawa mandarin whose mix of brilliant charm and political savvy made him an ideal match for the Reagan crowd when Trudeau appointed him ambassador to the United States in 1981. Peering myopically through circular glasses, Gotlieb looked every bit the pinstriped and bookish Canadian emissary. He was anything but. Instead of sitting in his office, operating through junior officers and waiting for his calls to be returned, Gotlieb decided to court the Reagan administration's power brokers. He arranged a birthday party for Michael Deaver, the president's much-trusted public relations and media manager, and sent invitations to everyone in the administration. Few declined to fete the well-liked and influential Deaver.

Whether because of our mutual connection with Trudeau or because I was a single man happy to fill a chair left empty by an unexpected cancellation, I enjoyed a lot of dinners on the embassy tab and was able to see the effectiveness of Gotlieb's strategy. Once the major players were in your dining room, the relationship became personal and the access much easier. It helped that Gotlieb was clever and engaging and that his wife, Sondra, was hilariously eccentric, as well as an accomplished hostess. She wrote an amusing column in the *Washington Post* about a mythical ambassador's wife who is overwhelmed by her life in the American capital. Everyone knew it was Sondra writing about herself.

Receptions and parties at their official residence became something of an after-work club for certain members of the Reagan administration, among them George Schultz, Caspar Weinberger, and James Baker. They did business and talked out differences away from the pressures of their offices, and it was not unusual to see senior figures, from Cabinet officers to congressional leaders, pulling one another aside for private chats. An invitation from Canada was the hottest ticket in town: People wanted to be there because they knew that others they wished or needed to see would be there too.

In Ottawa, Gotlieb had been considered almost an honorary member of the Liberal Party. In fact he was a professional public servant, and when Mulroney won the Conservative leadership, Gotlieb saw that he might soon have new political masters. Happily, he believed in the need for a continent-wide trade deal to protect Canada's crucial privileged entry into the American market, and so did Mulroney. Not long after, I was at another dazzling party at the Gotlieb residence when Ed Meese, then White House Chief of Staff, asked me about Mulroney. Over port and cigars, the big heavy-jowled Californian told me, "This is a man we can work with."

The White House let Gotlieb know they would welcome a visit. The subsequent Canadian embassy party was a hugely successful coming-out for Mulroney. In an unprecedented show of diplomatic courtesy to an Opposition leader, all of the top officials of the administration attended. Gotlieb took his career in his hands with this event. He made an effusive after-dinner toast in which he predicted a bright new era for Canada under a youthful new leader. The Trudeau camp was furious at this traitorous talk, but Gotlieb had made the right move.

Unfortunately, the Gotliebs' and Canada's star fell abruptly a few years later with a notorious incident on an evening in 1986, when the Gotliebs were hosting Prime Minister Mulroney and Vice-President Bush. The ambassador and his wife were under great stress to get it right at an event that could set the tone for the leaders' future working relationship. But there was a laughable error. To accommodate so many guests, the hosts had to cover the swimming pool with temporary flooring and fill the space with dining tables. I noticed after an hour or so that my feet were getting wet; someone had neglected to shut down the pool's running water. Then the vice-president was late in arriving, holding up the proceedings.

Apparently the pressure was too much for Sondra. For reasons that are not clear even today, she slugged the embassy social secretary, a well-known, elegant woman named Connie Conners. It was no gentle tap: Connie was knocked off balance and broke an earring. Such an episode might have gone unreported, but it happened on the front steps of the embassy in full view of a Canadian Press reporter, Julie O'Neill. It fell to my former Ottawa colleague Bruce Phillips, recently appointed as the embassy's communications director, to offer excuses for Sondra's behaviour. Although O'Neill had witnessed the whole fracas, her desk would not use the story. It ran the next day in the *Washington Post*.

Connie Conners could have sued for assault. A woman lawyer she and I both knew advised her to do so, but in true diplomatic style, Connie accepted an apology from Sondra and left it at that. It was rumoured that Sondra had also bowled over a reporter from *Women's Wear Daily* the same night. I knew Sondra to be a charming person who could become over-excited, and well remember chatting with her one evening over a drink when she suddenly turned and ran hard, right into a wall. Colourful behaviour made for a high profile, but Sondra's position as one of the city's foremost hostesses was forever lost. Washington society, where servants were called "assistants," could not tolerate bad manners and certainly not in public.

Nonetheless Allan Gotlieb continued to be one of the best-connected and influential ambassadors on the diplomatic circuit. The relationships he forged helped smooth the negotiation of the Canada-U.S. Free Trade Agreement (FTA) that came into effect in 1989. He also broke new ground by conducting an active lobbying effort with the politicians in the Senate and House of Representatives. This is common practice today, but he was among the first diplomats to use his credentials for access to more than the executive mansion.

When foreign reporters speak of covering the White House, it is understood that they are really talking about covering America, with all its magnificence, madness, and contradictions. The United States is really many nations bound together by myths, most of its citizens knowing as little about each other as they do about, say, Canada. As reporters, we dealt with an elite, a veneer on the population. Getting out of the capital and meeting Americans on their home ground was always rewarding and enlightening. The more I travelled the Union, the more my affection grew for this most complex and idiosyncratic of nations.

One such working trip changed my life. It was 1985 and I was in Florida covering the devastation of Hurricane Gloria. My cameraman and I were travelling fast and light, transmitting our material, including stand-ups and whatever interviews and video we shot, in bits and pieces to Toronto. There, it was sewn into a single coherent news item. The message I got back was that the young woman assigned to do this assembly and editing work was producing good stories for us. She was also pleasantly unflappable during our sometimes-frantic calls. Who was she?

I called on my friend Sandie Rinaldo for a bit of intelligence. The young woman's name was Anne-Marie Bergeron and she was in her late twenties. Sandie reported that she was blonde and the most beautiful woman in the CTV building. Whenever she stretched across the news desk to toss or retrieve copy, every man in the room stopped in his tracks to watch. Sandie also informed me that Anne-Marie was spending a lot of time with a senior writer on the desk, although whether or not the relationship was a romantic one was unknown. All this was enough to convince me that at the very least I could invite this colleague for a business lunch next time I was in the city, as thanks for her work on our stories. I was bowled over when we met a few weeks later. She was smart, cool, and reserved, clearly not someone who would cling.

My pattern with women was well established by this time. I had no problem with physical intimacy, but emotional commitment was a different matter. As soon as a relationship ripened into a demand for closeness, the inner voice told me to run. Childhood memory taught that love was about hurt and abandonment and it was preferable to choose companions who would not want to stick around. I was a loner who fooled the world into believing otherwise and was not yet prepared to confront the deception myself.

Not long before the Florida assignment, though, there occurred something like a Road-to-Damascus experience. My travels in Central America had taken me away from Washington for a month. I had been back barely long enough to do laundry and check in with friends before Don Cameron sent me down to South America. Another month flew by. Home again, I did not unpack before calling a woman from the World Bank I had been seeing. She had clearly moved on. "What about the Argentinian sweater I brought for you?" I inquired.

"Leave it at the front desk at the bank," she said.

I sat down before a tall stack of unopened mail and unexpect-edly burst into tears. It was not that I felt sad to be dumped; the truth was, I didn't care one way or another about her. It was the disconnectedness of my life that suddenly became clear. My glamorous, well-paid existence was an accident of circumstance, it seemed. Apart from meeting that day's deadline, I was without goals or objectives, living a haphazard life.

I liked who I was, but not what I was becoming. I had always believed that we create our own lives and that nothing prevents us from re-creating them at any point. Every person makes the choices that drag her into the abyss, as my mother was doing, or raises her to the heights. I saw that my determination never to put myself in a position of dependence on another person had cost me the achievement of real happiness.

Looking back, I believe that was the moment when I won the upper hand over the inner nuisance. He was not entirely vanquished and for some time after still insisted he knew my best interests. But I was starting to regard him as a false prophet.

After meeting Anne-Marie Bergeron, I thought it wise to have a conversation with the colleague who was dating her. No profit for anyone if I was interfering where I was unwanted. The two suitors held what amounted to a negotiation about the way ahead. Anne-Marie would make her own choices, but I wanted to know from my colleague whether I would cause offence if I pursued my interest in her. Not in the least, he assured me, adding that I was not the kind of man who would appeal to her in any case. We parted on the friendliest of terms, as we always had.

Anne-Marie moved to Halifax as the network producer covering the Maritimes, but we kept up a long-distance friendship. Whenever I felt the old urge to flee, she pulled me back. She was not someone who could allow herself to retreat from commitments. In 1986, and on her thirtieth birthday, we got engaged in a grass hut in Bora-Bora. By then her other swain had become so distraught and angry he'd quit the network. How different my life would have been had he been honest in his initial reaction.

When I told Mom, she did not respond with the joy I'd hoped for. She had always preferred my first wife over any girlfriend I introduced her to, as if each were somehow responsible for the breakup of my marriage. When she came to Washington with her sister for a visit, I made sure not to raise the topic, though it would likely not have made much difference. From the time she and Aunt Mary arrived, Mom was distracted and anxious in the great city. The two of them went for a walk one evening and got caught in one of those hot summer downpours that clear the air and then pass over quickly. Mary returned to the apartment alone, telling me Mom needed help outside. I found her lying in the gutter, rolling in the gushing rainwater and laughing, seriously drunk. That night I asked her what the hell she was after. She answered with a single, haunting word, "Oblivion."

⌒

Reagan will be remembered as the president who escalated and then ended the Cold War, the ideological conflict that had held the world hostage for four decades. In the early eighties, he condemned the Soviet Union as an "evil empire" and supported anti-Communist movements in Africa, Asia, and Latin America. Alongside vastly increased military spending, he proposed the

Strategic Defense Initiative, the infamous Star Wars project that was meant to create a defence shield for the United States against nuclear missiles.

The Soviet Union could not keep pace with this arms race and its economy was quietly stagnating when Mikhail Gorbachev assumed the leadership in 1985. As Trudeau had done years before, Reagan at last recognized that with a fresh generation of leaders at the helm of the USSR, diplomacy might have a role after all. He decided to try for significant arms reduction agreements.

I travelled with the White House press corps to the four historic U.S.-Soviet summit meetings between 1985 and 1988. At the first meeting, in Geneva, Switzerland, Reagan and Gorbachev broke the ice by recalling the cold in Canada. In spite of the chilly morning in the Swiss city, they agreed this was nothing compared with the frigid greetings they experienced on their first visits to Ottawa years before, when Reagan was on the speaking circuit and Gorby was the visiting Soviet agriculture minister. (I was still in the Prairies during his tour of western farms and, like everyone else, was surprised at this Communist's easygoing manner.)

The American intelligence agencies told Reagan, erroneously, that the Soviet economy was strong and sustainable. The foreign policy experts warned that he was being drawn into a trap. But Reagan believed Gorbachev was a departure from previous Soviet dictators, those dull and entrenched apparatchiks who kept dying every time he attempted to schedule a meeting with them. Reagan also believed that the command-style economy and incompetent bureaucracy were not delivering the goods to the USSR's citizens or even maintaining its military strength. He was convinced the structure was crumbling, and he decided to test his theory.

Star Wars was questionable, both technologically and financially, but to match it would break the bank of the Soviet economy. That drew the Soviets into negotiations about arms control with the bottom-line demand that no progress could be made unless Reagan dropped his scheme. By January 1986, in the face of Reagan's stubborn refusal to abandon the Strategic Defense Initiative, Gorbachev was begging Reagan to soften his stance. In an open letter to Reagan, Gorbachev promised unprecedented reductions in the Soviet nuclear arsenal if only Reagan would shut down Star Wars. The pressure on Reagan to do so came to a head at their meeting on a miserable, wet, and cold day in Reykjavik, Iceland, in mid-October 1986.

This was the big league and we all knew the game was down to its final innings. It was breathtaking to realize I was present and reporting on an event that could change the world—literally watching history on the run.

Both countries brought large delegations, but the actual face-to-face meeting took place in a small government building with most of the military and diplomatic experts waiting anxiously in rooms nearby. Those of us in the White House travelling press corps were staying at neighbouring hotels and set up our recording and editing equipment in airport hangars. The Americans had spent hundreds of thousands of dollars to floodlight the historic city centre just so their anchors would have an appropriate backdrop.

I had one run-in with Icelandic culture that could have caused me great embarrassment. The local welcoming committee had invited the correspondents to discover the delights of one of their sauna clubs. Naked as the day of our birth, we sweated through the bathhouse, whipped our backs with birch boughs, and learned that the obligatory next step was a run outdoors and down a wooden boardwalk to a bracing dip in the snow-covered ocean.

A brave reporter headed out the door so I followed but was too far along when I noticed that local news photographers were snapping pictures of the scene. There was no intention to cause us discomfort; they simply wanted to capture their Washington guests enjoying a bit of Icelandic hospitality. Clearly, these Nordic nature lovers did not share our North American horror of public nudity. Next morning the front page of the local daily paper carried a picture of the naked behinds of two reporters dashing from bathhouse to ocean. One of them was mine, and I was thankful the paper had spared readers a frontal view.

Whatever merriment this brought to the delegations, there was serious business going on and anticipation of a historic breakthrough, possibly a pledge to eliminate all nuclear weapons. But the talks foundered on Reagan's insistence that Star Wars testing be allowed to continue. The summit broke up in anger and accusations of bad faith.

For some reason of logistics I flew back to Washington on Air Force Two, normally used by the official delegation of negotiators, senior White House officials, and the American journalists. The mood was grim. It was easy to believe that a singular opportunity had slipped from our grasp and that the world was heading back into the darkest days of the Cold War. One adviser muttered that they had warned the president all along that this was a Soviet set-up. Another described how Reagan was visibly angry when he threw Gorbachev's ultimatum back in his face.

The recriminations included one presidential aide complaining bitterly that Star Wars was a nutty idea that his government should be able to jettison. They could not do so because "the old man" could not face the humiliation of killing it in exchange for Gorbachev's stunning arms reduction offer.

But the voice of one experienced Cold Warrior stood out for me. The Soviet offer had not gone down a black hole, he insisted. Informal talks with his Soviet counterparts had convinced him the country's economy was in dire trouble. It was in their interest to return to the bargaining table.

Just over a year passed before Gorbachev returned. There was no mention of Star Wars in his request for another summit, this one held in early December 1987. Gorby dropped the demand that had been the stopper. Reagan's stubbornness had paid off. Under the terms of the Intermediate-Range Nuclear Forces Treaty (INF) signed at this meeting, Star Wars was sidestepped and the two men agreed on massive reductions in nuclear weapons. For those who have not lived under the threat of nuclear war, the significance of that deal may be difficult to grasp. The warmth of the personal relationship between the two leaders, with its promise of broader conversations to come, shone rare a light of hope on the world. It led straight to the fall of the Berlin Wall, another unwelcome Cold War relic, and—to Reagan's considerable satisfaction—to the breakup of the Soviet Union once headed by his friend Gorbachev.

In the economic realm, Reagan's record is more controversial. His spending resulted in the largest budgetary deficits in American history up to that time. He cut taxes by an astonishing 30 percent on the promise that the wealth would "trickle down," a theory that has been largely discredited. The economic policy was essentially unfair, rewarding the rich at the expense of low-income and particularly black citizens. Strangely, Reagan seemed insensitive to this.

Despite fears he would be a dangerous right-wing zealot, Reagan governed as a moderate conservative. After five disappointing presidencies in a row, he restored the prestige and authority of that enormously important office. He also gave back to Americans their pride and self-respect. Reagan refused to accept the concept of an America in decline, a view widely held by the intellectual class at the time. If he was ever pessimistic, he never showed it through that endlessly cheerful demeanour.

I went to the White House press room to watch Reagan's goodbye speech to the nation in January 1989. The "great communicator" was never better. He told Americans he had only provided the voice for the ideas of a great nation. He stole that line from Winston Churchill, but who knew or cared. His closing lines were perfect. "We made a difference ... All in all, not bad, not bad at all." It was corny, certainly, but then so was he.

6

THE VULTURE BRIGADES

The life of the war correspondent is a disorienting, gypsy existence. A strange exhilaration takes hold, a fascination with the morbid. Life on the road seems more real than life back home. Situations that should be frightening become routine, leading to the easy embrace of ever-greater risks. Confusion and chaos are eagerly anticipated aspects of the job. Then one morning, if you are lucky, you wake up with the certain, sickly knowledge that if you keep pursuing death, it will catch you.

My foreign adventures were the dirty conflicts in El Salvador and Nicaragua, the tidy and relatively uneventful U.S. invasion of Panama, and a generally benign tour of duty in Argentina, where the greatest threat most of us faced was a bad bottle of Chilean wine. To report from Washington in those years was to report from these Central and South American hot spots, all targets of the Reagan administration's aggressive attention. I became a part-time member of the international vulture brigades, that club of broadcast and newspaper correspondents who specialize in wars and revolutions.

These men and women are a breed apart. Many have been

killed or seriously injured, and among those who do survive, marriages seldom last. It is a business for the young, kids fresh out of journalism school who pick up a videocam and set out to make their reputations. But so too are there greybeards, reporters and cameramen who have become hooked on the action. I have seen war photographers, in particular, perform courageous acts to get their footage, and then drink the night away. The fearless BBC correspondent Martin Bell was proud of telling me he had covered twelve wars without a scratch. Eventually he too was wounded—in Bosnia.

The brush wars in Central America were particularly risky for reporters because we operated on our own. We did not travel under the protection of large armies. There were no medics or field hospitals to minister to our occasional wounded. Nor were there any "friendlies." Government troops and rebel fighters alike abhorred reporters for separate but equally malicious reasons.

I owed my war experience in El Salvador to the Reagan administration's knee-jerk anti-Communism, an ideology that cost the lives of thousands in that country. Most victims were peasants, some were aid workers, and a few were priests dedicated to the tenets of liberation theology. Though officially denounced by the Vatican, this theology provided a moral rationale for Catholic priests and laymen to support the revolutionary struggle in the name of social justice.

In America, it was necessary only to brand such reformers as Communists to justify the corruption and human rights abuses of the U.S.-backed military regime or the actions of landowners who killed peasant farmers rather than accept change. The assassination squads of the Salvadoran security forces were free to do their work without interference, and the leftist guerrillas retaliated in kind; neither side gave any quarter in that butcher shop of a civil war.

In early 1980, the activist Catholic archbishop of San Salvador, Óscar Romero, was murdered on the steps of his cathedral. Shortly after, an American lay missionary and three Catholic nuns were likewise shot to death. The United States' position became crystal clear when Secretary of State Al Haig declared that the nuns were trying to organize farm workers and were caught in the crossfire with the military. His suggestion that they may have been engaged in a firefight with the Salvadoran army indicated how far the administration was prepared to bend the truth in order to defend its policies. In fact, the nuns and the archbishop were early victims of El Salvador's military death squads.

In one of his frequent efforts to wax Churchillian, Haig had also pronounced, "the final battle for Latin America is taking place in El Salvador." American intelligence officers whispered the party line in the ears of reporters. The Communists were no longer content with Cuba, we were told; first they would seize Central America, then Mexico. The administration was still retailing a shopworn domino theory. In their minds, El Salvador was another Vietnam, a test of American mettle that this time would not be lost to the Communists. The lessons of southeast Asia seemed to have been forgotten, and right on cue, a new generation of military advisers and mercenaries, official observers and covert spies, misguided lefties and well-meaning aid workers all headed south to witness the cataclysm. The reporters, photographers, and television crews were not far behind. True to form, Don Cameron intended to expose his viewers to the horror of war up close. He dismissed coverage of boring diplomatic manoeuvres and demanded front-line "bang-bang."

Such were our producers' orders when the CTV crew from Washington, equipped with bulletproof vests purchased from a Virginia arms dealer, landed at the airport in the capital city of San Salvador. The vests captured the attention of troops at the terminal, which was literally an armed camp. We were directed to a nearby police station, a steel wire–reinforced bunker about ten minutes' walk from the terminal building, to obtain the necessary photo identification and hand over our passports.

As we arrived, members of the notorious Treasury Police, distinctive in their shiny helmets, were leading out two men, perspiring and white-faced. The prisoners had their thumbs tied behind their backs with wire. While we were negotiating with the sergeant, two shots rang out, followed a few seconds later by two more reports. That told us the nature of the country we were entering: In the right circumstances, any policeman or soldier had the power of life and death over others. This rattled me somewhat, but the sergeant didn't even pause mid-sentence. Wired thumbs were favourite signatures of the Treasury Police; we were to see them on many corpses in the years ahead.

In every war zone, the foreign press tends to cluster at a favourite hotel. In El Salvador it was the elegant Camino Real. We were among the earliest arrivals, having landed in the steamy summer of 1981, before Haig raised the stakes and before American print and TV journalists descended in herds. The Real lobby, with its ensemble of reporters and whores, intelligence officers (from both the CIA and the Salvadoran army), and rebel sympathizers, resembled a tableau from Conrad's *Heart of Darkness*. All drank companionably in the bar and around

the pool, with booze and marijuana in ample supply. It went
without saying that the phones were bugged. We dropped our
bags, and then sought out our designated contacts.

It was clear that the Salvadoran Army was utterly untrained
and ill-equipped to take on any foe. A friendly colonel invited
us to accompany a patrol into the mountains near Palo Grande,
a guerrilla stronghold. The soldiers, some without boots, wore
ratty, mismatched uniforms and carried a variety of old and new
weapons. They were led by a drunken captain whom we plied
with beer for his friendship and approval in the eyes of the ranks.

The region, we were assured, had been swept clean of
guerrillas in earlier combat. However, no one had told the
guerrillas. We had marched the dusty, bug-infested jungle trails
for about an hour before we were suddenly ambushed. Two
nearby soldiers instantly fled. I felt it best to jump into a ditch
with my cameraman.

A ragged firefight ensued and continued sporadically for the
rest of the day until the army brought in an armoured vehicle. It
blasted away at the suspected enemy stronghold, but none of the
soldiers had any idea of their true target. A few yards from me a
soldier's helmet went spinning into the air. It had caught a bullet,
but the fellow beneath it was okay, save for a bad headache. We
videotaped dead and wounded soldiers being flown out in small
helicopters that were totally unsuited for the job.

Lying in the relative safety of my hole, I had time to
consider that this is what happens when people cannot settle
their differences: They kill each other. The last man standing
wins. The thought was not especially profound, but interesting in that I was seemingly lucid in the middle of a pitched
battle. Nausea and trembling always gripped me after the

incident. In the moment, one simply did what was necessary to survive.

A few weeks later, I attended a dinner party at the Canadian embassy at which Al Haig was a guest. He listened closely but grim-faced to tales of my encounters with the sorry armed forces of El Salvador. "Goddamn," the former army general declared, "we have to get those people some training." A massive military assistance and Special Forces training program was launched soon after, but I take no credit: The planning had clearly been under way for some time. Bolstering the Salvadoran regime kept it alive, but also extended the bloodbath until the end of the Cold War brought a lull in U.S.-Soviet rivalry.

In the meantime, we journalists entered into a deadly dance. One morning, just to remind us of the risks, the killing squads left the body of a local reporter lying in the parking lot of the Camino Real for all to see as we went out on our assignments. How much protection could we expect from our army-issued ID cards or the bold-lettered *Prensa* taped to the sides of our news crew vans? Not much, even for those of us from the West. At the hotel, we made a point of loudly praising the courageous struggle of the Salvadoran people against the godless commies. Letting anyone know what you really thought of the right-wing regime was dangerous.

Into this macabre atmosphere came a Dutch television crew who felt it was their duty to expose the corruption and depredations of the U.S.-backed government. We were all doing that in our satellite reports, but this bunch felt the need to broadcast their views publicly. They arranged what they believed to be a clandestine interview with the guerrilla leaders. Their contact was actually an army spy; all five members of the crew were shot in the jungle. An army investigation trotted out the old line that the victims had been caught in crossfire, but the evidence indicated they were set up. The incident was a sobering reminder of the consequences of bad judgment and misplaced trust in such circumstances.

While serving in Ottawa before the Washington stint, I had been a casual friend to an American diplomat. He was polished and smooth, very interested in Liberal government plans, especially energy policy. This was not unusual, since at the time a major objective of the United States was to ensure long-term supplies of Canadian oil and gas. But I suspected the diplomat was more than a simple embassy official, so I was not surprised when a contact in the Prime Minister's Office warned me that my friend was a CIA liaison officer. Even so, we shared an enthusiasm for skiing and we continued to meet socially until he called one day to tell me he was being transferred. We soon lost touch.

Later in Washington, before one of my trips to El Salvador, I met with a woman whom I'd hired there a year before as a translator. She was one of a community of Americans who were committed leftists and acted secretly for the Salvadoran revolutionaries—in effect, a rebel agent. I hoped she could help me arrange a visit to a guerrilla camp. I was given written instructions on how to link up with the guerrillas, directions I was to memorize and then destroy. (I still have the note; I didn't trust my memory.)

The details are reminiscent of a bad spy thriller, but in view of the fate of the Dutch film crew, I regarded them as deadly serious. I was to meet my contact in, of all places, a McDonald's restaurant. I should wear a sports jacket with a pin in my left lapel. I gave the translator my passport photo. The contact, who would introduce himself as Juan, would leave his left shoelace untied. When I pointed this out, he would reply, incongruously, "In my country, smart people keep their right shoelace loose." If there was any deviation from this script, I was to laugh at the remark and leave. We were to meet at 10:15 A.M. If no one appeared within half an hour, the rendezvous was off.

I waited an hour, but Juan did not show. On my return to the hotel, a well-dressed Hispanic woman bumped into me as I was crossing the parking lot. In the few seconds it would have taken to say, "Excuse me, *señor*," she said, "Another time; not safe."

That night a shot was fired through the window of the hotel room two doors down from me. The occupant, a female German radio reporter, was unhurt but sobbing hysterically as everyone in the floor rushed to see what had happened. She was much braver the next morning, displaying a spent rifle slug of the same calibre used by the Salvadoran troops. Hotel security claimed there had been fighting in the barrio nearby and the bullet was doubtless a stray one. I didn't think I was being excessively paranoid to wonder whether the local officials had intended to send me a message but delivered it to the wrong room.

Paranoia took full flight two days later. An official at the U.S. embassy in San Salvador had granted me a background briefing on the military and political situation. The embassy was protected by a wall of sandbags and bunkers, the ugly snouts of heavy machine guns poking out here and there. At the entrance, I gave the Marines the name of the political officer I was to see. Inside, I was escorted through a labyrinth of corridors and steel doors and into an office with a view out over the city. The window was made of thick bulletproof glass; embedded in a bubble halfway through the glass was a rifle bullet. Stranger still was the embassy staffer who came in to brief me. He sported a beard and had lost weight and seemed to have changed his name, but smiling back at me was my acquaintance from Ottawa. He warned me to hit the floor if an alarm sounded.

My acquaintance had the same charming manner and easy rapport as before. We might just as easily have been in Rome or London. But his tone changed as we said our goodbyes. He warned me to be careful about the friends I made in the country, driving home his point in unmistakable terms. "We are managing to exert some control over the army we trained," he cautioned, "but the paramilitary bunch are pretty much out of our hands."

With that he disappeared back into the bowels of the embassy, leaving me wondering if he knew about my aborted meeting. Could he have somehow intervened on my behalf? Or was I getting bushed, seeing spooks where none existed? He and I never met again.

Eventually, I did meet up with the guerrillas, though not through an arranged assignation. In 1982 the insurgents blew up a steel bridge spanning the Lempa River in west-central Salvador. They isolated a vast mountainous section of the country that they then declared liberated territory. It became their sanctuary and redoubt between assaults on government troops. The Salvadoran military, by then trained and equipped by American advisers, mobilized to clear the guerrillas out of the disputed territory. The operation was to be the army's first major assault of the conflict, and our CTV crew was sent to record the newly equipped troops in action.

There were four of us in the well-marked van: the sound and cameraman, an interpreter, me, and ABC News correspondent Jack Smith. Jack was the son of Howard K. Smith, one of America's pre-eminent foreign correspondents, who was famous for his World War II coverage for CBS alongside Edward R. Murrow. Jack had opted to join us that day because, as he had observed, the Canadians always had beer on ice in the back of their news vans, a luxury in that sweltering heat. I did not know Jack well but was intrigued by his nickname, "Sandbag Jack."

We arrived at the Lempa River where the bridge, a shaky edifice high above the river, had been repaired to allow a single vehicle to cross on makeshift steel runners. Our van crossed to await the army advance. The Salvadoran troops looked as if headed for a festive occasion. There were two hundred of them, all carrying M-16 rifles with yellow ribbons around the barrels. For many of these recruits, army boots had been their first shoes, and the ribbons would help ensure they were shooting at the proper targets. Assuming the army had a lengthy march into the countryside before it encountered guerrilla fighters, we drove on ahead.

To find the battle, if it could be found at all, we usually just headed toward the sound of gunfire. But this day there were no sounds beyond the running engine of our van. I had learned to be wary of war's silence; it usually preceded the unexpected explosion for which no preparation was possible. We drove slowly with an eye out for landmines, keeping the windows down in the intense heat as we made our way along a bumpy road half overgrown with weeds. We had progressed about ten miles when heavily armed men started to appear on the hilltops ahead; others popped up behind us. They were battle-hardened

fighters of the Farabundo Marti Revolutionary Front, obviously
waiting in ambush for the leading troops of the army to appear.
For a few seconds we considered whether to run for it but
abandoned that idea when the squad ahead levelled weapons at
our windshield.

We were ordered up against the van, arms spread across the
roof, rifle muzzles in our backs. In the only Spanish I knew,
I shouted that we were *periodista canadiense, no disparen.* I
was not being brave or lying for Jack's sake; I simply meant
to describe the group quickly and forgot about our American
companion. At that the tension eased slightly. The squad's
commander demanded the photo identity card that all journalists were required to carry, confirming their country of origin. To
my immense relief, he was satisfied to read mine alone, and he
handed it back with something resembling a smile. "Nicaragua,"
he said. I believed he must have been referring to the fact that the
Canadian government had refused to support the U.S. embargo
of the leftist regime in Nicaragua (thank you, Pierre). Then I
remembered Jack sitting in the back seat. I also remembered
that anti-Somoza guerrillas had shot to death an ABC reporter at
a similar roadblock not long before—in Nicaragua. The insurgents of both countries co-operated closely.

Fortunately, the chief was apparently satisfied that we were
all Canadians. In English he questioned me about the strength
of the army he was facing. No threats were necessary to elicit
what I knew. They had light tanks and heavy machine guns,
I said; his company was outnumbered. He seemed to appreciate that information. They took our watches and cash, *por la
revolución,* helped themselves to our cold beer, and sent us on
our way.

They let us keep the video we had shot of the exchange, so the day was not lost. On the return trip we drove in the direction of the approaching army like the proverbial bat out of hell. Until then, Jack had said not a word, but I have a memory of him exhaling audibly. Had they known he was an American, they would no doubt have killed or kidnapped him.

Jack had such a polite and cool demeanour that I was surprised to read in a later *New York Times* article that he was a combat veteran of the Seventh Cavalry in Vietnam. In fact, he was a survivor of the first large-scale battle between North Vietnam regulars and the U.S. army in the La Drang Valley in November 1965, when his unit suffered 93 percent casualties. Their position was overrun by a human wave assault; twenty soldiers around him were killed by machine gun bullets. Jack fired straight into the mass of oncoming Vietnamese until his gun was empty and he was knocked to the ground. He lay there surrounded by dying and wounded men, pretending to be dead. A Vietnamese soldier used Jack as a sandbag, mounting his machine gun on top of him. Jack told of how the gunner was, like himself, young and frightened; he could feel the man's knees trembling as they dug into his ribs. The Americans counterattacked and the soldier was killed in a grenade burst that left Jack wearing pieces of shrapnel in his head until his death twenty years later.

The prospect of being wounded in the jungles was a greater worry to us than death. Nothing could be done if one of us got killed, but a seemingly superficial injury could be fatal in those conditions. We did not even carry a medical kit, a situation that has since changed for television crews, who today receive weeks of military and first-aid training before assignments in dangerous places.

We were reminded of our vulnerability during a combat patrol with one of the specially trained Salvadoran units. A short firefight erupted as the soldiers moved in to push insurgents from a village. As happens too often, civilians were wounded and an army medic treated one of them, a young man, by the side of the road. There would be no medical evacuation for him, even if it had been available for the troops, which it was not. The medic moved on.

We watched all this from our own van. If we took the young man to the nearest hospital, roughly two hours away, his life might be saved. But we were not there to provide ambulance service, and who knew how many other casualties could claim our help among the villagers or the combatants. Here was a painful moral dilemma that we had no time to resolve. We decided to carry on and check again on the trip back. By the time we returned, the young man had bled to death. In this awful moment we could only repeat to ourselves the mantra that in the midst of death and calamity, reporters are doomed to be observers—that we cannot do our own jobs if we become involved. It was no comfort.

We could never predict who or what we would encounter in El Salvador. An unforgettable incident occurred one morning while we were on what we called "routine patrol" of the jungle roads. Hearing gunshots, we headed for the action. We came upon a group of soldiers circling the bodies of three teenagers. The victims' torsos were still smoking from wounds made by the high-velocity bullets that had torn into them as they knelt on the ground, hands tied behind their backs. The sergeant told us they were suspected members of a "Communist cadre" and so had been executed. But they were dressed in typical teenagers' clothing, jeans and T-shirts. One of them was a stunningly beautiful girl wearing flirty red-plastic shoes. That grisly scene haunted and angered me. So this was the professional army that American Special Forces were training.

In El Salvador I learned about the terrible gap that too often exists between policies enunciated at a White House news briefing and their horrendous consequences on the ground. I wondered, not for the last time, if the cost in blood and treasure of a war fought for a dubious cause didn't make for a pitifully hollow victory.

Nicaragua was a very different story. There the United States had no puppet government in place, and although the Sandinista regime was Marxist, the Reagan administration did not view it as a major continental threat. Consequently, it attracted less attention from the American media. As a Canadian crew, however, we visited frequently. Various Canadian aid groups and the Canadian Catholic church had been active there for years, and a number of Nicaraguans had attended Canadian schools.

It was difficult not to have some respect and even sympathy for the Sandinistas. In 1979 they had overthrown one of the most hated and repressive military regimes in the Americas, that of Anastasio Somoza Debayle. When it became known that Somoza and his cronies had pocketed millions in foreign aid following the country's devastating 1972 earthquake, Somoza's government lost any remaining moral authority in the eyes of the world and was eventually abandoned by the U.S. government under Jimmy Carter.

Prior to the successful revolution, the Sandinista National
Liberation Front, a coalition of socialist groups, had conducted a
guerrilla campaign of strikes, hostage takings, and armed insur-
rection against the Somoza regime. When the guerrillas finally
took control, the country was in economic ruin. Among the new
regime's first programs were land reform, grassroots political
organization, and measures to improve literacy, health care, and
working conditions.

The Sandinista leadership was a mix of dedicated Marxists,
practical socialists, and leftist intellectuals. By 1982 they
had imposed so-called emergency security measures that the
Reagan administration pointed to as a pure Communist dicta-
torship. It was true that Fidel Castro was a hero to many of
them, but the Sandinistas never adopted the nation-as-prison
pattern of the Soviet Union. They jailed the noisiest of their
political opponents and were not particularly gentle, but they
didn't routinely murder them. A degree of open criticism of the
government was permitted, including an opposition newspaper.

The leadership did, however, accept military and economic
aid from the Soviet Union. For that reason, the Reagan administration hoped to contain and even squash the Sandinistas before
they spread the Communist contagion to other Latin American
countries. The United States imposed a harsh economic
embargo and in effect bought itself a counter-revolutionary
army, the Contras, to wage another guerrilla war in the country.
Congress prohibited federal government funding of the Contras
in 1983, but the administration continued to finance its dirty
work through such covert schemes as the sale of arms to Iran.
The revelations surrounding the Iran-Contra Affair were the low
point of Reagan's time in office, though he himself preserved a

deniability of the essential details. The Contras never succeeded, and in 1984 the Sandinistas gained the legitimacy of election victory under their bespectacled, intellectual guerrilla leader, Daniel Ortega.

We in the CTV crew covered those elections and were moved by the turnout of thousands who lined up in the hot sun to cast ballots. One night the Contras attacked our hotel, the site of the government's election headquarters, with small arms fire. I threw my mattress against the balcony window to protect myself from shards of glass if the room was hit. Tim Kotcheff, who had come down to produce a special item on the elections, took a different approach. He phoned the front desk to complain about the noise and inquire how long it was expected to last. Not long. The army arrived and the insurgent band disappeared into the bush. Later we covered the impact of the embargo and the Canadian companies who continued to do business in Nicaragua in defiance of the American policy. Small local industries that were still able to sell abroad were endlessly thankful to Canada and happy to say so on camera.

Even during the worst of the bloody struggle with the Contras, Nicaragua never became the killing ground that El Salvador was. But it was a country at war, and tension was always in the air. In the capital, Managua, we sometimes dodged flying debris when Contra bombs were set off, a pathetic gesture in a city that had remained largely shattered and unrepaired since the 1972 earthquake. The war itself was hard to get to. The Contras were ineffective as an insurgency movement; their specialties were bombs and ambushes of Sandinista troops. All of this happened in the hills and jungle, and government troops would not allow us to join them on patrol. As a result, the most serious threat I faced in Nicaragua was a love affair that turned out to be a dangerous liaison.

We had hired a young American woman, clearly a Sandinista sympathizer, as our translator. The two of us became fast friends, very fast in fact, in that live-for-the-moment atmosphere. Such attachments had no consequences and, at that point in my life, I had no reason to resist urgent impulses.

One night she confessed that she was the mistress of the *commandante* of the secret police and warned me that he was quite jealous. I wasn't overly concerned; after all, the Sandinistas loved Canada. Spanish machismo would not be denied, however. Soon after, while she and I were quaffing a bottle of the best French champagne (at two dollars U.S. a pop, thanks to the black market) a posse of uniformed military men paid us a visit. I was invited to be an honoured guest at a noontime event at army headquarters the next day. With plans to travel into the countryside, I declined with regrets. These were not accepted. A military escort would pick me up on the morrow.

The following day I was taken not to the army base but to a flat concrete bunker that I knew to be the headquarters of the secret police. As I was marched down a long, dark tunnel, I speculated on how many had come this way before me, never to retrace their steps. We emerged into a drill hall and a gloomy scene. A crowd of several hundred people, about half in military garb, sat before three open coffins whose uniformed, bemedalled occupants had been killed a few days earlier in a Contra ambush. I was shown to a seat directly in front of the bier, cheek by jowl with the portly *commandante* in question. One after another, armed mourners approached their departed comrades and let loose with fiery orations. I understood nothing, but the meaning was clear: bloody revenge on the gringos. My host spoke not a word to me, though he seemed to eye me accusingly during his shift at the caskets. It was time to leave town.

There was one final coincidence, if it was one. In the airport waiting room, a military policeman motioned me to follow him outside. I clutched my passport tightly as he led me behind the terminal building. He stopped and then slowly drew out his pistol. Alarm turned to relief when I saw that he held the gun in his open palm like an offering. Would I care to buy his sidearm? I agreed the nickel-plated Smith & Wesson was an admirable weapon and the fifty-dollar price tag a fraction of its cost in Virginia. Rather than insult the policeman with an immediate rejection, I raised the issue of getting the gun through airport customs. He assured me that would not be a problem. In Miami, however, the officials might not be so co-operative, I reminded him. The policeman pleasantly accepted my refusal and let me go on my way.

Perhaps, like so many in that country in those days, he was just a fellow desperate for Yankee dollars. Or he may have been the accomplice of a jealous lover who needed a reason to arrest me. *El Commandante* went on to become a respected politician and poet in his homeland. I often wonder what became of our mutual girlfriend.

In the spring of 1982, Don Cameron dispatched me to Argentina to cover a rare modern-day shooting war between a former imperial power and a one-time New World colony. The dispute centred on the British-dependent territories of South Georgia and the Falkland Islands, three hundred miles off the coast of Argentina in the South Atlantic. Long claimed by Argentina, *Las Malvinas* provided the ruling military junta with a rallying cause for patriotic sentiment and a distraction for citizens who were chafing under horrific political abuses and economic mismanagement.

On April 2, Argentina's military forces invaded and occupied the largely agricultural islands. The inhabitants were easily overcome: Sheep outnumbered people, and the population had little more than a few shotguns to defend themselves. The strutting generals back in Buenos Aires had told Argentinians that the British lacked the moral courage to fight, that they were fat and lazy. This was a tragic misjudgment of Britain's Iron Lady, Prime Minister Margaret Thatcher. When diplomacy failed, she stunned the junta by sending a naval task force to retake the islands.

I arrived in Buenos Aires feeling, as many did, that this was some sort of Gilbert and Sullivan theatrical production that would amount to little more than a shouting match. Cameraman Malcolm Fox and I set up in the elegant Marriott Hotel in the city square across from the train station. Two blocks away, the trendy Florida Street shops were brimming with luxury fashions while inflation ran at exorbitant rates. For more than a month, I filed almost nightly stories, the satellite feeds transmitted from the top floor of the hotel.

At first it was a cakewalk of an assignment. We covered the shuttle diplomacy as efforts were made to head off a confrontation. Canada uttered the usual sighs and appeals for a fair and lasting settlement. Al Haig met with the generals, who appreciated that he was one of them, but he was unable to break the deadlock between the British and Argentinians. He told reporters that the situation was not looking good, and suddenly the mood toward the international press cooled appreciably. On the streets, people stopped to lecture us, and the ever-present police turned hostile.

Moreover, as we started to hear horrendous tales about the regime, our attention was drawn to Argentina's domestic politics. For four years, the military had carried out a war of extermination against so-called "leftist revolutionaries." In a highly organized campaign of state-sponsored torture and terror, they had murdered an estimated three hundred thousand people, most of them young men and women. When mothers and grandmothers mounted a public campaign to find the "disappeared ones," some of them too were killed. Accounts of thousands of people thrown to their deaths from aircraft and of torture cells inside the Navy Mechanical School, not far from the elegant shops and theatres of downtown Buenos Aires, were chilling to hear.

More shocking was the knowledge that leading business-people, journalists, and Catholic clerics silently and in some cases actively supported these crimes. I realized how ignorant I had been of the realities in a country proud of its cultivated ways but permeated by fear. A lawyer invited me to his home for dinner and behind closed blinds and in a voice barely above a whisper confessed his agony over what was happening to his country. He was a sophisticated, well-educated man who explained that everyone he knew was afraid to speak out against the military bosses. He provided eye-opening and invaluable grist for our reports back home.

Like caricatures of Chaplin's *Great Dictator,* in riding boots and elaborate uniforms, the junta leaders could have stepped straight out of a comic book, but they were far more dangerous. Their florid televised speeches about blood and honour echoed the excesses of the Third Reich. Indeed at informal social gatherings, I frequently heard opinions expressed that were strongly reminiscent of Nazi and Fascist propaganda. People spoke of a cancer eating at their society. Just as surgeons must cut out not just the tumour but all the flesh surrounding it, so too was it necessary to eliminate undesirables to save the body politic.

In the days before hostilities erupted, Argentinian officials worked to win the sympathies of the foreign press corps. I went to cocktail parties with known killers, suave in their monogrammed jackets and ties. On one occasion I attended a house party with a man I had met at a government social function. I was surprised to find myself the only foreigner at the event and thus the centre of considerable attention.

Talk naturally turned to the imminent battle. Who would triumph? Some of the guests were silent, but most agreed with my host who, using the conflicts in Vietnam and Northern Ireland to buttress his opinion, declared that soldiers from democracies were drawn from the lower classes; like their leaders, they lacked the moral fibre to fight for a cause they believed in.

A young man wearing a naval coat of arms on his jacket pocket challenged me to predict the outcome. My view was that the Argentinian conscripts, however brave, could be no match for the professional British troops, among the toughest and best-trained infantrymen in the world. I said the challenge would be much more difficult than taking on a few hundred sheep farmers and added that no one could remember the last time Argentina's forces had done any serious fighting. We had been speaking

English, but the young man exploded into angry Spanish. I retreated to another part of the room, leaving behind me shouts and the sound of a struggle. Two of the fellow's companions were restraining him from inflicting physical damage. The person who brought me rushed us down the elevator and drove me back to my hotel in silence. I was lucky. Within days, men in civilian clothes driving the infamous Ford Falcons were picking up foreign correspondents off the street. Reporters were roughed up and dumped naked in the barrios to intimidate the rest of us.

None of us seriously expected open warfare, perhaps anticipating that a show of force by the British would bring a negotiated resolution. Instead an amphibious assault recaptured South Georgia Island and a British submarine sank the Argentine cruiser *Belgrano,* taking 323 lives. That night I sent out my report on the sinking, and afterwards a friendly hotel waiter suggested it might not be wise to go out at night thereafter. Our Argentinian translator and those who worked for other networks suddenly quit, and the locals shunned us. Getting reliable information became difficult, especially since any material given out by the army was laughably inaccurate. Sometimes they would provide the same photo, claiming it to be two different locations, or a bit of film that obviously predated the damage caused by British attacks.

After a second month, I was ready to return home to Washington and my day job covering the Reagan administration. Toronto sent a replacement who had advertised his intention to become a full-time foreign correspondent. I got him settled, briefed him on the most useful contacts and the best bars, and waited for him to get to work. But he wouldn't leave his hotel room. Every time I tried to drag him out, he went into a cold sweat. Days passed while he dithered. Finally, he told me that he felt his life was threatened, that the danger was too great. It was getting a little rough on the streets, but the war itself was a thousand miles away. The poor guy confessed to me that perhaps he was a coward. In fact I think he was a highly intelligent person with a too-active imagination. You can't cover war up close if you dwell on the personal risks. Inevitably, he demanded to be sent home. We hired a security man to accompany him to the airport.

The next candidate was the indefatigable Pamela Wallin, then host of *Canada AM*. Don Cameron had hired her from the *Toronto Star*, where she was a reporter in the Ottawa bureau. Wallin remained on the scene until the Argentinians surrendered. A photograph of her covering the fiery postwar riot in the square facing Government House is a tribute to her courage. I suspect she even enjoyed her first taste of tear gas. Cameron had warned Wallin that she was a test case; the network had not often sent women into wars. She did her gender proud. Nothing demonstrated Wallin's talents as more than a drawing room anchor than her performance under literal fire in Argentina and elsewhere. Soon afterwards, she was named the network's Ottawa bureau chief.

Waiting for my plane out of Buenos Aires, I sat in the airport bar and considered how such a highly cultured nation could have slipped so easily into barbarity. When the country returned to democracy after the junta was defeated, Argentinians made little effort to examine what had happened. Germany faced its sins and learned from the Nuremberg trials; South Africans did the same with their reconciliation courts. In Argentina trials were few, and later on the worst of the convicted killers were pardoned in the interests, citizens were told, of national unity.

In 1989, I took the most expensive airport taxi ride of my life, from the terminal in Panama City to my hotel, paying five hundred dollars for a journey of roughly twelve miles. I arrived just days before the American invasion that ousted President Noriega, once a U.S.-supported strongman but recently accused of international drug trafficking. The Panama Canal could not be allowed to fall under the control of a narco state, and the Americans were mobilizing to bring down Noriega.

Fighting had already broken out downtown, and the route from the airport was littered with burning tires and evidence of shooting. Not unreasonably, the cabs were refusing to take passengers, and only the promise of a hefty fee got me to the hotel. There I found the power cut off and had to make my way up fourteen storeys by candlelight. No sooner had I located my room than the Toronto newsroom telephoned, asking for a voice report. That story was written and read by stuttering candle flame.

A discouraging number of young Americans with military haircuts were staying at the hotel, obviously members of an advance intelligence unit preparing for the invasion. But their presence made all of us North American reporters seem like marked men to the Noriega gang. Sure enough, as the crew and I were returning from a late dinner, armed men pulled us over in our car. They were in civilian clothes, which was a bit worrying. Again, as in El Salvador, it was out of the car, arms on the roof, and guns pushed into our ribs. And, thankfully, once again, when they learned that we were Canadians, we were allowed to go without further trouble. Shortly afterwards, the Americans invaded, a brief spate of intense fighting took place in the city centre, and it was all over.

We did a few reports on the dismal outlook for Pineapple Face, as the acne-scarred Noriega was called, and then quit the scene. A nice, neat little war. Great rum, good restaurants, and nothing to contribute to sleepless nights.

7

RETURN TO THE RIDEAU

Pierre Trudeau had submitted his second and final resignation from the leadership of the Liberal Party while I was in Washington, and I admit to watching those events with less than professional detachment. Constant rumours of his possible retirement had circulated for several years, a period that marked a widening gap between dispirited party members and their preoccupied standard-bearers in Cabinet, yet no one (except perhaps William Casey) could discern the prime minister's intentions.

By January 1984, party president Iona Campagnolo felt it necessary to report on the state of the party to its leader. The party's constitution provided for such a report, but Keith Davey refused to allow it, and the faithful Prime Minister's Office staff blocked every attempt to arrange a meeting between Trudeau and Campagnolo. Finally, Ted Johnson scheduled a lunch for February 28. It was snowing when Campagnolo arrived at the prime minister's residence, precisely on time. She and Trudeau sat down to a salad lunch during which they discussed each of the party's regional organizations. She told him that there was a general sense in the ranks that the Liberals would lose the next election and the party recommended he leave office before, rather than after, such a defeat. He should go out as the champion, not the vanquished, as had happened in 1979. The party desperately needed rebuilding, but Trudeau had no interest in that task. It followed that he should consider resignation at a time of his own choosing, but soon.

After lunch, Trudeau and Campagnolo travelled back to Parliament Hill together in what had become a full-blown storm. Before they parted, she told him that Canadians would expect some sort of drama to be attached to his decision, and he said he would let her know his thinking by morning. That was the night of the famous walk in the snow. Campagnolo also took a stroll in the wintry capital, agonizing over whether she had been too candid and blunt in relaying the feelings of party members. Promptly at ten o'clock on the morning of February 29—a leap year day and hence the element of drama Campagnolo had anticipated—Trudeau's letter of resignation was delivered to her by hand.

Not long after, Trudeau was in Washington to accept an award and invited me to his hotel for a visit. I told him I could not travel without a camera. Obviously he wanted to get a few things off his chest because he agreed to be interviewed during our get-together. He was miffed that the Turner-led Liberals were starting to blame his stewardship of the country and party for all their problems. "If they don't shut up," Trudeau declared, "I will come back and run against them." After that remark was broadcast on the national news, his detractors stopped complaining.

Trudeau was gone, but unlike so many pensioned-off politicos, he was not one to fade away gently. He never lost his ability to influence the country. In 1987, he came out of the shadows to campaign against Mulroney's Meech Lake constitutional deal and was instrumental in turning the country against it. Around the time he made a brilliant anti-Meech speech to a special House and Senate Committee, I met him at a gathering of the canoe group and told him I thought he was mistaken. I believed Meech might head off an inevitable and painful confrontation with Quebec. He shot me a hard look and got a laugh from the others by announcing that his friend Oliver was in need of remedial reading on constitutional issues. I'd hoped Meech and new leadership might bring closure to those endlessly perplexing issues.

Years of covering American politics and the Reagan administration, its good and bad features, had taken the edge off my youthful convictions about progressive politics, and although I was no late-blooming Republican, I was intrigued to see how far to the right Mulroney might try to shift my own country. But I was content to follow it from afar, even when Don Cameron asked me to replace Pamela Wallin as chief of the Ottawa bureau in 1988. She was returning to Toronto as a national correspondent and occasional news anchor.

As happens to all Canadian reporters who live and work there, Washington had expanded my horizons. The thought of returning to the often-suffocating nitpicking of Parliament Hill did not inspire me, but Cameron dispatched Tim Kotcheff, my canoe partner (as Don well knew) and his senior news executive, to deliver an ultimatum. Business was business, after all, and the message was come home or ship out. Tim and I talked during a long and well-fortified dinner in Georgetown until he committed to a generous financial offer, putting it in writing on a paper napkin. When I received my first paycheque, the figure did not jibe with my fuzzy memory of the amount specified, and either I had misplaced the paper napkin or Tim had carefully retrieved it. The matter remains unresolved to this day.

Back in Ottawa and once again in the business of managing people, I took a leaf from the Reagan playbook. Perhaps I should have felt less confident than I did, but the simplest thing in the world seemed to be to hire people smarter and more talented than myself, then provide a supportive work environment in which they could succeed. If, as part of the bargain, their accomplishments made me look good, that was fine too. I was able to hire a bevy of new individuals, many of whom went on to enjoy distinguished broadcasting careers. One of the first new faces was Kevin Newman, whose work as the network correspondent in the Maritimes had long impressed me.

Newman was a must-have, but the bureau I inherited from Wallin was all male and the testosterone levels were way too high. By the next election four years later, fully half the editorial and reporting staff were female. I had always found myself comfortable with women colleagues and with a consensual style of operating, rather than a top-down hierarchy.

Head office in Toronto was as demanding as ever. Yesterday's triumphant scoops were soon forgotten if today's CBC or Global coverage delivered an angle that we had not. We were under pressure to match our broadcast competition story for story, even when we suspected, but could not prove, that their pieces were faulty. If we fought off the national assignment desk and were proven right, this too was forgotten at the next skirmish.

Management obsessions had not evolved much during the near-decade I spent in Washington, but political Ottawa was undergoing a sea change. More and more I found the capital on the Rideau resembled its counterpart on the Potomac. There was less civility and more partisanship, although in some ways this made for livelier coverage. Conflict is a good fit with television and television now drove the coverage at all the bureaus. If a newspaper broke a story, it lay virtually dormant until it was broadcast on television. Certainly the atmosphere was made more stressful by the sudden arrival of new and numerous ethical dilemmas. Daily, it seemed, we were called upon to balance the demands of special interests or fierce partisans with journalistic truth and fairness.

Not long before I departed for Washington, two friends, Mike Robinson and David MacNaughton, had left their jobs in the office of a Cabinet minister to set up a consulting firm. I offered them lunch and some fatherly advice: Don't do it. That kind of business might thrive south of the border, but it will never work in Ottawa. So few individuals actually make the decisions in this town that outsiders have no need of consultants to knock on doors. How wrong I was. Today both of these men are millionaires, and reporters are buffeted by swarms of industry flacks and private lobbyists.

Within government, communications specialists and press aides became equally aggressive. Sometimes the approach would be presented as well-meaning concern. A Mulroney press assistant inquired solicitously whether I might be troubled or puzzled by a particular issue, lest lack of information affect my presentation of the government's position. How could they help? Sometime later, it was widely believed that Mulroney had

intervened with the friendly owners of another news organization to sideline a reporter whose columns on the prime minister
were notably inflammatory.

My worst experience of this kind happened during the
Chrétien era and involved a communications officer whose
minister seemed constantly to be in hot water for a series of
misdeeds. Naturally the CTV bureau was reporting the minister's travails for all to see. In an effort to shut down our coverage,
the press aide decided to go nuclear. The network was in the
process of applying to the Canadian Radio-television and
Telecommunications Commission for a raft of new television
licences. I was told outright that if we did not cease our unflattering news stories, the minister would see to it that the network's
applications were rejected. Of course the CRTC is supposed to
be an independent semi-judicial body, but that did not seem to
restrain the press aide.

I pondered how to deal with this. I did not have the
conversation on tape, so a denial was entirely likely. Indeed, I
did not know for certain that the politician involved had even
uttered such nonsense. I decided to go directly to the source
and requested a private meeting with the minister. He expressed
astonishment that a member of his staff would make such a
gross threat. Within a few weeks the fellow was quietly let go,
although not without one final and delightfully obscene phone
call to me. He was not the first or last of his ilk, and although
the threats were rarely that flagrant, his style of operating with
the media became much more commonplace. The trend began
with the first Mulroney government, when a cadre of influential
political assistants took up residence in the corridors of power,
all with their own urgent agendas.

The presence of lobbyists also intensified. Not long after he had led the Conservatives to an unprecedented majority victory in 1984, Mulroney invited his political supporters to belly up to the trough, promising that no Liberal would get a cent until every deserving Tory had been looked after. After that kick-start, friends and party hacks poured into town. They set up consulting firms that offered little more than a promise to open Cabinet ministers' doors—for a price. The right Tory connections won millions in government contracts and commissions, a sorry imitation of the practice in Washington, where Ronald Reagan's pals grew rich as lobbyists. Much of this was going on well behind the scenes, and the press gallery did its best to keep on top of it. The same applied to the RCMP, one of whose top criminal investigators told me he was well occupied following up on suspected financial hanky-panky in the awarding of contracts, some of which led to the laying of charges.

Mulroney's connections to doubtful money were evident very early on in the contests he waged against Joe Clark for the leadership of the Conservative Party. It was at the party convention in Winnipeg in January 1983 that Mulroney effectively won the prize, filling the floor with delegates bused in from Quebec. I recall watching these confused men and women disembark from their buses and follow their minders to the voting booths, all the while being instructed to vote against Clark's leadership. We were doing exit polls, so I asked one of these delegates how he had voted and he replied, "to get rid of Clark." His minder leaned in with a word in his ear. The delegate then corrected himself to say he had voted to keep Clark. The result was that our exit numbers projected much greater support for the leader than actually existed and set up high but ultimately false expectations among Clark's workers. The actual tally of 66 percent in Clark's favour was deemed too low—at least by Clark—and he called a leadership convention that we all knew Mulroney would win.

Reporters wanted to know who was bankrolling this questionable and expensive operation. That Sunday, on the long-running CTV interview show *Question Period*, Conservative stalwart Dalton Camp revealed that the money to defeat Clark had come from offshore. He was referring to German businessman Walter Wolf, who later sought contracts with the government and who also introduced Mulroney to Karlheinz Schreiber, another German businessman.

My personal relationship with Mulroney did not start well. In 1976, he had emerged the bruised loser in his first leadership contest with Clark, but he was already thinking ahead to next time and was determined to maintain a high profile. That year he attended the annual Parliamentary Press Gallery Dinner. It was precisely the kind of venue at which a hungry, upwardly mobile self-promoter like Mulroney would feel comfortable, mingling with the Governor General, the prime minister and the leader of the Opposition, and the most influential journalists in the country.

At the pre-dinner cocktail party, Mulroney and I chatted together over drinks. Evidently Mulroney was still nursing resentments at his leadership defeat. Before I could offer words of commiseration, I spotted Jim Munson, then a private radio reporter, vigorously shaking a bottle of beer and approaching Mulroney from behind. Munson had a wild look in his eyes. I dropped my drink and reached over the shoulder of the startled target to try to disarm Jim Munson. Too late. He shoved the foaming brew down the back of Mulroney's tuxedo. Mulroney turned and lunged at him, shouting, "I'll kill you, you little bastard." Munson was a famously aggressive reporter as well as a prodigious hockey scrapper, but the future prime minister would have floored him had I not stepped between them. I tried to make the preposterous argument that Munson had accidentally stumbled with a beer in his hand. Mulroney understood I was not involved, but he associated me with the incident and was too proud a man to forget such a humiliation.

At least Munson was nonpartisan in his assaults. On one occasion when then prime minister Pierre Trudeau was trying to dodge the media after a Cabinet meeting, Munson pushed a microphone into his face. Trudeau bounced him back with a judo hip toss. Undaunted, Munson countered with a hard check. Trudeau was coming off the boards with a snarl when his RCMP bodyguards intervened to prevent a brawl. Munson's bosses were mortified and intended to fire him, but when Trudeau heard of it, he insisted that he, not Munson, had started the fracas and that the reporter should not be disciplined on his account.

Brian Mulroney never learned the wisdom of ignoring slights and insults from lesser mortals, and seemed incapable of understanding that settling scores is a waste of energy better spent achieving the goals that are the ultimate revenge. He appeared supremely confident, but I often wondered if he suffered self-doubts that sprang from his working-class boyhood on the north shore of Quebec. An amateur psychologist might conclude that these insecurities explained Mulroney's desire for the approval of others and the reassurance of positive exposure in the media. His daily question to his staff was, "What are the boys saying about me?"

Ronald Reagan, Mulroney's mentor and friend, knew by training and instinct that overexposure could be fatal. Yet

Mulroney had to associate himself publicly with every minor issue or crisis. When his government ran into trouble, as all governments do, he became the lightning rod for Canadians' frustration and anger. In Mulroney's first term in particular, scandal dogged his Cabinet colleagues, but the ignominy stuck to him.

Adding to Mulroney's image problem was his tendency to overblown rhetoric and galloping hyperbole, excesses that his advisers could never rein in. He overacted on the public stage, leading many to question his sincerity and authenticity. I was astonished by his actions at the Shamrock Summit in 1983, where it appeared to me that he dragged a reluctant Ronald Reagan into their famous duet, "When Irish Eyes Are Smiling." Others were offended by Mulroney's attachment to wealth and showy consumption. Tales of extravagant spending by his wife, Mila, were rampant, whereas her dedicated fundraising for the Canadian Cystic Fibrosis Foundation was unfairly dismissed as a public relations gimmick.

I returned to Ottawa just as the Conservative government was ending its first term in 1988, and I prepared the bureau to cover what we knew would be a historic election on the issue of free trade with the United States. I assigned myself to cover the prime minister's campaign.

By this time the relationship between the Prime Minister's Office and the press corps was poisonous. Most of my colleagues hated Mulroney, and they seemed to seek out stories to justify their opinion that his was a dishonest and unworthy government and that he himself was unfit for leadership. Typical of those were the rumours regularly published by *Frank* magazine—now defunct—suggesting that Mulroney was under treatment for alcoholism. Everyone seemed to know someone who knew someone who had shared a room in a drunk tank with the prime minister. These stories were so persistent that our own desk in Toronto asked me why we were covering up Mulroney's alcoholism. Time and again I asked those who repeated these claims for a name, a source of any kind, but the trail invariably led nowhere. One of my bosses once called and said ABC in New York had a witness who had seen Mulroney being admitted to an alcohol treatment facility in Miami the preceding Saturday. Could I dig around Ottawa and find out whether he was in fact out of town? "No need," I replied. I had dined with Mulroney at Harrington Lake that Saturday, along with Don Newman and Charles Lynch. Unless the prime minister had sent his double to dinner, he could not have been in Miami that night.

Of the many elections I covered, including presidential campaigns, none was more arduous and gruelling than that of 1988. Those of us in the media understood that the outcome could transform the national economy and change Canada's relationship with the United States in ways that might not be clear for years to come. Mulroney hit the road as if the hounds of hell were pursuing him. In fact, he was chased only by an unruly pack of Liberals led by John Turner, who upped the ante by declaring the election the fight of his life and free trade a threat to the nation's sovereignty.

I had spent countless hours with Turner, discussing politics and economics over many a Scotch and soda. Turner believed in and tried to live by old school virtues: loyalty to the cause, devotion to duty, and most of all trustworthiness. This put him at a tactical disadvantage against Mulroney, Trudeau, or Chrétien, whose teams were far less fussy about such matters. Turner was rusty when he returned to politics in 1984 after years spent in Toronto's corporate boardrooms. He was badly out of touch with real people's problems, as were the advisers he gathered around him, and he discovered that the parliamentary press corps was no longer a cozy gang. When he asked me to explain the new rules, I had to tell him there were none anymore. In 1988, his campaign against free trade was courageous, but it put him at odds with his own instincts and, even worse, those of many in the Liberal Party.

Those late November days on the campaign trail began before sunrise and ended not with the final evening election rally or the filing of the latest story, but back on Mulroney's plane. He insisted on travelling to the location of the next day's events during the night before. En route, the press corps devoured cold hamburgers and beer and napped fitfully. Once arrived, we checked into hotel rooms in the middle of the night. Many mornings my first act on waking was to phone the front desk to inquire what town I was in.

The stakes were huge and so were the crowds. Noisy anti–free trade demonstrators showed up at every appearance. I had to admire Mulroney's cool and restrained manner when debating them from the stage. Heading into a rally in PEI, Mulroney was accosted by a man who jumped the rope line, thrust his face inches from Mulroney's, and shouted, "Fuck you!" Mulroney turned to him and said, "And a good evening to you also, sir."

Private moments on the tour revealed a delightful candour from Mulroney. His blunt and obscene characterizations of his opponents were hilarious, the parodies sharp and well timed. But he was utterly committed to the fight. At one packed rally,

I took a back stairwell to escape the crowds and ran into him leaving with his RCMP bodyguards. Still sweating and flushed with excitement, he grabbed me by the shoulders and, as if I were an audience of thousands, exclaimed, "It's going to be a new Canada, Craig. A new Canada!" He won that election with a second majority, a result that was most accurately predicted not by any pundit in the travelling press entourage, but by the driver of Mulroney's campaign bus.

The U.S.-Canada Free Trade Agreement, which was signed with much fanfare in January 1989, was a necessary, but painful, transition. It forced an unprepared country to acknowledge the realities of global competition and ultimately guaranteed Canada access to the world's richest economy. And it was just one of Mulroney's ambitious national initiatives.

Mulroney had undertaken the Meech Lake Accord in his first term in an attempt to bring Quebec into the constitutional fold. In the days leading up to the June 23, 1990, deadline for ratification, the premiers gathered in Ottawa for a final round of tense negotiations. At one point, the CBC announced that a historic deal had been struck. They were wrong, and I reported the pending failure even as they reported the opposite. My sources were two premiers who had unwittingly tipped us off when they were overheard by a source sitting in a washroom stall. We had enough of the true picture to allow us to pursue the balance of the story. When Manitoba and Newfoundland failed to sign on, the deal was officially dead.

In this case, Mulroney had helped sink his own ship. He boasted to a *Globe and Mail* editor that he knew exactly when to apply pressure on the premiers, suggesting that he had deliberately created a crisis atmosphere at the negotiating table and picked his moment to "roll the dice." The notion that he had gambled with the future of the country infuriated Canadians.

Mulroney tried constitutional change again in 1992 with the Charlottetown Accord, but it too was rejected, this time by a national referendum. He paid a high price for putting the country through a constitutional meat grinder that, had his efforts succeeded, might have resolved a still-existing threat to national unity.

In 1989, he introduced the goods and services tax, a useful if unpopular economic tool that the Liberals of the day loudly decried. Can Liberal senators ever live down the picture of so-called Honourable Members blowing whistles and sounding horns in the Senate chamber in an effort to stall passage of the legislation? Mulroney enlarged the Senate to push through the legislation, and the tax came into effect in 1991. When the Liberals returned to power in 1993, they broke their election promise to scrap it. Likewise when Mulroney undertook the privatization of a raft of money-wasting state enterprises. The Liberals railed against these measures while in Opposition but did not reverse them once they formed the government. The Liberals eventually defeated the Conservatives, yet they retained Mulroney's economic policies and enlarged upon them. In many respects, Mulroney was the architect of the historic Liberal victories in the decade that followed, preparing the way for the prosperity that marked the Chrétien years.

In pushing these major initiatives, Mulroney, it could be argued, was more forthright and open with the country than either Trudeau before him or Chrétien after. The GST, free trade with the United States, and the Meech Lake and Charlottetown accords were all subject to vigorous public debate. It's also true that no leader since Mulroney has put forward significant policy ideas; our leaders have become fearful of national dreams.

At his best, pressing the case against apartheid in South Africa at the United Nations or offering long-overdue compensation to Japanese Canadians for their losses during the Second World War, Mulroney was as statesmanlike as any prime minister in our history. His understanding and command of the detail and nuances of foreign policy won him high regard and the status of an equal among other world leaders.

In private, he could be charming, engaging, and generous. I was not the only reporter who received a congratulatory phone call on the occasion of some personal celebration, in my case on the day my daughter was born, when Mulroney offered the loan of a baby carriage. His equally quick expressions of comfort to those who had suffered grievous losses were legendary. Had Trudeau done this, reporters would have swooned. With Mulroney, such gestures were regarded as ingratiating, if not deeply suspect.

The flip side of an attentive regard for others was Mulroney's apparent belief that every person had his price. I may have experienced a touch of that. We were both attending a lengthy social event in the House of Commons one night in Mulroney's second term. He invited me to his office for a chat while he changed his shirt. During our conversation, right out of the blue and with no preamble, he said, "Maybe I should put you in the Senate one day."

The offer was made casually enough, but I wondered if Mulroney was holding out the prospect of that comfortable red chamber should my coverage be sufficiently obliging. Had I wanted the appointment badly, I would have been on the hook for years. I replied with some truthfulness, "No, thanks. I can't afford the cut in salary." We both laughed off the remark and no more was said.

By late 1992, public and media distrust of Mulroney was widespread and his standing in the polls at a historic low for any prime minister. That fall, during another conversation in his office, Mulroney commented mournfully that he could rely only on his close family and a few old friends for support. Clearly he was considering a departure from office, so I started to look for hints of the timing.

At a canoe reunion in February 1993, I chatted with Bill Fox and his admirable wife, Bonnie Brownlee, both former staffers and close friends of the Mulroneys. They could not stay because they were rushing to a dinner with the prime minister. That would not have aroused my curiosity greatly, except that the next day I ran into another Mulroney family friend who had been at another 24 Sussex dinner. She told me everyone at that event, which included close Montreal pals, understood it was something of a farewell party. Without explanation and uncharacteristically, Mulroney was not in the Commons for Question Period the next day.

I called one of his aides who would not lie to me, I knew, because of our longstanding friendship. Was something up? "I can't talk about this," he said, and signed off abruptly. I sent a camera crew to 24 Sussex to keep watch and, within a few hours, they reported the arrival of several Cabinet ministers' limos. Working my contacts, I found someone who would have to know if Mulroney were leaving. He was reluctant to be the source of any leak, so we made a peculiar bargain: He would not have to volunteer anything. I would count to five and if he did not interrupt, I would take that as confirmation. He waited through the count, and then wordlessly hung up.

That night Lloyd Robertson and I broke the news to the nation. Of the hundreds of reporters covering Parliament Hill, no one had a whiff of the story. Robertson asked on air what I would do if Mulroney did not resign. I replied that if he did not go, I would have to. As Mulroney went in to inform his caucus of his resignation the following morning, February 24, he shouted boldly to the crowd of reporters, "Oliver better start looking for a job." That gave me a few minutes of panic until word leaked out.

If there is a lesson for aspiring reporters in this exclusive scoop, it is the importance of working one's sources and developing personal contacts. Ours is not a business for misanthropes. It's important too to establish the ground rules and stick to them. Do not allow yourself to be compromised by promising that certain information will not be used. No statement is off the record; only the timing of its release may be in question.

Many a source will ask for anonymity on a story that is worthy of public knowledge, and that is fine with me. But I will always want to understand the source's motive. I have declined more than one supposed scoop when the person offering it was looking for political gain and nothing more. For me, the value of personal connection with newsmakers and those around them has always been about depth and perception, the ability to bring context and insight into my reporting of events and individuals.

Many Canadians wanted to believe that Mulroney, or "Lyin' Brian" as he was called, was a crook. Long after Mulroney left office, revelations surrounding his cash-in-envelopes dealings with Karlheinz Schreiber became the subject of parliamentary committee hearings and a federal inquiry, and lent credence to those who shared that opinion. Long-time political allies felt betrayed and asked themselves what Mulroney could have been thinking. For years Mulroney's friends had drawn on their own ethical capital to defend him against charges of just this kind of questionable behaviour. In my view, Brian Mulroney became the Richard Nixon of Canadian politics. He could claim significant domestic and foreign policy achievements, but fatal flaws in his character brought him down.

One long-time colleague summed up Mulroney this way: He was deeply wounded by a childhood of poverty and a resulting low self-esteem. His experience left him with a desperate need for money and status, which ruined him.

Many Canadians have come to regret another legacy of the Mulroney years. Bitter over the rest of Canada's rejection of the Meech Lake Accord, Lucien Bouchard quit the Mulroney Cabinet and formed the separatist Bloc Québécois, which went on to win fifty-four seats and take over as the Official Opposition in the 1993 federal election. Bouchard's departure caused me to question his character. At a lunch not long before he jumped ship, the then environment minister waxed eloquent about his commitment to Canada. To hear him that day, you would have concluded Canada was the perfect union.

The presence of the Bloc in the Commons destabilized our national politics, making it extremely difficult for any national party to form a majority government. As well, through nothing less than blackmail, the Bloc used its leverage to secure disproportionately large financial transfers from Ottawa to Quebec. If in future Quebecers once again send separatists to Ottawa, English-speaking Canada may question Quebec's commitment

to the larger interests of the country. In another Quebec referendum on independence, the rest of the country might well say,
*Let's end this thing as amicably as possible and get on with building
a strong and prosperous nation.* What one separatist leader once
called "the knife at the throat"—that is, Quebec separation—
will perhaps have lost its value as a threat.

After Mulroney's departure, Kim Campbell narrowly won
the Conservative leadership and the prime ministership from
Jean Charest. But in the election Campbell called for October
1993, Mulroney's once-successful coalition of Quebecers and
Westerners could not hold, nor could Campbell overcome the
electorate's lingering distaste for the Mulroney government. A
week before the election, Bob Rae, then premier of Ontario,
called me in the studio. "Are you ready for the biggest defeat of a
government in our history?" he asked. He predicted the government would lose all but twelve seats. I told Rae I doubted it, and
of course we were both wrong. The Tories returned only two
Members to Parliament, one of whom was Jean Charest.

It is easy now to forget Kim Campbell's political star power
before that disastrous election. Even before the campaign, large
crowds came out to see Canada's first woman prime minister,
and they were not disappointed. At her best, she could make a
dazzling impression: witty, original, a charming and disarming
woman with a good, though occasionally unfocused, mind. I
was in the room when she sat down with Bill Clinton at the G7
summit in Tokyo in 1993. She attracted considerable interest at
that gathering and impressed reporters with her command of the
issues. The American president was thoroughly smitten. "Turned
on" and "eager" is the only way to describe his demeanour.
When his one-on-one with Campbell was over, he insisted that

they share his limo for the return trip to the conference meeting hall. If he did not make a grab for her in that armoured car, I'd be surprised.

As an election-time leader, however, Campbell was ill served by inexperienced advisers imported from her home province of British Columbia. She sidelined many of the Mulroney-era hands who could have saved her from herself. Nor did she win hearts among the media when she explained that she intended to run a campaign that would be beyond the understanding of old troopers like myself.

There were public gaffes aplenty and complaints that Campbell was undisciplined. Members of the Cabinet griped that they could not get Campbell's attention, and one commented bitterly that the prime minister was spending too much time closeted with her Russian boyfriend. Her staff defended the anti-Liberal ad that ridiculed Chrétien based on his personal appearance until public opinion forced them to pull it. After that debacle, I was chosen to ask the first questions at Campbell's news conference and naturally raised the issue of attack ads. She sat in stony silence for one question, then a second, until another reporter took his turn with a different line of inquiry.

One of the great what-ifs of recent Canadian history is whether Campbell might have defeated Jean Chrétien had Mulroney left earlier and given his replacement a year of seasoning before she faced the electorate. In the event, the economy was sagging, the Free Trade Agreement had not yet begun to show positive results, and Canadians were reluctant to endorse a prime minister they had not had time to figure out. That famous bare-shoulders portrait of Campbell sent the wrong message. At that point, Canadians needed to see gravitas, not cleavage.

The final humiliation for Campbell was that she had trouble finding work after the election defeat. Chrétien sent her to Los Angeles as the Canadian consul since, as Eddie Goldenberg remarked, we could not have a former prime minister on unemployment insurance, even if she was a Conservative.

The Tories attempted to rebuild over the next ten years under the leadership of Jean Charest, one of the most genuine people I have met in politics, and then under the good soldier Joe Clark in his second tour of duty. Neither could stop the tide of change demanded by the hard right from within the party ranks.

Political influence comes in many guises, and we in the media don't always recognize a game changer when we meet one. In the late 1990s, a political outrider, a man the press gallery gently derided as "Parson" Manning, undeniably shaped the national agenda. His utter faith in the rightness of his views and the conviction with which he expressed them seemed very like sermons from the pulpit, but I expect history will give favourable reviews to Preston Manning, if only in a sidebar.

The issues that Manning chose to push into the spotlight—taxes, the deficit, crime, and tough love for Quebec—became the country's major political preoccupations for nearly a decade. He created a space in the public arena for serious discussion of ideas that were barely mentionable by the mainstream parties. At the close of the twentieth century, the reigning Liberals were once again happy to co-opt the positions popularized by their rivals, and Manning succeeded indirectly in shifting the country to the right. His railing against government debt fed public concern, which allowed Chrétien and his finance minister Paul Martin to take the drastic measures they did to straighten out the nation's finances.

Preston's father, Ernest C. Manning, was the Social Credit premier of Alberta during much of my tenure as a CBC reporter covering the Prairies. Beloved by Albertans for his famous *Back to the Bible Hour* radio show, Ernest was to me an austere, humourless figure who barely tolerated reporters and rarely spoke to them. Communicating with the press was not a part of public duty as he saw it. We were a pack of peeping Toms, and how he ran his government was none of our business.

I expected the worst when in 1987 Preston was chosen to lead the newly created Reform Party of Canada at its founding "assembly" (not convention) in Vancouver. First impressions from the stump seemed to reinforce the hard-line schoolmaster image, so it was a surprise to discover a very different man in person. Preston Manning had a quick laugh and, unlike so many political leaders, was a keen listener. As for the party he created with a corporal's guard of discontented Westerners, it was a modern version of the traditional agrarian protest movements of the 1930s, with the added feature of a strong right-wing religious component.

But Manning was thinking beyond regional grievances. He believed real change was possible only by taking hold of the levers of power at the national level. If Reform's activism were confined to one or two provinces, its ambitions would be frustrated. In the early going, even after Reform had won its first federal seat with Deborah Grey's victory in a 1989 by-election, most of us in the national press corps regarded the party as a prairie fire that would burn itself out as quickly as it had ignited. I began to pay more attention when two old Vancouver friends confided that they had become financial supporters. One was my cousin, Tony Allen, a criminal lawyer and long-time NDP supporter; the other was a wealthy businessman and a Conservative. These were no Prairie rednecks.

While I may have been late seeing Reform coming, Brian Mulroney was not. During Mulroney's second term, his office called me to advise that the prime minister would be making a keynote speech to an audience of heavy hitters at the Palliser Hotel in Calgary. Recognizing that Manning posed a serious challenge to the Tories in the West, Mulroney focused in his speech on the evils of Reform. He hinted strongly that the Reformers were a nest of racists and bigots, and warned that an economic policy based on massive tax cuts and deficit elimination would break the country and destroy its social fabric. No doubt he also recognized that this upstart movement could undermine the western pillar of the coalition that sustained his own success. When I spoke to audience members afterwards, I was surprised at the hostile reaction to Mulroney's words from individuals whom I expected to be loyal Conservatives.

No better rule obtains for a reporter than to go and see for himself. In the fall of 1989, I went on the road with Manning, touring Manitoba and northern Ontario. Not since the days of the CCF in Saskatchewan had I witnessed such earnest grass-roots politicking. There was almost no advance work beyond renting a hall, and there was no attraction beyond a slight man with a Prairie twang, owl's glasses, and a stock speech that was long on detail and short on bombast. Yet he packed them in. All it took were handwritten notes nailed to telephone poles or circulated in stores and the crowds appeared out of nowhere.

Manning was a preacher, sure enough, though personally anti-charismatic. The power was in the message. The crowds were not jaded enough to dismiss his ideas—direct democracy, an elected Senate, no special status for Quebec—as impossible objectives, though they seemed like pipe dreams to hardbitten reporters.

I found Manning sometimes irritable with reporters but also candid in his relationships with them. He was not a man to tell an easy joke, but he did not lack a sense of humour about himself. The CTV cameraman assigned to Manning's first national campaign, Bill Purchase, had a great talent for mimicry and his imitation of Manning could fool the leader's own staff. One day Purchase was re-enacting a speech in that familiar high-pitched drawl when the man himself walked into the press room. Purchase froze, but Manning immediately picked up the recitation where Purchase had left off.

In public settings, Manning was serious and occasionally distant. Fortunately for him, his wife, Sandra, possessed an outgoing friendliness that helped warm her husband's image. The three of us went horseback riding together in the Alberta foothills and I could not help but be impressed by Manning's obvious delight in his wife. At dinner in the ranch house later, Sandra took the lead in the conversation around the table, while Manning listened with respect and admiration. They made a good team, each complementing the other's personality.

After the 1997 election, when Reform ousted the Bloc Québécois to become the Official Opposition, friends who represented a Canadian Jewish organization visited me in my office. We made small talk while I tried to guess why they'd wanted to see me. Finally, after some delicate tap dancing, they came to the point. I had covered Manning and his party for some time, they noted. Was there, as some believed, an anti-Semitic bias in the leader and the organization?

Though the party had its share of right-wing zealots and haters of gays and lesbians, Manning used precious political credit to heave them out. No party can control the private prejudices or statements of its members, but I never heard from Manning or any of his senior people even a whiff of anti-Semitism or intolerance of any kind. Those few closest to Manning were thoughtful and honest characters, fired up with the need for change. They included the wise Ray Speaker, the acerbic Rick Anderson, and the rough-hewn but fair-minded Jay Hill. All were moderates from the centre right but far from typical among the early Reform MPs.

My impression was that most of these rookies had never visited eastern Canada, let alone travelled abroad. They brought a fierce partisanship and a stiff moralism that verged on the sanctimonious. To them, Ottawa was Sodom and Gomorrah on the Rideau, full of soft-on-crime judges, lazy civil servants, spendthrift Liberals, and a complicit national media. They were the "antis"—anti-gay, anti-abortion, anti-government, and anti-Quebec.

In time, however, more than a few of the rookies showed themselves as susceptible to human frailty as the rest of us. During the sixteen years between the arrival of Manning and the Harper government's second re-election, quite a number retreated from politics after finding public life more than they could handle. Some left to save their marriages, others abandoned their families for the doe-eyed assistants who provided the admiration they did not get at home. At one point I estimated that as many as 20 percent of the 2010 Harper Cabinet had left their spouses,

openly taken lovers, switched sexual preferences, or otherwise
been undone by lonely nights and alcohol. None of this was new
to Parliament Hill; the difference was that their fellow MPs did
not pretend to moral superiority.

Manning at least was flexible and open to ideas. While he
was a dedicated Christian fundamentalist, he did not wear his
religious heart on his sleeve. For that reason, few thought he
would try to impose his personal moral beliefs on the country,
as might some of his caucus.

In the moment of Canadian history that Manning inhabited, he may have done the country a great service in another
way. The Western provinces and the Prairies in particular nursed
a cauldron of resentments and grievances against centralized
government and eastern Canada. Manning could have exploited
and inflamed those sentiments; instead, he chose the slogan
"The West wants in." By doing so, his movement caught the
voice of the West, but also spiked the guns of growing Western
alienation and Western separatism.

In 2000, the momentum to unite the right led to the
formation of the Canadian Alliance, a coalition of Reformers
and a few prominent members of the Ontario Progressive
Conservative Party. The Alliance chose Stockwell Day over
Manning as party leader, assuming the youthful, photogenic
Day could win the new entity votes in Ontario. But Day
communicated a message that most Ontarians didn't want
to hear, backed up by a perceived record of anti-gay, anti-
abortion, pro-gun, and pro-hangman rhetoric—all of which
his opponents put to devastating use in the election campaign
later that year. The party seemed headed for the extreme right,
rather than the political centre that Manning had steered for

and where the vast majority of voters in eastern Canada felt comfortable.

Had Manning contested the 2000 election, I have no doubt he would have been a formidable challenger to Jean Chrétien. Normally we hope for too much from fresh arrivals on the political scene: We want perfection and they inevitably disappoint. With Preston Manning, it was different. Little was expected from him at the start, but by the time he left in 2001, I felt that Manning and his wife, Sandra, had lent a fleeting grace to the political life of the country.

It would be hard to say as much for Kim Campbell or Stockwell Day. They are the unforgiven, never to be forgotten for taking their respective parties into the abyss. Both soared unexpectedly to the top of their parties' hierarchies, even though they were relative newcomers. They barely knew the key aides and advisers they'd inherited, inviting mistrust on both sides, and their campaigns were hobbled by infighting. The contrast with their common rival, Chrétien, who had operated for thirty years with the support of a savvy kitchen cabinet, could not have been greater.

Certainly Campbell and Day had charisma. They looked like leaders, and in the early going, their glibness was taken for profundity. Unlike Campbell perhaps, Day was never a serious contender, especially after a devastating CBC mini-documentary featured his evangelically inspired view on evolution. Canadians began to believe Day was simply an oddball, possibly a dangerous one. He had embarked on a campaign with all the superficial elements in his favour, and then talked voters into defeating him with a series of embarrassing pronouncements. On election day 2000, the Canadian Alliance added two seats to their Opposition ranks, but the breakthrough in Ontario never materialized.

Thereafter the internecine struggle to oust Day was a circus of intrigue and betrayal. Almost daily, willing caucus sources kept me informed of the latest plans and timetables to remove the leader. My informants will remain unnamed, as Stephen Harper later gave many of them plum Cabinet posts. Day at least had the satisfaction of becoming one of the most competent and media-friendly members of that front bench and of shifting attention away from the most contentious of his early beliefs.

Harper elbowed aside all comers and won the leadership of the Alliance in 2002. After that one of his closest advisers, John Reynolds, admitted they were watching greedily when, on May 31, 2003, Peter MacKay won the leadership of the Progressive Conservative Party. The defeated candidates, including Jim Prentice and Scott Brison, were furious when it emerged that MacKay had secured the backing of another rival, David Orchard, by signing an agreement promising never to merge the party with the Alliance. The race was tight, and MacKay captured it only on the fourth ballot amid accusations of duplicity. By that August, polls showed that his personal standing with Canadians was in the low single digits and support for the party near an all-time low. None of that much mattered, because before long MacKay took the party and his own leader-ship of it and smothered both in the cradle. In mid-October 2003, following a series of secret meetings, Harper and MacKay shook hands on a deal to merge the two parties.

As far as anyone could tell, MacKay had thrown away his party for a song. He did not even drive a bargain for the post of deputy prime minister in any future government, which left many believing he had been badly outmanoeuvred by the more cunning Harper. In March 2004, Harper took the helm of the united Conservative Party, having dropped the "Progressive" from its name, and pulled off a historic coup.

Soon after my return to Ottawa, Anne-Marie Bergeron and I were married. Little more than nine months later, enough to claim truthfully to her parents that Anne-Marie was not pregnant at the ceremony, we had a daughter, Annie Claire.

This time around, the role of father was a revelation. In the sixties, when my son, Murray, was born, the hospital would have considered my presence in the delivery room peculiar, if not medically unwise. But in 1989 I was there as Annie emerged into the world. She was silent for the first few seconds, but my apprehension ended soon enough and then it was bawling all around. Like all fathers at this moment, I was awestruck—a brand new life, safely delivered, and from where? I understood the mechanics of the process, but the train of events that had created a human being totally unique among the billions of others in the world remained a mystery. Albert Einstein was right when he observed that God does not play dice with the universe.

Unfortunately, the joys of second fatherhood coincided with my mother's accelerating decline. Her depression had led to heavy drinking bouts and recurring health problems. Every attempt I made to spend time with her ended in calamity, as if she couldn't bear to be with me for more than a few days. Perhaps my presence reminded her of the years we spent apart in Rupert, a period she was unwilling to confront or explain.

At my wedding, she became inebriated and created a scene by shouting racy obscenities at me during the after-dinner speeches. This was acceptable behaviour at most of the weddings I had attended in Prince Rupert, and Mom was truly funny, but my in-laws must have wondered what their daughter was in for. Even then, Mom's self-loathing was such that she refused to appear in any of our wedding photos.

Two years later, there was a less forgivable incident when Mom came to Ottawa for Christmas. My wife and I went off to work leaving two-year-old Annie in Mom's care. When I tried to call at noon to see how things were going, I got no answer and rushed home full of foreboding. I found Mom drunk and out cold on the floor, my daughter howling beside her. Fortunately, Annie had not crawled away or come to harm elsewhere in the house, but the incident was enough to shatter my composure. I shook Mom violently to wake her up and then refused to help as she crawled up the stairs to her room on her hands and knees. To this day I regret my reaction and wish I had understood more about the nature of manic depression. In the years following, Mom sent wonderful gifts and delightful books to Annie, but I was too frightened ever to have her in our home again.

I made a last attempt to save Mom from herself. She realized that the time had come to leave the stifling confines of Rupert. All her closest friends had died, many of them too soon from cancer. Sometimes I wondered if the heavy pollution of the air and water by a once highly toxic pulp mill might have contributed to so many early deaths. I bought Mom a two-bedroom condo near Vancouver's Jericho Beach, where I hoped she might find some peace and serenity. For a year or two, she seemed to manage, but the old demons eventually returned. Once again she was incoherent in phone calls, even as she tried to persuade me she was not drinking. Then came messages from well-meaning friends with reports of "falls" at the golf club and fender-bender car accidents.

I proposed an evening together in Vancouver on a working trip. She seemed enthusiastic. When I arrived at the condo, I found Mom's car parked outside with her beloved dog locked inside, gasping in the heat. There was no response to the buzzer, so I summoned the building security man who had to force the door. We found Mom face down on the kitchen floor, unconscious and intoxicated. More was to follow, including warnings that she was trying to kill herself. Twice she overdosed on pills and alcohol. On one occasion she refused to go with the ambulance attendants. There was no reasoning with her, nor would she accept professional help. Her two-pack-a-day habit inevitably led to lung cancer and a series of surgeries.

Like many in their late fifties, I found myself caring for a parent at long distance while coping with the needs of my own family and a demanding professional life. Mom's parting words on her last visit to Ottawa had been, "You will never have to look after me." I feel still a keen sense of guilt in confessing that, in my heart, I had hoped she was right.

~

Before leaving Washington, I had drawn another significant inspiration from the example of Ronald Reagan. His Saturday morning ritual of a horseback ride at Camp David and the obvious joy it brought him recalled for me those carefree summers on horseback at the ranch in Williams Lake. I decided to reclaim that pleasure permanently. Over the next few years I took winter vacations at guest ranches in Arizona and Texas, avoiding the big resorts in favour of small operations that focused on horsemanship rather than golf. Adherents of the equestrian sports insist there is scientific evidence that the four-dimensional movement of a horse releases a chemical in the brain that creates a feeling of well-being. It certainly did so for me.

For my fiftieth birthday, Anne-Marie bought me a fifteen-hand Chestnut mare named Katy. She was four years old and we had a lot to learn together, but after years of lessons from an Austrian riding master, I was able to compete in amateur horse shows, jumping fences. Charging at a three-foot fence on a cantering horse was almost as exhilarating as heading into a swirling rapid, except that hitting the ground was considerably more painful than plunging into the drink. The challenge became greater as my vision dimmed, but Katy was a natural Seeing Eye horse. I found the physical relationship between horse and rider so intimate that it seemed I had only to think about our direction before she responded as if reading my mind.

An engagement with horses also brought me closer to a colleague. Lloyd Robertson and I had been friends since his earliest days at CBC, but any time together was usually work related. That changed in 2002 when Lloyd was invited to be parade marshal at the annual Calgary Stampede, an honour extended in the past to sports heroes, Hollywood celebrities, leading politicians, and even royalty. Lloyd was unfamiliar with horses, so he was expected to ride in an open convertible. I thought this would make him look like some effete entertainer or politico, and I held out for horseback. When Lloyd put this to the organizers, they proposed to put him in the saddle but have his horse held by a cowboy walking ahead. This was even worse, the eastern dude being pulled along by his nose.

Although the stampede folks were thinking purely of Lloyd's safety, they did not know him. He took himself to a western-riding school near Toronto and spent hours learning to get comfortable in the saddle. When the day of the stampede arrived, Lloyd was greeted with roars of approval from the crowd, especially when the horse got it into his head to turn around and go back to the stampede barn. With a command reminiscent of John Wayne himself, Lloyd calmly reined in the animal and legged him on. Lloyd had found his sport.

Thereafter we took many horseback vacations together at a ranch I had frequented in the Alberta foothills near Bragg Creek. The Homeplace Ranch is owned by one of Alberta's leading horsemen, Mac Makenny. One day he took us on a mountain ride with trails so steep we had to climb up, leading the horses behind. Reaching a stone outcropping at the peak, we were able to view the mountains on all sides and found that our voices echoed across the valleys. Lloyd could not resist shouting to the peaks, "Good evening, I'm Lloyd Robertson and this is the news."

It was one of countless delightful moments in a friendship that has deepened with the years. Both of us experienced hard times and dysfunctional families growing up, but we learned to look to the future rather than regret the past. After such a start, we agreed, life could only get better, and it did.

8

NORTH OF NORTH

Whatever upheavals or changes might attend their professional and personal lives, the members of the Rideau Canal and Arctic Canoe Club continued to meet faithfully in Toronto, by the Rideau and, come high season, in the Arctic. The Far North offered incomparable obstacles but abundant rewards. With the confidence of a decade's adventures behind us, we joked that anything south of the Arctic Circle might as well be the Mexican Riviera.

The Arctic is still one of a few places on Earth where entire mountain ranges and ecosystems remain almost as they have been for millennia. Many people imagine a winter scene all year-round; in fact, even near the pole, there is a fleeting and urgent summer. The ephemeral nature of that season is what gives it its intense beauty. How sobering, then, to realize that global warming threatens the seasonal rhythm of life for all Arctic dwellers and may end the isolation that has been the region's best protection. Our generation could be the last to experience this terrain in its largely untouched, pristine grandeur.

Not that the conditions are always heavenly. Mosquitoes and other biting insects are plentiful, kept somewhat in check by the relentless winds, though being wind-bound is itself a dismal prospect on a canoe trip. Days pass in a monotonous cycle of sleeping, reading, talking, and cooking. It's not uncommon to have to tie the tents to the canoes, which are in turn weighted down with small boulders. The decision to resume a trip is taken after judging the ferocity of the flapping inner and outer flies against the tent skin or, worse, the sound of nylon ripping. The din inside the tent rises and falls like an audio barometer—so loud it can be hard to carry on a conversation. Having to shout at your companion tells you it is pretty bad and likely means more hours confined to quarters.

At the conclusion of the Hanbury trip in 1979, while our canoe group waited out brutal conditions until our plane could pick us up, Peter Stollery pulled a bad practical joke. He was out of sight in his tent while the rest of the group collected at the riverside camp. Peter shouted in despair that he could take no more and let off a pistol shot. After a moment we laughed, though one of the group murmured that Peter never was a great shot.

Even in fine weather, paddling in the Arctic meant that our routines had to be especially well disciplined and thorough. The first order of business on reaching a campsite was to look after personal matters—erecting tents, laying out sleeping bags, finding dry socks. Group responsibilities came next, with the canoes dragged into a semi-circle as counters for the cooks, while a stove, rather than a fireplace, was set up. In the Barrens there was no wood.

L'heure de bonheur found me at my customary bartending duties, but the pre-dinner gathering was more than a social nicety. It was the first group meeting since breakfast and an opportunity to rehash the events of the day. Plans and maps for the following day were reviewed and a consensus reached on the critical question of how many miles must be covered and what hour we must start out.

Any complaints were aired and debated. Once a chronic grumbler was told that we were to pass an outfitter's lodge the next day. He would be left there and arrangements made to fly him out. When tempers cooled overnight, he asked whether a few mitigating words might be said on his behalf prior to the punishment's being carried out. He was allowed to stay with the group. On another occasion, in Alaska, we held a trial when someone let a fresh catch of salmon—the evening's meal—slip into the river and disappear. The sentence, summarily enforced, allowed each person to throw a ball of mud at the defaulter from a distance of five yards.

As members of our all-male group married or settled into long-term relationships, the question of breaking the gender barrier arose. Any number of capable wives and girlfriends would have eagerly come along. But we could never overcome the issue of numbers: As long as the regulars signed on faithfully, our crews were large and logistically cumbersome enough. Responsibility for everyone's safety was also a constant concern.

We had learned that one cannot bluff a rapid. No amount of bravado or blind stubbornness can compensate for lack of skill, and in big and remote whitewater, the ability to overcome fear is equally essential. To go for it—what Hemingway described as "the final lunge at the bull"—becomes the elemental moment of truth. I was able to overcome my early fear, but it never quite left me: the dry mouth, the urge to urinate. Once we were committed, the butterflies lifted. But on many a restless night, I lay listening to the ceaseless roar of a rapid I would meet in the morning. Would it be my last? Was I, as someone once unforgettably told me, a drowner?

Drowning takes only a few minutes, fewer when strong currents are tumbling you end over end, preventing you from finding air at the surface. I dumped seriously only once, in the swollen Rouge River in Quebec during spring runoff. I could not keep my head above water; the standing waves and surging cross-currents kept sucking me under. I could feel the blood throbbing in my ears. Within seconds, the near-freezing water turned my hands into claws. My fingers lost the dexterity to grasp or hang on to the rocks that swept past.

Fortunately, one of my companions was Judd Buchanan, six foot five and strong and lanky. He raced ahead along the shoreline, waded out into the rapid as far as his tall frame allowed, and snared me as I tumbled by. Just below that point the river presented a sharp turn and even greater speed. I was glad I did not have to face those odds against my survival.

There is a hanging moment of suspension at the top of a big chute or rapid. The lead canoe team makes an irrevocable decision about whether to enter and what line to take, then contends with whatever faces it. The options can never be accurately judged from a far shore or a high point above the obstacle. At a distance, the forces are almost always underestimated. Modest standing waves become monsters at water level; ledges are deeper and rocks much wider at their base. In that blood-rushing moment of risk and excitement before the rapid, nothing else exists, no past and no future, only that instant of crazed exhilaration. And when it is over and safety is reached, who would not succumb to feelings of triumph and relief? Or discover again a sense of balance with the natural world and joy in the camaraderie of sharing it all with like-minded friends? John Godfrey once described any canoe trip as a legalized reversion to adolescence. Indeed, ours kept us young.

Our education in river running never ended entirely, nor could we allow ourselves to believe we were invincible or beyond accepting assistance when needed. That lesson was reinforced in 1982 when we completed an arduous and mishap-plagued trip down the Korok River in subarctic Labrador. Our put-in point on a lake near the headwaters in the Torngat Mountains was too high and we discovered there was not enough water to float the canoes. We spent the first three days dragging fully loaded vessels down shallow creeks, an ordeal that inflicted the usual injuries to feet and ankles.

Matters got worse when we finally reached the main stream. Canoe driver David Silcox and his bowman, John Godfrey, went over a ledge and into a souse hole. When the two abandoned ship, the canoe sank bow-first like a submarine going into an emergency deep dive. We could see it clearly lodged under a rock six feet below the surface as if preserved in aspic. Nothing could budge the canoe, which no doubt will remain in plain sight to amaze and puzzle future travellers for years to come.

The loss meant a dramatic change in transport accommodations. The two boatless paddlers, plus their baggage, had to be distributed among the three canoes still afloat, which left those vessels overloaded and less seaworthy. In two of the craft, the guests sat in passenger class, propped amidship against the backpacks. This was not good since we would shortly have to make a run for it across a wide stretch of open water. Ungava Bay is a vast expanse of water, but still small enough that winds can quickly whip it into a whitecapped frenzy. Before then, however, we had to run the last series of heavy rapids where the river crashed down out of the Torngat Mountains into the bay.

Tim Kotcheff and I now had on board David Silcox, an expert sternsman in big water. This was not unlike a third person interposing between a happily married couple. As we descended the rapid, David could not restrain himself from shouting instructions as to the safest course through the waters. But he was not in command in this vessel and often his choice was the opposite of ours. We soon had a full-scale domestic quarrel on our hands. For the first time in almost a decade, Tim and I began to argue with each other, and David, about technique. Decisions had to be made quickly as rocks loomed up fast in the steep rapids. Now we were three individuals countermanding one another instead of a team of two operating as one. Others remarked that we sounded like a brass band coming down the river.

That night we camped at salt water on the shoreline of Ungava Bay with David sharing our accommodation and peace restored at last. The view to our north looked very like open ocean. In the morning, we found the shoreline had receded, leaving our canoes high and dry. Ted Johnson had inadvertently left the tide tables on the charter plane. Had it been a flood tide, we would all have been twenty feet under, although Ted reassured us that the water lapping at our feet would have awakened us soon enough.

The route that morning took us across the mouth of a large bay to a point of land where we had to turn south, hugging the east coast of Ungava Bay until we reached our pickup point at the Inuit hamlet of Kangiqsualujjuag on the George River. About halfway across, we were engulfed in a pea-soup fog that came rolling in from the bay without warning. The fog was so impenetrable it was impossible to see a canoe more than ten feet away. We resorted to shouting out at intervals of five minutes or so to keep the three canoes from drifting apart, following a compass heading with a declination wildly off true north. All of us were only too aware of the risk that we might miss the point and head out into the open bay. That could be a serious misstep in overloaded open canoes designed for running rapids, not navigating heavy seas. Our relief was immense when, after about three hours, a rocky outcropping loomed up out of the fog. The compass perched on the canoe pack in front of me had not failed us, though the temptation to second-guess the needle in dodgy situations is hard to resist.

But this was not the end of our problems. When the fog dissipated, it was followed by persistent rain and a wind in our faces so strong that we were barely able to move forward against it. Worse yet, we obviously were fighting a twenty-foot outgoing riptide. I vowed to reduce Ted's rum ration as punishment for losing those tide times. The combination of wind and tide was pushing us farther out from shore where waves were blowing up, tall and ice-cold as only salt water can be.

The occasional wave started breaking over the gunwales, but it was impossible to stop paddling and bail. To do so in the high winds would have put us at risk of losing control of the canoe and broaching. We were the last canoe in line, and we knew if we went over we could endanger the lives of the others who might try to turn around and paddle back to us. A few years earlier, Pierre

Trudeau had underscored that truth as some of our group had been forced to cross a choppy lake on the Hanbury trip. When someone asked what to do if the canoe behind swamped, Trudeau's reply was chilling but realistic: "Sing louder and keep paddling."

Fortunately, salvation arrived in the form of an Inuit hunting party and their lifeboat-sized freight canoe. They came alongside and, with typical Aboriginal understatement, asked if we needed help. That was putting it mildly. In my judgment, we were well beyond the margin of safety. Some of our crew disagreed, but no one declined the offer of a lift. The Inuit took our canoes in tow and we, shivering with wet and cold, piled into their boat and found space between the hunters and three freshly killed caribou.

When we were safe in our lodgings, one of the Inuit men came to see me and asked, somewhat shyly, if I would consider selling our canoes. They were valuable commodities, and for him to buy them in Montreal and ship them in would be prohibitive.

I suggested he make an offer and he started at three hundred dollars each, fully expecting I would try to bargain higher. Instead, I countered with two hundred each. He looked at me as if to ask what kind of white man's trick was this. I figured our lives were worth a few hundred dollars.

As we boarded our charter flight the next morning, the Inuit brought us a stack of frozen caribou meat, a delicious treat we later enjoyed at that year's annual canoe reunion.

~

After a dozen years of paddling challenging rivers, everyone in the group had capsized except Tim Kotcheff and me. We attributed this to my limited vision. In running whitewater, both ends of the canoe have to act in unison, each paddler using whatever strokes are required to perform the necessary manoeuvres. Any confusion, disagreement, or delay can be fatal. Since my eyesight was not reliable enough to make calls of my own from the stern, I responded without question to whatever moves Tim initiated up front. We thought we were invincible—not just the Affirmative Action Canoe but also the OK Canoe, the one that always ended the trek intact. Unfortunately, that boast did not survive an incident in 1987 on the fierce Isortoq River in northern Baffin Island, when we lost everything but our lives.

In aerial photos and maps, which showed the Isortoq flowing some thirty-three kilometres southwest into Foxe Bay, it appeared doable. It had never been canoed, so there were no eyewitness accounts of conditions at river level. Ted Johnson, David Silcox, John Macfarlane, Peter Stollery, Tim Kotcheff, and I could not resist the call to be the first to record them.

From the moment we gazed down on the river from the windows of the aircraft delivering us to the starting point, however, we knew we were in over our heads. The riverbanks were solid stone, with hardly any sand or pebble beach to land canoes. Where the river wasn't a roiling torrent, it narrowed into miles of unnavigable cascades between sheer walls. It was too late to back out, so we soberly considered what lay ahead as we camped that night in bitter cold, directly across from the Barnes Ice Cap, one of the last remnants of the great glaciers that had covered the better part of the continent ten thousand years earlier.

Next day, we paddled where we could through waves reminiscent of Atlantic rollers. Whenever we encountered an impassable obstacle on one side of the river, we ferried to the opposite shore, one canoe at a time. For a few heart-stopping minutes, those waiting their turn watched the crossing canoe disappear into the waves as if swamped. David Silcox and his bowman, John Macfarlane, pulled ashore after one traverse as if sitting in a bathtub, their canoe full to the gunwales. Another ten feet would almost certainly have cost them their balance and dumped them into the churning rapids. David's face showed both anxiety and triumph. John silently lowered his forehead to his resting paddle as if in thanksgiving prayer.

Where paddling wasn't possible, each two-man crew pulled its canoe from the safety of the shoreline by manipulating the bow and stern lines. At the best of times, lining is a tricky business. Though you are off the water, life jackets are worn as padding against frequent falls on slippery boulders. Oftentimes it is necessary to run and jump to keep up with a canoe caught in a charging current. Twisted ankles and bruised feet are expected, but the worst outcome is a cracked head. When falling, heads up is the rule.

In some places through the canyons, there was no passage on either side, only steep granite walls. We did not know it, but we were engaged in a hybrid sport called "canyoneering," a combination of rock climbing and canoe lining. We crept along the walls, gripping whatever ledges and crevices our boots and free hands could find. Our other hands held lines to the bows or sterns of the loaded boats, pitching and tossing in the rapids five to ten feet below. In a balancing act worthy of the Cirque de Soleil, we teetered on narrow ledges while controlling the tension on the ropes that held the boats. Occasionally, an unexpected tug or a loss of balance meant one of the team had to throw away his line rather than risk a fall. The lone hanger-on then had to manage the charging vessel single-handedly until his partner had recovered his balance. The thundering river was frigid and the possibility of rescue, should someone slip, frighteningly slim.

Two days of this was enough to convince us that the enterprise was madness. The volume of the river was immense, greatly increasing the danger of its rapids. The unrelieved tension of physical effort was exhausting. Hands and feet were cut, ribs bruised from falls, nerves frayed. My mind has done me the kindness of erasing from memory whether it was Tim or I who stumbled and dropped his lead line. The current bit into our canoe's stern like a ravenous animal and ripped the line from the other man, who could not hang on to what was now a two-ton torpedo. I watched sick and disbelieving as our canoe flew downstream fully loaded and upright with no one aboard. It disappeared into a cauldron of piled-up water and waves.

Even now, many years later, I search in frustration for a favourite item of clothing or equipment. Then I remember. Was it Proust who said the hours of our lives are embodied in material things? I grieved the loss of personal possessions lovingly collected and cared for over many years. On the other hand, Tim and I were not in the canoe; we were alive and the trip was over. Fortunately, the accident occurred near an ancient riverbed lined with hard sand. This was one of only a few times we used Ted Johnson's emergency radio transmitter to contact a passing pilot.

There was a postscript. As luck would have it, the spot where we ended our expedition marked the last significant drop in altitude on the Isortoq. Just past that point, the river flows into a series of calm lakes that lead all the way to Foxe Bay. The following year, a few of the group insisted on completing the balance of the river. They found our canoe, its gunwales and guts ripped out. Nothing else surfaced except two bottles of our best wine, buried in the sand alongside the shell of the boat. Happily they were intact, and all of us enjoyed them in urban comfort at the club reunion a few months later.

Another opportunity for canoeing notoriety presented itself in 1992 when we made for Ellesmere Island and the Ruggles River. Ted Johnson had dreamed of this expedition for years, whereas Peter Stollery was game for anything; Eddie Goldenberg had probably never been so far away from Jean Chrétien; John Godfrey was supremely nonchalant, whatever the risks. We had invited two first-timers that year, perhaps hoping for fresh conversational material. Bill Fox filled the bill with his story-telling gifts, and Ross Howard, a *Globe and Mail* reporter and experienced outdoorsman, was stimulating company.

On Ellesmere, in a delightful reversal of roles for a television reporter, a dozen European tourists with video cameras captured our party's departure as we set off in canoes across Lake Hazen. In our remote locale, this was news: We were the first to attempt a descent of the Ruggles, the most northerly river in the world and the sole outlet for Lake Hazen.

The early signs were not encouraging. Though located in a rare thermal oasis that usually gives it some two months of frost-free days annually, the lake that year was a solid mass of white candle ice at the height of summer. Harnessed like beasts of burden, we had to drag our loaded boats nine miles across the lake to the narrow band of open water along the far shore. Behind us, some fifty snow-capped mountain peaks formed a phalanx from one end of the horizon to the other. Halfway across, I began to sink through the thin ice and I threw myself into the canoe. Tim upbraided me for stepping on the tomatoes. Apparently the fresh vegetables held a higher priority than I did.

Our plan was to follow the Ruggles' course to Chandler and Conybeare fiords and Lady Franklin Bay and the Arctic Ocean beyond, then paddle a few days north to Fort Conger, the long-abandoned jumping-off spot for several doomed nineteenth- and twentieth-century expeditions to the North Pole, only a few hundred miles beyond.

But the objective was beyond our reach. We were only a few days down the rapid-filled but relatively shallow river when ice walls began to appear on both banks, making it difficult if not impossible to go ashore if a canoe were upset. Farther along, large chunks of ice that had broken off from the walls floated by, prompting thoughts of the *Titanic*. We pressed on until a helicopter from the Federal Parks Department swooped down on us with a warning that the river ahead was treacherous, full of ice bridges and deep holes. They advised us that even if we made it past these hurdles, the ocean itself was solid pack ice. Moreover, heavy winds were forecast. Did we have ice screws with which to anchor our tents and equipment?

Not wanting to relive the grim fates of other adventurers from Sir John Franklin to Robert Edwin Peary, we gave up on further advance, hunkered down in our tents, and awaited the helicopter we had summoned by emergency radio. The winds were as advertised: During the day we had to sit in the corners of our shelters with our backs against the walls to hold them down. We slept that way as well, with the tent walls constantly hammering our heads.

During that long wait for the chopper, Bill Fox and I decided to go for a hike to ease the boredom. We climbed up a long

traverse to the top of the river canyon and walked south for
several hours. By then the cold was biting and we began the
trek back to camp. We'd walked a long time until I told Bill
I no longer recognized our trail. I had brought a map but no
compass, and neither of us had a clue where we were. The map
was of little help in this flat horizon, especially since we had
become completely disoriented.

The issue was simple: Had we walked past our takeout point,
or was it still ahead? We trudged on a few more kilometres and at
intervals I fired distress gunshots but heard no reply. We found
a high point from which we could gaze down on the river, but
everything looked the same. Night was settling in and a decision
had to be made: keep going or turn back. I elected to turn back
and Bill accepted that decision, God bless him. I was just uncertain enough that had he disagreed strongly, I would have pushed
us farther into the wilderness.

Finally Bill spied one of our companions standing at the top
of the campsite's ridge. Another few seconds and he might have
disappeared back down to camp. I will always wonder if Bill and
I could have missed the takeout path for a second time. The
headline *Lost in the Arctic* came to mind. But who would have
won top billing? Bill Fox, the high-profile former Mulroney
staffer, or Craig Oliver, an obscure reporter?

Taking the whole party out was not a rescue mission, of
course. If anything, we were oversupplied and knew our exact
whereabouts. But it was a few days before the winds died down,
allowing the chopper to land. By then the supply of rum was
falling dangerously low. I dared not tell anyone, but the disappointment at failing to reach Fort Conger was worth that scene
of departure at the outset, surrounded as we were by lights and

cameras and exclamations of admiration. For a fleeting moment, I understood why Franklin and the others had done it.

⌒

Sometimes I felt that the greater risk to our lives was taken not on the rivers but on the chartered flights in and out. In the early days, we had to rope canoes to the struts of the aircrafts' pontoons. We tied them carefully because the burden on one or both sides of the plane affected its aerodynamics. If a canoe came loose, the results might be fatal. Today the Department of Transport forbids that practice and canoes are nested into one another inside larger planes, usually Twin Otters.

For the inexperienced, charter flights into the Arctic wilderness are still white-knuckle flying. There are no prepared landing strips. The aircraft, some of them fitted with oversized tundra tires, find a flat spot in the landscape or a hard-packed sandbar on which to land. If pilots are uncertain whether or not the landing surface can bear the weight of the loaded aircraft, they put it down under full power, then circle back to judge how deep the wheel tracks are.

Trying to fly from Yellowknife to Banks Island one summer, our canoe group turned back three times when ice buildup on the wings exceeded the capacity of the heaters. As we were finally approaching the island, the pilot had to fly at ocean level to escape a low ceiling. Breaking out of the fog, the plane was headed directly for a beautiful blue iceberg, which the pilot avoided only by a quick reaction. That particular flyer was the one who had dropped a metal canister containing a message of protest onto the deck of the American supertanker *Manhattan* when that ship sailed through the Northwest Passage in 1969, challenging Canada's claims to Arctic sovereignty.

On another occasion we flew through a narrow valley in the Brooks Range in Alaska with granite mountain peaks to either side of the wings. I became worried when heavy weather closed in, stealing visibility in front of us and behind. Should we try for more altitude? "Nope," replied the pilot laconically. We would fly blind, supposedly reassured by the fact that the valley broke through the mountains straight ahead of us and it was simply a matter of maintaining the same compass course.

Venturing to some of the most remote places in the world frequently put us beyond the reach of ready help, at least until the invention of the satellite phone. Everyone was aware that a heart attack or a stroke that might easily be survived in a hospital would probably be fatal in the Barrens. On balance we regarded such risks as worth taking. More worrisome perhaps was what might happen to those back home when we were not there to help.

In 1998, we were dropped off in the east-central Barren Lands of Nunavut to paddle an isolated section of the Back River. We canoed for weeks with no sign of the outside world. The river lies below no major flight paths, nor did we pass any communities. From hilltops we could see the permanent pack ice shimmering in the sun, and eventually we reached Starvation Cove, a desolate island of shale and rock with nothing to sustain life. It was here that Inuit found the remains of the crew of the doomed Franklin Expedition. The desperate men had made their way south in a ship's whaler and their skeletons were discovered huddled together beneath it.

The sounds of the Arctic night and day had become so familiar to us that everyone was startled one afternoon to hear

the faint drone of an engine. As the distant speck grew into a
Twin Otter, our resentment over the intrusion turned to anxiety
when the aircraft flew past us and then circled back. Now it was
losing altitude as if to land, except that the small point where we
were camped could never provide a safe landing spot. Apparently
the pilot was looking for us; a flight to this speck on the map
would cost thousands of dollars and was no joyride.

We were all apprehensive. Allan Rock, then minister of
Health, put his hand on my shoulder. "Someone has died," he
said. "There could be no other reason." The group stood in a
circle, each with his private thoughts. A tragedy seemed about
to befall one of us, but whom?

"If it is one of my kids, I will never forgive myself for not
being there," said a voice.

"If it's for me," replied another, "it has to be that serious
because my wife and I agreed that if our parents died, she'd keep
them on ice until I returned."

A grisly discussion of death's pecking order followed. Would
a brother or sister mean cancellation of the trip, or just that of
a spouse? Should all of us fly out or only the canoe member
involved? Was a violent death more urgent than a death from
natural causes?

The noisy Otter made a run out to sea and then turned
toward us, flying just above the waves. As the plane roared
overhead, a hatch opened in the belly and a steel canister
dropped out, plummeting a few yards from our camp. We
scrambled to retrieve the message, which was greeted with near-
incredulity. The aircraft was on its way to fight fires in the south
and happened to see us. It belonged to the charter company due
to pick us up a week hence, and the pilot merely wanted us to

know that a spit of hard sand about forty miles ahead would make an ideal pickup spot.

One paddler turned away and wept in relief. It took a moment for all of us to collect ourselves. The tension was broken with a laugh when we recalled what had happened many years before when our pickup plane arrived to retrieve us after three weeks on the Nahanni. The pilot was barely out of his cockpit before we asked for news of the outside world. What had transpired in our absence? "My God, you mean you don't know?" he gasped, clearly astonished that lost souls such as ourselves could be unaware of the news he possessed.

"Elvis Presley is dead!" he announced. I appreciated once again that in the real world, news priorities differ.

⌇

Around the campfire one night on the Thelon River, Trudeau asked me why I had not yet taken my son on an Arctic trip, surely a tremendous adventure for a young man. Coming from anyone other than this dedicated father of three sons, I might have taken exception to the implication that my canoe partners were more important to me than my own child—a hurtful notion, though I doubt Trudeau intended it that way. But he was right, I thought. Perhaps it was time for what was then called a "bonding experience."

It took two years to put together, but in 1981 I organized a shared family trip with former finance minister Don Macdonald, his daughter Althea, and his courageous wife, Ruth, who was fighting the cancer that eventually took her life a few years later. David Silcox joined the group with the teenaged son of a friend,

Ian McPhail, who would be close in age to fourteen-year-old Murray. Denis Harvey, eager to escape his desk in Toronto, also threw in with us; it was the first trip we made together.

We had chosen the Coppermine River, a mecca for northern canoeists. This stunning Barren Lands river finds its source in the Great Slave Lake region and gathers steam as its heads north-west into Coronation Gulf on the Arctic Ocean. About nine miles south of its mouth lies the famous Bloody Falls, where in 1771 explorer Samuel Hearne recorded the ambush and murder of a group of Inuit by his Chipewyan guides.

Two years before our trip, a canoe team led by a friend of mine had found a body on a sandbar at the end of the Rocky Defile rapid on the Coppermine. My friend learned later that the victim had dumped in the rapids, but his companions could not find his body. They headed downstream to summon police, and in the meantime the body surfaced and was found by my friend's party.

Conscious of the hazards, David Silcox and I planned to run the empty canoes of the inexperienced paddlers through the trickiest rapids, leaving the others to portage with their packs. We would be an odd crew, not knowing one another well and all travelling with private purposes of our own. Unlike the friendly though ever-competitive all-male outings, this trip proved to be a more relaxed venture, thanks largely to the presence of the two women. Watching three young people discover the magic of the Arctic and the midnight sun renewed my own sense of awe at an environment that I'd almost come to take for granted. If I missed the intense camaraderie of the club's wilderness excursions, I found focus enough in my personal agenda.

. This was a chance to restore some balance in my relationship with Murray, with whom I had not lived since leaving
home when he was five years old. I had done my best to stay
connected, taking him on European holidays, spending every
Christmas with him, even when it meant sleeping on the couch
in my former wife's apartment, and phoning him every week.
Now when I tried delicately to raise my fears of losing him, his
reaction was the wry amusement one might reserve for a daft
uncle. I was worried about a problem that did not exist, he told
me to my surprise, and that was that.

An incident on that trip gave me the confidence that father
and son did share a mutual understanding; indeed, it brought
a sense of overall cohesion to our disparate party. I made a bad
judgment about heading into a wide lake-sized section of the
river one afternoon. In spite of a stiff wind, the river seemed
calm enough to go for it. Halfway across, the wind shifted hard
behind us and the river erupted into whitecapped rollers, threatening to broach anyone who lost control of the stern. Ninety
percent of fatalities on canoe excursions occur not in rapids but
during crossings of large bodies of flat water. We had no choice
but for every man, woman, and teen to dig in hard for the far
shore, and I so instructed the crews.

When we'd completed the passage, Don Macdonald was
understandably upset with me for putting his family in such
peril. I had to accept his criticism, but could not help but appreciate the effort that all had shown in pulling together. I found in
Murray a determination and strength I had not known. He saw
a father who could do more than simply babble on television.

Later we were winded for three days, unable to leave camp.
Don constructed a sheltered fireplace on a narrow rock ledge

ten feet above the river. He warned all of us not to step back too
far, lest we lose our footing on the ledge. Not more than a few
minutes later, there was a great splash when the six-foot-six giant
forgot his own advice. That night Don, who had also served
as defence minister, showed everyone how soldiers under fire
roll over the ground on their elbows. Thousands of kilometres
from anywhere, we tried it ourselves, rolling about with gleeful
abandon on the tundra. Next morning, two bottles of Scotch
were missing. Only the evidence of screw-tops around the fire
convinced us adults that we had consumed all the Scotch. All in
all, the voyage was one of the most memorable of my paddling
career, and everyone who was there fondly and gratefully recalled
its joys for years after.

~

Every trip holds memories, but at a campsite halfway across an
unassailable set of rapids on the Hood River, I experienced one
of those moments of understanding that come all too infrequently in a lifetime. I awoke in my tent at three in the morning,
and in the half-light of the midnight sun I hiked a few hundred
yards up a granite-strewn bluff high above the river. While I sat
there in a silence so profound as to be almost indescribable, I
could appreciate why the natives of the western plains regarded
their landscape as an extension of the Great Spirit. To them the
plateaus, mountains, prairies, and rivers were the embodiment
of that spirit, and they held them sacred.

It came to me that there was a timelessness to this place, but
also a terrible vulnerability. Warnings of environmental depre-
dation suggest that the rivers may not run forever, nor the pack

ice anchor us to the pole. If we fail to protect the Arctic, we are doomed; the North calls on us to acknowledge and preserve the interconnectedness between ourselves and the land that lies at the heart of our very existence.

Looking back toward our campsite, I saw in our little group a metaphor for the country. One misstep could have swept any of us away had we tried this adventure on our own; it had taken the skills of all to ensure the well-being of the whole. We are a nation of survivors, but we need each other to do it.

9

UNCIVIL WARS

Of all the prime ministers I covered, shadowed, or otherwise harassed for more than a half-century, Jean Chrétien was the most impressive when judged by the objective measure of victory at the polls. His record is unassailable, and although he was the ship's captain when the sponsorship scandal broke in 2002, he was never implicated personally. His pressure on a government banker to rescue an investment in a golf course and hotel in his hometown are largely forgotten today. Since leaving office in 2003, Chrétien has grown in stature and reputation, just as Pierre Trudeau did. The difference is that Chrétien was regarded with immense affection in his heyday, whereas Trudeau commanded awe and respect.

Even former political rivals acknowledge Chrétien's achievements. This was brought home to me at an Ottawa Senators hockey game shortly after Stephen Harper's Conservatives came to power in 2006. Chrétien was in the stands that night, as were several newly appointed members of the Harper Cabinet. I was surprised to see these eager ministers arrange themselves in a respectful queue to shake Chrétien's hand.

Later, I chided Monte Solberg, who had just been named immigration minister, reminding him that he wasn't supposed to pay homage to the man who had kept the Conservatives in Opposition for so long. It was not about personal homage, Solberg said. "We were admiring three consecutive majorities. After all, that's how those of us in politics keep score, and he hit home runs."

Chrétien's detractors say he had it easy because the political forces against him were divided—Progressive Conservative vs. Reform/Alliance, Green Party vs. the NDP—or regionalized, as in the case of the Bloc Québécois. He was able to take his Liberals up the middle between a fractious right and a weak left and win every time. Those detractors are not crediting the fact that Chrétien kept his opponents off balance and successfully played to public suspicions of what the Conservatives in particular might do once in power, all the while calibrating his own policies to the public's fickle mood.

Jean Chrétien created a persona for himself as the "little guy from Shawinigan" and had enough modesty to his biography that he was allowed to play the part of a common man even after he became a millionaire. His slightly garbled speech patterns only added to his Everyman appeal. Listeners sometimes strained to follow an indecipherable pronouncement, then smiled in relief when Chrétien ended with a solid point and a witty and insightful one at that.

What I saw in Chrétien was a fellow survivor. His father, a tradesman in a rural Quebec town, had struggled to give his nine children an education. Jean spent years at a gritty boarding school where, as he is fond of telling people, he had to win a fight every day on the ice rink or in the playground. He was

single-minded and hard driving in pursuit of a law degree
from Laval University and became a dedicated worker for his
hometown Liberal organization, battling the corrupt local ward
healers of the Duplessis regime. Inevitably he was elected to
Parliament—at the age of just twenty-nine.

When I first met Chrétien in 1974, he was a junior minister
in Pierre Trudeau's Cabinet and, even then, a popular political
figure with the public. A close friend of mine, Judd Buchanan,
mentored Chrétien, who would eventually follow in Buchanan's
footsteps as minister of Indian Affairs. Chrétien and I saw a
lot of each other on the social circuit and he became a likeable
regular at my annual Christmas parties. He spent time listening
and absorbing information, rather than attempting to dominate
the conversation. He was clearly aware that Parliament Hill
reporters could influence his career, and he was quick to tell
self-deprecating jokes about his poor English. Nonetheless,
he seemed to me almost preternaturally shrewd and seriously
ambitious. Like the best populist politicians, he could analyze
complex issues with street-smart intuition.

In those early years of Cabinet tenure, Chrétien ingrati-
ated himself with the more powerful ministers and with their
canny deputies, many of whom would be surprised years later
to find themselves working for him. Among the elites close
to Trudeau, Chrétien was regarded as a charming hick, with
his thick accent and down-home humour—certainly an intellectual lightweight. My sources in the Cabinet told me that
Trudeau did not hold Chrétien in particularly high regard,
although he recognized him as a loyal ally with genuine
political value in Quebec, if not beyond. Judd Buchanan,
however, believed Chrétien had the potential to win over

English-speaking Canada, where voters found him sincere and unthreatening.

Perhaps Chrétien's greatest asset then was an immense self-confidence that allowed him to have the courage of his convictions. He hired strong staffers and knew when to follow their lead, and he did not mind being underestimated in the short term. He was looking ahead to the future. Some in the Trudeau entourage—although not the prime minister himself, it must be said—lived fast and loose lives in those years. Plenty of attractive young women, not to mention abundant booze and drugs, were available to any upwardly mobile young man so close to the seat of power. Possibly his basic nature would not have allowed it, but Chrétien did nothing that could later come back to haunt him.

A character as earthy and colourful as Chrétien could not escape the attention of my mother. She made quick and instinctive judgments about people that were seldom wrong, and I often relied on her trenchant observations. She met Chrétien at one of my Christmas get-togethers in the late 1970s and was attracted by what she regarded as his common touch. She also sensed something in him that I never did: a vulnerability born of his childhood brush with Bell's palsy, a disorder that left him with a partial but permanent paralysis of the left side of his face. She formed a strong attachment to him and never wavered in her admiration. After he became prime minister, any criticism of Chrétien by our bureau brought a swift call from Mother, questioning my "fairness."

Occasionally Mom's partisanship caused me embarrassment, as during the spring 1984 Liberal leadership campaign when Jean Chrétien and John Turner were duking it out for the party's

top job. I was assigned to cover Turner's campaign and was with
his entourage in Terrace, B.C., on a day when Chrétien was also
expected to arrive. Mom decided to pay a surprise visit too, and
she appeared in time to interrupt my lunch with a group of
Turner's senior advisers. Before I could make introductions, she
demanded to know why I was working for "that jerk, Turner." I
explained that I was covering Mr. Turner, not working for him,
to which she replied, "It was damn hard to tell the difference."
She then turned to the astonished company and announced that
Turner wouldn't be prime minister for long, if ever; Chrétien
would make the better leader for the country. Turner's staff fled
in horror, but Mom's prediction turned out to be prescient.
Turner won the party leadership yet later that year served as
prime minister for less than three months.

But worse was to come that day in Terrace. When Chrétien's
plane landed an hour after the lunch incident, my mother
ran across the airfield and wrapped her idol in a bear hug as
he stepped onto the tarmac. The photographers had a field day
with that shot, and it was Chrétien and not Turner who won
the picture of the day in the national newspapers. One of the
other reporters travelling with Chrétien wondered aloud, "Who
was that crazy old gal the local Liberals had rolled out?" I had
to admit she was my mother and she didn't even live in the city.

After two electoral defeats at the hands of Brian Mulroney,
John Turner resigned the Liberal helm in 1990. At the convention that year, Chrétien bested Paul Martin for the leadership
of the party, inheriting an organization that was in disarray and
near bankruptcy. By 1993, however, with the neophyte Kim
Campbell heading the Conservatives and the NDP no threat,
Chrétien led the Liberals to a resounding majority, winning seats

across the country, including twenty in Quebec, this despite the strength of the Bloc, who formed the Official Opposition. He and Martin, his capable and admired finance minister, proceeded to slash spending to reduce the national deficit, with no apparent long-term ill effects on the Liberals' popularity.

One of Chrétien's great strengths was his ability to read the electorate's mood on domestic issues. And while he was taking the temperature of public opinion, he fuzzed his answers about where the government stood. He got away with a lot, making fractured off-the-cuff remarks that would have discredited other politicians. Reporters tolerated Chrétien's tortured syntax in both languages, in part because of his childhood illness, in part because they understood he was slightly dyslexic. Most of all, his malapropisms were funny and made good copy. An example: Until he had finally mastered the word, he would refuse to answer questions that he deemed to be *hypo-political*. The suspicion never left me that Chrétien used these wacky expressions as diverting and intentional obfuscations.

The technique was less successful in the area of foreign affairs; indeed, his poor grasp of the nuances of foreign policy generally caused him grief more than once. His first foreign trip as prime minister was to a NATO summit in Brussels, where his remarks were invariably naïve and out of sync with longstanding Western alliance positions. At one point he told reporters that Canadian peacekeepers should act like members of the Red Cross, only with guns. His artful press aide, Peter Donolo, attempted damage control, asking me to do a one-on-one interview that might cover some of the same ground and allow the prime minister to correct his earlier remarks. Reporters would then be obliged to write their stories based on the revised version. I refused, saying

that I did not want to serve as a patsy for the Prime Minister's
Office. Donolo replied that if I did not agree, I would never be
granted another exclusive interview with Chrétien as long as he
resided at 24 Sussex. Considering that Chrétien's government
appeared to be destined for a long tenure, I caved in. I rational-
ized this surrender with the excuse that the prime minister was
only recently elected, that he'd had no previous exposure to the
grand strategies of the NATO alliance, and that it was only fair
to give him a chance to find his feet.

Seven years later, however, Chrétien was still unsteady. In
April 2000, he undertook a twelve-day trip to the Middle East
that was so marred by gaffes and errors that I dubbed it "the
debacle in the desert." Every day the accompanying foreign
affairs officials had to hold off-the-record briefings with reporters
to explain that what the prime minister had said wasn't really
what he meant. When Chrétien met with Yasser Arafat in Gaza,
the PLO leader told him that he might issue a unilateral declaration of independence for the Palestinians. Chrétien agreed this
would be a good idea. Reporters ran to their computers to write
stories about the implications for Quebec sovereignty. Even as
his government jet was lifting off, Chrétien held a hasty news
conference to backpedal from those remarks. In Ottawa, the
Opposition Reform Party demanded that the prime minister
return home before he started a new Middle East war.

As the tour progressed, the relationship between the reporters
and Chrétien's staff deteriorated from frosty to hostile. At one
point the elegant and usually unflappable chief of staff, Jean
Pelletier, stormed into the press room and accused me of being
the ringleader of a press lynch mob. "I am tired of your shit," he
declared. "You must be on a different trip than I am."

Once back in Ottawa, Pelletier was gentleman enough to call me and apologize for his outburst. I told him I understood and admired his loyalty to his boss. Chrétien however was not so forgiving. At a cocktail party soon after, the prime minister approached me in a crowd and in a voice low enough that no one else could hear asked, "How do you manage to look yourself in the mirror every morning?" As he turned on his heel, he may not have caught my attempt to defuse the tension between us: "Actually, sir, I'm barely able to see myself in the mirror."

Midway through his first mandate, Chrétien suffered two events that might have unnerved lesser mortals, but that summoned his survivor's instinct and sent him back into the fray with added steel. The first was the 1995 Quebec referendum, perhaps the lowest point of Chrétien's prime ministerial career. At the outset of that contest with the separatists, Chrétien was full of confidence. All we have to do to win, he assured me, is to keep the federalist position low profile and avoid provoking the *yes* vote. In speeches across the country, he counselled Canadians not to say or do anything that might give ammunition to the other side. Pierre Trudeau was told to stay mum in Montreal. In the first weeks of the campaign, I suggested to Chrétien that, as they say in old westerns, things were too quiet out there. Was trouble brewing? He insisted that a do-little strategy would win the day.

The separatists had found themselves a charismatic new champion in Lucien Bouchard, and soon matters were not unfolding as official Ottawa had predicted. On the night of the vote, October 30, I was at federalist headquarters in Montreal. Minutes before the results began coming in, I received a call from Ted Johnson who was helping out at Chrétien's headquarters in

Ottawa. He was distraught, his voice heavy with emotion. "We are going to lose the nation tonight," he told me. "The tide is running against us." During our short conversation I choked up myself and found it difficult to go on air. For the first time in my professional life, I felt emotionally overwhelmed, too personally involved with a news story. My country seemed on the brink of dissolution.

The night ended with a victory for the federalist side, but only by a heartbeat. A few thousand votes could have ended the Canada we had known, and Chrétien would have been responsible. White-faced and obviously shaken, he went on national television and promised to make changes to the federation. That he did, but not quite the changes many Quebecers had expected. Reform Party leader Preston Manning had been preaching tough love with Quebec. Tell them the price of independence, he urged. Chrétien and his advisers picked up on those ideas and added a few of their own in drafting the so-called "Clarity Bill" and then testing its legality in the Supreme Court. Never again would Quebecers be asked to take a leap into the dark. They would know the consequences, including the fragility of their own borders, if they chose independence. Which I doubt they ever will.

Sanctioned in 2000, the Clarity Act was one of several initiatives that divided Chrétien and Paul Martin. Martin opposed it, fearing it would arouse a backlash against the federalist cause in Quebec. He was wrong, but his trepidation infuriated Chrétien and reinforced his view that Martin was an easy mark for the separatists. A more immediate but highly questionable response to the near-miss of the referendum was the attempt to reinforce the federalist vision in Quebecers' minds with a little-known "sponsorship" program. If Quebecers knew better what Ottawa was doing for them, the reasoning went, they would better appreciate the federalist option. It proved to be a misguided scheme that would loom larger in the fates of the two men.

Chrétien faced a more personally threatening event just a few days after the referendum vote, on the night of November 5, 1995. I learned of it the next morning, when a telephone call from the Prime Minister's Office caught me just as I was heading out for a trail ride. The caller was Eddie Goldenberg, prepared to hand me a stunning scoop provided no one knew that it had come from the PMO. According to Goldenberg, an intruder at 24 Sussex had tried to kill Chrétien and his wife, Aline, the night before. The knife-wielding culprit had reached the hall outside the couple's bedroom before Aline discovered his presence, retreated behind the bedroom door, and raised the alarm. RCMP officers then took several minutes to arrive at the scene, during which the Chrétiens, barricaded into their bedroom, prepared to defend themselves.

The red-faced Mounties were trying to cover up the incident, claimed Goldenberg, and were planning to put out a simple statement that a man had been arrested following a minor incident at the official residence during which no one was hurt. Their intention was to gloss over a potentially fatal failure of the prime minister's personal protection detail. Goldenberg was furious at their evasion of responsibility.

At that moment the prime minister was two hours away from boarding his government jet for an official visit to Israel, where he would attend the funeral of Israeli prime minister Yitzhak Rabin, assassinated scant days before. No doubt I cut a comic figure as I rushed into the military airport, clad in riding breeches, boots, and spurs. Colleagues from the press gallery who were waiting to board Chrétien's plane were mildly amused, then incredulous, when I told them that I intended to ask the prime minister about an attempt on his life in the early hours of the morning. Peter Donolo was astonished and declared my tale "plain crazy." He turned to me with that look of concerned pity one gives to a person who has gone over the edge. "Craig, I'm sure the prime minister will not comment on any such nasty story, even if it were true." Shortly after, a sombre Jean Chrétien arrived and confirmed the harrowing tale.

Much later I learned that during his RCMP interrogation, the would-be attacker said he would certainly have stabbed Chrétien in the chest had Mme Chrétien not come to the door of the bedroom. He said he didn't know exactly where Chrétien was and assumed that Aline was a housemaid. Both the prime minister and his wife needed time to overcome the psychological trauma of the attack, and Aline underwent weeks of counselling.

Then a few months later, in February 1996, Chrétien was involved in another bizarre event. In full view of the cameras, Chrétien put a chokehold on a protester who stood his ground as the prime minister made his way through an unfriendly crowd at a Flag Day ceremony in Hull. It was an unwarranted assault by the prime minister, whose dark glasses and fierce grimace made him look like a mafia hit man. Peter Donolo begged me not to overplay the incident, suggesting that Chrétien's behaviour was an instinctive reaction to the lingering intruder incident, an explanation that might have been accepted. Later, though, that line was dropped and replaced with the excuse that the protester had aggressively tried to block the prime minister's right of way. The media's interest was soon diverted amid jokes about the "Shawinigan Handshake," and Chrétien didn't suffer in the opinion polls. Still, the episode had revealed the street fighter not far below the surface of *le petit gars*.

In the period that followed, the former easy charm was less in evidence. Chrétien agreed to much heavier security protection and seemed to become both more isolated and less tolerant of criticism. His government began to take a harder line on justice issues and, in barely noticeable increments, adopted an uncharacteristically arrogant and nasty tone. Chrétien seemed much more stressed than before, sometimes saying bizarre and unaccountable things. His defence of the Mounties' use of pepper spray on protesting students at an Asia-Pacific Economic Co-operation (APEC) meeting in Vancouver in 1997 was flippant and combative. His government's abrupt shuttering of the Somalia Inquiry into the brutal actions of a rogue military unit in Somalia flew in the face of Chrétien's insistence on a full investigation when he was Opposition leader. In 2000, he reacted badly when an internal audit uncovered massive incompetence at the huge Human Resources Department, where bureaucrats looked like the gang that couldn't count straight. Were these examples of rare testiness or was the mask slipping?

Chrétien had won another election in 1997, and with two back-to-back majorities for the history books, he would, almost everyone believed, relinquish the leadership and leave politics at the end of his second term. Certainly that was the expectation of Paul Martin's supporters. While Chrétien was busy governing the country, Martin and his troops worked to gain control of key posts in the party hierarchy and to win the loyalty of the rank and file. But Chrétien was enjoying the job and, as he once told me, "My worst day as prime minister is better than

my best day as Opposition leader." Three years into his second
term he showed no signs of moving on, and so the Martin forces
made an attempt to oust him at the 2000 national convention
of the Liberal Party in Ottawa. The convention erupted when
someone leaked the plan to organize a vote against Chrétien on
the convention floor—one he might have lost.

Chrétien wrote his own keynote address to the delegates,
heavily promoted in advance as a statement of the prime minister's vision for the future of the party and the country and the
blueprint for the Liberals' next election platform. Yet he delivered a rambling dud of a speech. Astonishingly, many delegates
wandered out of the hall while Chrétien was still at the podium.
My report that night focused on how pedestrian the address had
sounded to me. Moreover, I drew attention to a grim truth for
the prime minister: that Paul Martin was clearly the star of the
convention, outdrawing Chrétien in applause time after time
that weekend. I observed that Chrétien seemed weary and listless
and wondered aloud if he was ready to quit.

Martin called off his troops and allowed Chrétien to win a
pro forma vote on his leadership, but only after Jean Pelletier
had assured Martin that the prime minister would not seek a
third term. Whether this was an educated gamble on Pelletier's
part, designed to head off an open revolt on the floor, or whether
Chrétien had instructed him to deliver the message, we never
knew.

At the news conference closing the convention, Chrétien
refused to answer my questions about his personal future and
glared at me darkly as he left the room. The depth of his disap-
proval was made evident the following Monday morning, when
my luncheon meeting with a Cabinet minister close to Chrétien

was cancelled at the last moment. In the weeks to come, calls to normally helpful sources in the government went unreturned. A friend in Cabinet eventually took me aside and warned me that, as he put it, in the coming death struggle between Martin and Chrétien, I was regarded as having joined the ranks of the enemy. This was how the prime minister's camp spoke of its own finance minister.

My friend and canoe partner of many years, Eddie Goldenberg, sent me to Coventry. He avoided me at social gatherings and did not respond to my phone messages. Eddie felt that I had betrayed him personally by what he regarded as unfair coverage at the convention. Conveniently, however, he renewed our friendship shortly before the next election. I always knew when an election was in the offing, well before my colleagues in the press gallery, because Eddie would call with an invitation to dinner, complaining that it had been too long since we'd got together. Over a fine meal, Eddie would do his best to persuade me that the Liberals had done a magnificent job and deserved to be re-elected. It was usually I who paid the bill.

Sensing that the new Reform Party leader, Stockwell Day, was vulnerable, and feeling the hot breath of the Martinites on his neck, Chrétien called a snap election for late November 2000, well before the end of his second mandate. It earned him a third consecutive majority and the everlasting enmity of the Martin faction. Yet Chrétien had undeniably run a flawless campaign. His experienced team, headed by Senator David Smith who had once worked for Lester Pearson, ran rings around the hapless and unprepared Day. Our national campaign coverage reflected that reality, and soon I was back in the PMO's favour. I was not surprised when, following our annual year-end television interview with the prime minister in December, Lloyd Robertson and I were invited back to 24 Sussex for a seasonal drink or two.

The prime minister settled into a comfortable sofa in front of the fire, with a glass of white wine in his hand, and held forth on life and politics. As he spoke, I could not avoid making comparisons with the likeable young pol I had met years earlier. Chrétien had become self-absorbed, edgy, and devastating in his criticism of his opponents. Any topic of conversation was soon narrowed to focus on him. This may be the inevitable result of years in power, of being the centre of attention of all who surround you.

His wife, Aline, sat close beside him on the sofa, clearly enjoying her husband. She is a warm, engaging woman who has worked hard to overcome her innate shyness. She was a beauty in her youth and those stunning good looks have been inherited by her daughter, France, who, as Chrétien is fond of telling people, is married to a son of the wealthy Desmarais family.

After four decades of marriage, the Chrétiens seemed almost extensions of each other. Both were in their sixties at the time of our chat, but the sexual attraction between the two was palpable. Aline is a woman of real character. She never wavered in her love and support for her adopted son, Michel, who suffered several courtroom exposés leading up to his imprisonment for sexual assault and confinement. Friends say Michel is probably a victim of fetal alcohol syndrome. In 1990, Aline and Chrétien, then Opposition leader, were present throughout a trial in which all the lurid details of Michel's case were made public. I have always been impressed that the television networks and even the tabloids gave very little attention to the story, leaving the Chrétiens to their private grief and personal agony.

But on the occasion of our year-end chat in 2000, Chrétien was in a belligerent mood. The Martin camp was restive yet still unsuccessful in its efforts to unseat Chrétien. The public opinion polls had never shown higher approval ratings for the Liberal Party or for Chrétien personally. At the start of a new decade, he said, he was doing what he wanted to do: spending time with his wife and grandchildren and golfing with old cronies, many of whom had no connection to politics. Chrétien was sending a message, thumbing his nose at his party rivals, at the Opposition, and at the pundits who had discounted and underestimated him for so many years.

He wagged his finger and scolded me for telling Canadians that there was a race on for his job. "I am here to announce there is no race." But Aline interjected, "What do you mean, no race?"

Then Lloyd and I learned something significant. It was Aline as much as anyone who had kept her husband in the prime minister's chair. Before the 2000 convention, almost everyone inside Chrétien's circle believed he was ready to retire and leave the job wide open for Martin. Afterwards, however, a fierce debate took place among Chrétien's closest advisers, including John Rae, Eddie Goldenberg, Allan Rock, and David Collenette, about whether or not to call an early election. In one crucial meeting, Collenette had warned Chrétien, "If we wait too much longer, Martin will have your balls for breakfast." It was Aline who swung the argument. She had never forgiven Martin for his aborted coup attempt at the convention, and she resented the pressure the Martin forces were putting on her husband to take his leave. Chrétien revealed that she told him to run again and to hell with Martin.

I was emboldened after a few glasses of Scotch to tell Chrétien that one of his ministers, a Martinite, had lamented to me that the third victory was "the worst thing that could have happened to us. Another goddamned majority!"

I did not report that another of Martin's fanatic advocates had wanted me to do a story on how the prime minister was losing his mind, perhaps had Alzheimer's disease, which I did not believe for a minute. "Yes, Chrétien is crazy," was my response. "Like a fox."

It is said that a year in politics is a century, and in the late fall of 2002, when Lloyd and I were once again at the prime ministerial residence for a private drink, we found much had changed. Chrétien's government was awash in allegations of financial skulduggery, some of it involving his former ownership and mortgage of a golf course and hotel in his hometown. The sponsorship program designed to foster warm federalist feelings in Quebec was revealed as a cash cow for a number of Liberal-friendly ad agencies in Montreal. Several Cabinet ministers had been fired for ethical lapses. And the previous August, the Martin gang had forced Chrétien to announce his resignation as prime minister, though he declared he would not actually go until February 2004.

For weeks in television reports, I had been indirectly chiding Chrétien for his insistence on this long goodbye when the party and the country were clearly impatient for his departure. A few days earlier, I had referred to him as a political dead duck. But he had won a parliamentary vote on the Kyoto Accord just the day before and was able to throw that remark back at me. "Some dead duck," he said and laughed uproariously. He jabbed a finger in my direction and demanded, "Why don't you resign? You look older than me and Lloyd put together!"

Though Martin had been out of Cabinet for months, Chrétien railed against him, recounting how often he had had to stiffen the indecisive minister's spine in a crisis. Apparently Chrétien was reluctant to step aside because Martin was not tough enough to take on the separatists. "They are just waiting for me to leave," he said, "because they will make a strong comeback with Martin as the leader." But he was equally concerned that if he stayed, his caucus, dominated then by Martin's supporters, would turn against him. There were rumours that some MPs might refuse to support Chrétien in the Commons. "Let them," he declared defiantly, "and as always I'll go to the Governor General and ask her for an election, and who the hell do you think will win it?" A Liberal MP later told me that Martin had better tread carefully: "The crazy bugger just might do it."

In all my years on Parliament Hill, I had never had a Cabinet meeting leak of any importance. On May 30, 2002, I received two of them. The first was a call from a familiar ministerial voice, uncharacteristically tense, telling me that at that morning's Cabinet gathering, the prime minister had given a very pointed shut up or ship out order to the dissidents in his ranks. Looking directly across the table at his finance minister but without addressing him by name, Chrétien had demanded that anyone who wanted to campaign for the leader's job do so from outside the government. Knowing the wily Chrétien as well as I did, my bet was that he must have orchestrated this leak, since once I'd reported the news on television Martin would be forced to make a public declaration one way or the other.

Within the hour another caller, this one a Martin loyalist, also broke Cabinet secrecy, claiming remorse for the breach but saying he was too angry to help himself. "That son of a bitch Chrétien has just invited Martin to leave the Cabinet! We have taken all we can stand from this guy."

That night I told the country that one of the most popular finance ministers in Canadian history had likely bought himself a ticket out of government. The following morning Martin would say to reporters only that he was considering his options. Of course, he knew he had none, and nine years after joining the government he was gone; whether as a result of firing or resigning, we never knew for certain.

The internecine battle was out in the open after a long history. Chrétien and Martin had been undeclared rivals for the Liberal leadership from the moment Martin was elected to Parliament in 1988. The two could not have been more different in background. Martin was a wealthy and handsome patrician, highly successful in business before he entered politics and, as the son of a Pearson-era Cabinet heavyweight, Paul Martin Senior, a member of the Liberal aristocracy. Both he and Chrétien had inherited the friends and the enemies of earlier incumbents: Chrétien had the party's Trudeau-era veterans on his side, while Martin was backed by John Turner's former supporters, still bitter at Chrétien's backroom machinations after Turner won the leadership in 1984. But Chrétien's team had the greater experience in the trenches, and at the first formal match between the two rivals, the 1990 leadership vote in Calgary, Martin found himself outmanoeuvred. Chrétien claimed victory on the first ballot.

Nowhere is defeat more an orphan than in Ottawa. Martin returned to the Opposition benches with a less-than-promising political horoscope, his confidence rattled, according to friends.

When I ran into him on Parliament Hill one day shortly after the convention, he seemed something of a lost soul. He asked whether I was free for dinner that night, which as it happened I was not. Back at the office, however, I had second thoughts and rearranged my schedule.

Over dinner he spoke passionately about two subjects that rarely evoke emotion: the economy and the national debt. Under the Conservatives, the latter had soared to unprecedented levels. Martin convinced me as no one had before that Canada was heading into deep financial trouble. Without urgent action, he predicted, Canada's public finances could face the equivalent of insolvency. For more years than I can remember, I have heard politicians declaim the grand legislative agendas they will enact if ever they get the chance. That night, Martin outlined for me an impressive roster of monetary and fiscal measures that he deemed essential; a few years later, he put them all into place as minister of Finance.

After that, I had dinner with Martin from time to time and occasionally our wives joined us. In our many conversations, I had to accept Martin's self-restraint on the topic of Chrétien's faults. If his facial expressions were any indication, the effort to stifle comment seemed almost physically painful. Yet his sense of mission and basic human decency inspired admiration.

Martin had never had to play hardball to achieve his political ambitions, but after 1990 his advisers told him it was time. He learned fast and gave his troops their head. No one would be allowed to remain neutral; everyone would have to choose sides. Even Jean Pelletier, brought to Ottawa as Chrétien's chief of staff in 1992, was asked to declare his loyalties. When he stuck by his new boss, he was, he said, added to Martin's enemies list.

Distinctions were made among journalists as well. After Allan Rock, another obvious contender for the party's leadership, made a northern expedition as a member of my canoe group, it did not escape me that phone calls and messages to Martin's finance department were not being returned. Martin himself seemed perpetually unavailable. This was a problem: As bureau chief, I needed access to the minister and his officials in a department that was at the centre of government and an important news source. Worse yet, my competitors at the CBC were getting stories that I wasn't.

Through a trusted intermediary, I arranged a dinner meeting with Martin at an expensive French restaurant. Neither of us raised any specific problems between us; rather, we gossiped and laughed over current events. As the evening ended, I told Martin as casually as possible that I had always thought it a mistake for reporters to take sides with political parties or indeed with individual political candidates. With a broad smile and a wave of his arm, Martin swept away such concerns, assuring me he had never doubted my fairness. The next day a finance official called and invited me out for lunch. Apparently I was back in Paul Martin's good graces.

Martin and Chrétien were nonetheless notorious for their ability to hold a grudge, and the ill will between them caught scores of colleagues in the undertow. Once when asked to help out a mutual friend who was down on his luck and seeking a government job, Martin replied that he would try. He warned against letting Chrétien find out about his efforts, however, since the prime minister would almost certainly quash any such appointment.

Party president Iona Campagnolo had earned the affection of

the Chrétien camp in 1984 when she told delegates at that year's leadership convention that although John Turner had won their votes, Jean Chrétien was first in their hearts. A few years later, Campagnolo concluded that time had passed Chrétien by, and she signed on as co-chair of Martin's leadership campaign. Although she had given the Chrétien camp no commitment of any sort, her support of Martin was seen as a betrayal not to be forgiven. She was one of the few Liberal party presidents never rewarded with a Senate seat, despite being a popular national figure.

Chrétien's animosity likewise affected reporters. For a time, then *Globe and Mail* bureau chief Edward Greenspon and I shared hosting duties on *Question Period*. Whenever major newsmakers came on the show, we interviewed them together, taking turns asking questions and signalling each other under the table when we wanted to hand off to the other. In 1996, Greenspon co-authored a book titled *Double Vision* with Anthony Wilson-Smith of *Maclean's*, which the Chrétien crowd condemned as nothing but a puff piece for the finance minister. Chrétien had agreed to an appearance on the show, but shortly after Greenspon's book launch, the Prime Minister's Office called with a new proviso. The interview could proceed, but only on condition that Greenspon not be part of it. I rejected that condition and the interview never happened.

Once out of the Cabinet, Martin was in great demand as the prime minister-in-waiting. The political cognoscenti were abuzz with talk of no one else. Liberal candidates across the country wanted to have their pictures taken with Martin, and since they would all be delegates at the next leadership convention, he was pleased to oblige. At a public reception at a golf course in Hartland, New Brunswick, the scene was one of full-scale

Martin mania. Next day, making an unannounced stop for a coffee at an Irving gas station in Nackawic, Martin was greeted with a spontaneous standing ovation from the customers when he came through the door.

His "consultation with Canadians," as Martin called it, took him across the country in triumph. The strategy was to create an aura of inevitability around his ascendancy to the top job and to discourage all other comers, chief among them Allan Rock, John Manley, and Sheila Copps, whom the Martinites particularly disliked. The PMO could only fume as Martin developed policy and expressed positions on topical issues, curried favour with an eager media, and built a leadership campaign war chest. He was creating a parallel Liberal party, one that seemed able to embrace his native Quebec, rural Alberta, and conservative Bay Street.

I had to blast my way through layers of self-important staffers to win a one-on-one meeting with Martin. I felt as if I were being ushered into an audience with a head of state when I arrived one rainy night at a ritzy restaurant across the Ottawa River in Hull. Martin was waiting for me in a private room with two fidgety aides just outside the door.

As always he greeted me warmly, but he appeared to be suffering jangled nerves. He had agreed to this sit-down, no doubt in his mind for future considerations, though his nervousness—perhaps a fear of making some verbal gaffe that might cost him the prize—was palpable. Martin peppered me with questions, shifting focus frequently, though always concerned with my work and interests, as if trying to avoid hard questions or to eat up the allotted time.

Eventually Martin spoke about the processes of managing government and public policy, which he believed was being done in a haphazard and unintelligent manner. I reminded him of Pierre Trudeau's near-fatal excursion down that road. Trudeau and Michael Pitfield, Clerk of the Privy Council, had spent their first term in the engine room, determined to make the machinery of government run better. But there was no one up on the bridge, plotting the ship's course. I thought to myself that Martin seemed to love the details of policy more than the tough business of making decisions. He left the crucial but messy business of politics to others, preferring the tidier precincts of planning and process.

Behind the scenes, the Martin gang was using strong-arm tactics to sweep aside anyone with the temerity to challenge their man for the leadership. Those who might be tempted were made to understand that there would be no jobs, no contracts, and no access if they did so. The smart ones, like Brian Tobin, Allan Rock, and Frank McKenna, knew it was hopeless and did not try. Sheila Copps was enough of a renegade to leave her name in the ring in what many regarded as a foolhardy but principled bid to stop the Martin juggernaut. Martin always pleaded innocent when such things were brought to his attention.

No one doubted that Martin would make quick work of the hapless Stephen Harper. Some commentators debated whether or not the massive majority they expected Martin to win in his first election as prime minister might skew the political balance in Ottawa for years to come. So it was that in November 2003, Martin was essentially crowned leader with 94 percent of delegate votes.

Up in the broadcast booth at Toronto's Air Canada Centre, Lloyd Robertson asked me for an assessment of Martin's acceptance speech. Amid the clamour of victory celebrations, I could not bring myself to rain on the parade and replied rather lamely that Martin had done what he had to do. In fact, I felt it was a speech devoid of any vision for the country. In his moment of triumph, Martin had offered nothing of substance that might reveal his convictions or values in government. Later we learned that the address was the work of a committee whose members couldn't agree on its content. He had left this pivotal statement in the hands of others and the result was an inconclusive mess and a harbinger of worse to come.

Chrétien took his leave earlier than he'd initially announced, giving the prime ministership to Martin on December 12. At the same time, Chrétien handed Martin a poisoned chalice. For some months Auditor General Sheila Fraser had been preparing a report on the sponsorship scandal; in February 2004, she released her findings that approximately one hundred million dollars in federal funds had been misspent, some of it ending up in the hands of Liberal supporters in Quebec. Chrétien's supporters insist he was prepared to take the heat and make the report public before Martin took over. He would simply have handed it to the RCMP, who would have buried the story for at least a year. In the event, the report was scheduled to be made public two months into Martin's watch, and many insiders claim that Martin's brain trust deliberately chose the timing. They considered handing it to the Mounties too, but all the research showed that Canadians wanted to put Chrétien behind them, if not to punish him and his minions. Martin needed to be seen as the agent of change. The strategy was to lay all responsibility on the departed Chrétien, creating a sharp delineation between the two Liberal regimes.

Martin then made the decision that ultimately doomed his

government. His key advisers debated fiercely about whether or not to launch an inquiry. The most experienced of the Quebec MPs were set against it, as was the national director of the Liberal Party, Steve McKinnon. On the Friday before the Auditor General's report was to be released, Martin seemed to have been swayed by their arguments. By Monday, however, he had changed his mind and the government went into damage control, announcing both a judicial and a parliamentary inquiry. Justice John Gomery would head the former, and his commission hearings in Montreal soon became the hottest ticket in town.

Despite other measures designed to demonstrate swift and righteous retribution against the architects of the sponsorship program, including the firing of the presidents of the Business Development Bank, Via Rail, and Canada Post, the polls showed that in the minds of most Canadians, Liberals were Liberals. Martin's government never did succeed in distancing itself from its predecessor on this issue.

A wise observer of politicians and a friend of Paul Martin's once told me he sensed in Martin an insecurity at the centre that made him easily manipulated by those who advised him. To me, it appeared that Martin had never been his own man entirely. Was he the creation of other people, a son who had captured the mantle that had eluded his illustrious father, or a respectable face for a group of ambitious policy wonks bent on their own purposes? Others less charitable saw Martin as an instrument of the giant Power Corporation of Montreal for which he once worked and that backed him politically all the way to 24 Sussex Drive. (Ironically, that company had backed Chrétien as well in his time. John Rae, a long-time political adviser to Chrétien, was also a senior executive with the firm. "Power," as everyone calls it, came by its name honestly.)

Once in the prime minister's chair, Martin handed over considerable responsibility and influence to a crew that was dubbed the "Board," a group that in other administrations might be known as the "kitchen cabinet." Many of them had no official position in government; one was Michael Robinson, a long-time intimate of Martin's and a principal at Earnscliffe Strategy Group, then one of the most powerful lobbying firms in Ottawa.

Lacking confidence in his own political instincts, Martin farmed out the necessary plotting and strategizing to this inner circle and in the process, some believe, he also relinquished his better judgment and principles. These dozen or so aides, pollsters, and assorted hangers-on prescribed the direction and recommended the decisions that guided the political agenda of the Martin government, but the need to settle old scores and punish old enemies forever influenced their counsel. They prolonged the hostilities within the party and the caucus.

Those who held positions both as close advisers to the prime minister and employees of lobbying firms also drew attention. One deputy minister told me of his astonishment at finding himself answering to Martin aides who worked full-time as private-sector lobbyists. Naturally, bureaucrats were reluctant to discuss privileged government plans in front of individuals whose clients could potentially benefit from inside information. The relationship was so intimate that on a number of occasions when I called the PMO to ask for certain people, I was transferred directly to the reception desk at a prominent lobbying firm.

Eventually the Gomery Commission exposed the dark underside of the Liberal Party in Quebec and cost Martin his popularity with Canadians. Martin called an election for June 2004, too late according to his critics, who believed he should have gone to the polls before the commission's revelations provided the new Conservative leader, Stephen Harper, with the rope to hang him.

The campaign was bruising, with Martin's coterie desperate to hang on to the majority they'd inherited from the despised Chrétien, and Harper eager to make his mark in this election debut. Both leaders made extensive use of strategists, spin doctors, and consultants for whom this campaign was not just about policy and platforms but about their very jobs. Victory meant access to government contracts and saleable influence worth millions. Bad press coverage could endanger the financial futures of scores of the party faithful in both camps. Knowing that I would have to deal with whichever party formed the government, I was determined that our CTV coverage and my commentary be fair and above partisan reproach. No chance of that. The Liberals turned on me with a fury after the nationally televised leaders' debate.

I had been chosen as the leadoff questioner, and Martin had won the draw for the first question. I knew that the hotheads of Martin's media operation would never forgive anything but a softball question, but I could not bring myself to throw an obviously easy lob. I asked Martin why anyone should believe that, as a finance minister from the province of Quebec, he knew nothing about the payoffs and skulduggery among Liberals in his home province. He stammered out a weak reply and was on the defensive for the next two hours.

In my post-debate on-air chat with Lloyd Robertson, I opined that Harper had won the night, and I should have left it at that. But I had been impressed with Harper and went on to say that perhaps Canadians should get used to the sound of "Prime Minister Harper." A contact in the Liberal war room told me there were shouts of derision and obscenities at that suggestion, and many of my colleagues also roundly condemned me for the remark. Still, I was only one election away from being right.

I knew I would have to pay for my outspokenness, and the consequences were not long in coming. At a campaign rally the next day, Martin greeted reporters with handshakes but had none for me. I received a baleful stare as he carefully grasped the hands of reporters to either side of me. For the balance of the campaign I was persona non grata with the Martin crowd. Old friends apologized for declining to have a drink with me in public. Every other reporter with a camera was granted a one-on-one interview with the prime minister, but Martin refused to appear on *Question Period*. As for the Harper Conservatives, they loved me for a brief time only. After I had savaged Harper for his ludicrous charge that Martin supported child pornography, the Conservatives too felt I had done them serious harm.

The Liberals survived with a minority that June, but drifted badly over the next eighteen months. Martin became known as "Mr. Dithers" and was resoundingly rejected by the electorate in January 2006, losing to Stephen Harper.

Out of office, Martin bears comparison to U.S. president Jimmy Carter as perhaps the best former leader we've ever had. In retirement he has proven the sincerity of his former government's commitment to improved health and education for Aboriginal peoples by using his private wealth and his fundraising abilities to launch innovative programs. His twenty-first-century policies concerning cities, national daycare, and centres of excellence and research are, some maintain, sorely missed. These were important initiatives advanced by a good man who, everyone believed, possessed the intelligence, character, and experience to become one of the country's outstanding leaders.

Yet thousands of loyal Liberals sat out the 2006 election or voted for other parties. The Martinites left town blaming not themselves, but the media and the machinations of backroom plotters within their own party ranks. After the dust settled, one Chrétien strategist told me, "They thought they were better than us but they weren't. We won." My thought was that in destroying their party's unity, both sides had consigned the Liberals to defeat for years to come. How many years remains to be decided.

Political combat is high drama, if not pure entertainment, for reporters on Parliament Hill, but in those years we were frequently reminded that conflicts of a far more serious nature were affecting Canadians. Four significant foreign wars arose during Chrétien's time in office: Kosovo, the first Gulf War, the war in Iraq, and finally Afghanistan. Canada was involved in three of them.

The exception was Iraq, and I felt the whole country breathed a sigh of relief when Chrétien rose in the House of Commons on St. Patrick's Day in 2003 and announced that Canada would not join the U.S.-built coalition against Saddam Hussein. His decision to reject President George Bush's request for participation by

Canadian troops in the disastrous invasion of Iraq was a bold assertion of our independence. The pressure exerted by the president
was intense. Chrétien himself told me that when the two men had
met shortly before the invasion at the opening of a new border
crossing at Windsor, Bush had physically dragged him into a room
alone and told him, "I must have Canada." Chrétien replied, "If
you don't have the United Nations, you don't have Canada." I
could forgive Chrétien a great deal for that gutsy act alone.

A year earlier, I had been with my son, Murray, when news
came of the first Canadian casualties in Afghanistan. Murray, then
in his thirties, was living and working in Kampala, Uganda, as a
reporter with *The Monitor*, the lone independent daily newspaper
in that country. Their columnists and editors were regularly
jailed for their opinions and stories. Murray was among the first
to report on the invasion of the Congo by Ugandan, Rwandan,
and other African forces from 1996 to 1997, which was designed
in part to carve up pieces of that mineral-rich failed state. Three
million died while the world barely noticed. Later Murray signed
on as African correspondent for the CTV News Service, and the
dreadful and the harrowing continued to be his beat.

During a two-week visit in April 2002, Murray and I hiked
for hours through the jungle on the Congo-Ugandan border to
get within twenty feet of a family of gorillas. Looking one of the
big males in the eye, I had the strange sensation of staring into
the past at an ancient ancestor and could almost believe that in
his level gaze was a similar sense of recognition. Our campsite
was outfitted with a bathtub and BBC reception, and on
April 18 I was stunned to hear a broadcast announcing the
deaths of four Canadians and the wounding of eight others by
American friendly fire near Kandahar. Four months before, I had

covered the departure of those troops, watching the emotional scene as they marched out of CFB Petawawa's drill hall and onto buses that would take them to their military flights from Trenton. Now four of them were dead, and Canadians could not imagine the losses that lay ahead.

From that day, a younger generation of reporters, very few of whom had ever worn a uniform of any kind, found themselves doing work they likely never dreamed of in journalism school: covering a war. The daily news diet had changed for all of us after the events of 9/11, although until the deaths started mounting in Afghanistan, Canadian news people felt somehow immune. That changed when reporters started to accompany the Canadian forces outside the wire of the heavily defended base in Kandahar in the heart of Taliban territory.

During the Second World War campaigns in Europe and later in Vietnam, correspondents were able to move around the countryside with acceptable risks, linking up with military units when and where they chose. London and Saigon were always available for rest and recuperation. There is no such space in Afghanistan. Roadside bombs are everywhere and anywhere, and to be captured by the enemy is to face near-certain death.

In the early days of the war, many reporters—my son, Murray, and his cameraman, Tom Michaluk, among them— donned Afghan garb and ventured out of the compounds, without military minders, to chase their own stories. By then, Murray had worked in some of the most lawless areas of Africa, far more alien and dangerous terrain than any I had experienced in Central and Latin America, so he did not need any professional advice from me. He had developed well-tuned instincts regarding risk, and I was not overly worried about him.

But as the Taliban's presence grew in strength and deadli-
ness, most correspondents were ordered by their bosses to stay
behind the protection of the walled camp, while a few others
simply refused to take chances for personal reasons, covering the
conflict from the safety of a fortified bunker. One cannot fault
them for their individual choices, often influenced by spouses
back home.

In fact, the only reasonable way to cover this war is to be
embedded with the army, which means accepting the necessary
compromises that effectively place a news organization and its
reporters under military command. Reporters are, and should
be, skeptical of authority and many find their dependency on
the military uncomfortable to say the least. Doubtless, the
military are likewise discomfited by the presence of the media
in their midst.

CTV reporter Lisa LaFlamme, who has since taken over the
national anchor desk from Lloyd Robertson, made four trips to
Afghanistan and spent months in the field with the troops. She
found that once she had established a relationship of trust with
the soldiers, they always told her the truth; in her view, it was
a fair exchange for the limits imposed on her as an embedded
journalist. Travelling with the soldiers on combat patrols, she
allowed viewers to see what it was like to fight off scorpions
along with enemy insurgents, sleep in gravel pits, and drive
through mined areas; all taken together demanded psychological
as well as physical courage. She describes her weeks buttoned up
in an armoured car with ten men as the closest one can get to life
inside a hockey bag.

The risks are real: In August 2007, two CBC journalists,
Patrice Roy and Charles Dubois, were badly injured when their

armoured personnel carrier struck a roadside bomb. Dubois lost a leg. In December 2009, *Calgary Herald* reporter Michelle Lang became the first Canadian journalist to die in Afghanistan, when a similar device destroyed the vehicle that she and a party of Canadian troops were travelling in south of Kandahar. Four soldiers also lost their lives.

Earlier that year, in March, CTV had lost an invaluable Afghan contact named Jojo Yazamy, who had arranged for everything from translation to transport to actual film footage in and around Kandahar City. Somehow operating between the Taliban and Western reporters, Jojo had seemed invulnerable, with his access to the powerful on both sides and his apparent ease as an all-purpose fixer. Eventually one side or the other concluded he was a spy or at least a threat, and he was assassinated in Kandahar City by a shooter who pulled up beside his car at a stop.

For the record, in 2009 I tried to find my own way to experience this controversial and still-uncertain conflict. I had growing doubts that we could ever achieve our objectives there, even if the struggle were winnable from a military perspective or at a political cost acceptable to the Western nations involved. Counter-insurgency wars are more often lost on the home front than in the field.

Since the war was the subject of many reports and commentaries I filed, I felt obliged to go and witness it for myself. I will confess too that the thought of being up close to a shooting war again got the old juices flowing. The network gently but firmly turned down this suggestion, my poor eyesight counting me out in their estimation. That was the only occasion on which disability put me on the sidelines.

10

SPARRING WITH HARPER

Whether the assignment is city hall or Parliament Hill, it's critical for a reporter to know the key players, and that means keeping ahead of the casualties by spotting the comers who will one day take centre stage. It was obvious to me in 1993 that Stephen Harper, a newly elected Reform MP from Calgary, was a cut above the rest, good-looking, smart, and—unusually for someone representing a Western constituency—bilingual. He was an intensely private person, a trait he shared with Pierre Trudeau. He was also seriously intelligent, but he lacked Trudeau's charm and ability to project personal warmth. He was not a backslapping, hand-grabbing, press-the-flesh politician; in fact, he was stiff and awkward in social situations. Even informal photos caught him ramrod straight, barely tolerant of physical contact beyond the obligatory handshake. Nonetheless, while Preston Manning could be more congenial, he would never win the Prime Minister's Office for his party. It seemed to me that Stephen Harper might.

Shortly after Harper had lost the 2004 election, his first as leader of the Conservative Party, a mutual friend asked if I would meet with Harper to try to persuade him to be more open and approachable with the media. I agreed, hoping that a frank conversation might serve reporters on the Hill generally, as well as those in my own bureau. Such one-on-one sit-downs were not uncommon in my experience, especially with Opposition leaders. These informal and usually private encounters offered an opportunity to suss out the essential character of the individual, free of the protective wrapping usually held in place by the image-makers.

Harper and I met alone at his office and had a conversation that was remarkable for its candour. He did not disguise his distrust of reporters, citing a long history of Parliament Hill journalists leaving the press gallery to work for the Liberal Party. I raised the fact that many in the press gallery and in his own caucus were unhappy with the performance of Caroline Stewart Olsen, Harper's press assistant. Although she was a creditable woman, she had no training for the position and clearly did not like reporters. (Harper later appointed her to the Senate.)

I urged Harper to follow the examples of Trudeau and Chrétien, leaders who had relied on press officers with very different personalities from their own. He should not hire individuals who would only reinforce his own aloofness. I probably went beyond propriety in suggesting that Harper had already demonstrated the right instincts in his choice of Laureen Teskey as his wife. Here was a woman who was garrulous, witty, and wore her endearing eccentricities on her sleeve—almost Harper's opposite, and certainly a great asset. He chuckled but was unconvinced.

While frankly acknowledging his own frailties, Harper obviously would never feel entirely comfortable with representatives of the national media, many of whom he believed to be biased against politicians of the Conservative stripe. I thought Harper wrong in his conviction that the public shared his low opinion of those who covered politics and said that I had yet to see a successful leader who did not have at least a civil relationship with the men and women in the press corps. Indeed, I have known many who suffered hostile relationships with reporters and subsequently went down hard. The Canadian public may have a healthy suspicion of extremists in the media, but they give credence to most of what they read and see in the national press.

We chatted for perhaps half an hour, Harper waving off one obviously scheduled interruption halfway through the conversation. He listened, but he did not concede. I rose to leave, not wanting to take up any more of his time.

"I enjoyed that," he said. "Would you give me a call? I'm not very good at calling people myself."

That intimation of vulnerability made me feel differently about the man, if no less wary of the politician. Curiously, though, that session was the first of a series of infrequent one-on-one talks between us that continued into Harper's first term as prime minister. And Harper did call a day or two after he was elected in January 2006.

"So, what advice do you have for me?" he asked.

I replied that he should guard against overexposure; that people soon tire of politicians who are constantly in their faces.

"Great," he noted. "The next time you ask for an interview, I'll turn you down."

I enjoyed the quip and actually looked forward to our first encounter after Harper was sworn in as prime minister, but complications soon arose.

In February, Harper travelled to Afghanistan to view the Canadian and allied war effort for himself. U.S. president George W. Bush had been there just days before, and undoubtedly the sight of Harper dressed in similar quasi-military garb struck the prime minister's communications staff as a chance to portray the new PM as a resolute leader, clearly in command.

The day the prime minister returned to Ottawa, I received a call from Caroline Olsen, who offered me an interview for *Question Period*, the first interview Harper had granted to anyone since coming to power. My mind raced ahead. Obviously, there were a lot of issues to be raised: Harper's legislative agenda for the new Parliament, his budgetary priorities, even the makeup of his Cabinet, announced before the Afghanistan visit. But there would be virtually no preparation time. The aide said the prime minister would be available within the hour for a ten-minute taped interview.

We readied the studio and the set was in place when Caroline Olsen called again. The prime minister was prepared to entertain questions concerning the war in Afghanistan and nothing else, she said; I was restricted to that topic and that topic alone. She reminded me that I was being honoured with the first interview given by the new prime minister.

From a news point of view, the interview was a coup. But clearly this was also the first test of a new strategy by the Harper communications staff to alter the relationship between the prime minister and the parliamentary press gallery. They intended to change the rules, to challenge the influence of columnists and reporters, and to subject them to the same centralized control that they would exert on the Conservative caucus and on government bureaucrats. If the disparate and often-quarrelsome members of the press gallery could be thought of as a union acting as an intermediary between the politicians and the rank-and-file public, Harper's advisers hoped to decertify it.

Much as I wanted an exclusive interview, I knew that making side deals to save politicians from difficult questions was a betrayal of the public trust. Ms. Olsen was astonished when I rejected her offer. With some trepidation, I then notified CTV's head office, which might have been displeased that their Ottawa bureau chief had risked alienating the prime minister within weeks of his taking office. News vice-president Joanne MacDonald not only supported the decision, but also said that had I agreed, she would have overruled me.

At the time, I felt no resentment toward Harper or his staff over this, regarding it as simply another skirmish in the eternal battle between the media and the politicians, and I was pleasantly surprised that Harper himself did not seem to bear a grudge when I was placed in an embarrassing position a year later.

Harper was making a high-profile visit to Mexico and agreed to an unrestricted interview for *Question Period* on the final day of his summit with the U.S. and Mexican presidents. In its never-ending attempts at penny-pinching, the network insisted we hire a local Mexican technical crew rather than fly in one of our own. Unfortunately, the complexities of putting the signal up to a satellite and connecting with our studio were beyond the locals. We tried frantically to complete the connection while the prime minister sat waiting, as did his anxious entourage, eager to take off at the airport. After an hour, we finally had to admit it was hopeless. I later sent Harper a note apologizing for our failure, which got me a quick personal call, in which he assured me the incident was unimportant.

This and other small incidents left me with contradictory impressions of Stephen Harper. I have never been able to rationalize the mean-spirited, secretive, and autocratic nature of his government's conduct in its first two terms with my many personal encounters with an invariably polite and thoughtful individual.

Oftentimes, small events, easily passed over, signal the particular stamp that a leader will put on his administration. Six months into office, Toronto Conservative Garth Turner was suspended from the party caucus for committing the sin of criticizing the prime minister on his blog, which eventually led to Turner's being harried out of the party altogether. Harper's same failure to read the dynamics of personal relationships had led another Conservative MP, Belinda Stronach, to cross the floor to the Liberal benches the year before, thereby saving Paul Martin's government from defeat for a brief time. Harper's message of zero tolerance of criticism only reinforced what his detractors in and out of the government soon labelled a rigid and controlling leadership style.

However, a more serious flaw in Harper's personality detracted from his considerable capabilities. He seemed to carry a burden of resentments, accumulated hurts, and complaints that occasionally caused him to boil over. In April 2006, Harper nominated the respected oil and gas industry executive Gwyn Morgan to head a new public appointments commission, a body that would ensure the transparency and quality of government appointments. The intention was certainly praiseworthy. But when a Commons committee failed to ratify Morgan's nomination, Harper was embarrassed and miffed. Rather than name another nominee, he declared the position dead and dropped the idea of the commission altogether. There was a complexity to Harper that led him to throw obstacles in his own path, even when he was at his most innovative and brilliant. Like a character out of Dostoevsky, he seemingly feared success, feeling that it was undeserved.

Observing Harper's occasional antics, I wondered if they might stem from a childhood plagued by asthma, a condition that isolates children from other kids and may have kept Harper in particular from joining in the roughhouse games that foster male bonding. At the risk of playing amateur psychologist, I think such individuals compensate for their fear of rejection by exerting an unwarranted control and authority over those around them. Harper could not be a hockey player, but he could make himself an expert on the rules and history of the game, thus giving him authority over those who played it.

This distance from others, while not preventing Harper from gaining the respect and obedience of his parliamentary caucus, did not always bring him affection. At the same time, his critics could not deny that he possessed many of the qualities of a natural leader. He was not afraid to lead and brought a stubborn grittiness to the pursuit of his objectives. He projected strength and determination, which Canadians have always favoured in their leaders. Finding a likeable person in Harper was possible, but one had to work at it.

By 2005 I had been CTV's Ottawa bureau chief for seventeen years. It was a seven-day-a-week job that involved divining the direction of government and Opposition manoeuvres, assigning reporters and producers, staying in touch with sources, and stickhandling endless calls from Toronto headquarters. During that time I had hired more than a score of talented reporters, among them Kevin Newman, Lisa LaFlamme, Dawna Friesen, Joy Malbon, Paula Newton, Roger Smith, and the indefatigable Jim Munson, plus a host of bright young producers who went on to run their own shows at U.S. and Canadian networks or, in the case of Joanne MacDonald and Tom Haberstroh, rose high in the network's executive ranks. It was exhilarating to work with these journalists, but enervating to carry the administrative load.

I asked for a change and Robert Hurst, president of CTV News and another of my hires some two decades before, was quick to grant it. I recommended that he approach Robert Fife, the canny bureau chief for Canwest News Service and the *National Post* who had been scooping everyone on the Hill in recent years, to be my successor. I asked that I be allowed to return to my first love as chief political correspondent. In that role, I would happily pursue political stories, offering where possible more than the facts of breaking news. I had long provided the national news with "thumb-suckers" or "talkbacks," as the networks call them, giving background to, along with interpretation and commentaries on, the events and personalities of the day. Presenting these thoughts without the appearance of bias, while still saying something worth listening to, is not simple. In Ottawa, views on what is really happening and why can vary sharply.

I continued as co-host of *Question Period* alongside Jane Taber, senior political reporter and columnist for the *Globe and Mail*. The longest running political news show in the country, the program first went on air in the 1960s. It was taped on Friday afternoons and broadcast on Sunday mornings, a two-day hiatus that was safe in those days of a much slower news cycle, when the whole world seemingly took the weekend off. By the end of the millennium, however, *Question Period* was looking tired, and audiences were dropping away on the full network. It was taken off the air in 1999.

In 2001, I suggested to the network's president, Ivan Fecan, that we revive the show by taking it live to air every Sunday. Without a moment's hesitation, Fecan said simply, "Do it." There were no lengthy committee meetings or study groups, no audience surveys or marketing studies. Fecan's words were holy writ at the network, and when I went to the money people for a budget and a new time in the schedule, I had only to repeat those words and all resistance fell away.

To describe Ivan Fecan as a broadcast genius is not too much. He built CTV into an immensely profitable operation through a series of acquisitions, including the money machine TSN. Although he was a committed Liberal and major fundraiser for Jean Chrétien, he never once interfered with the coverage decisions of his most important bureau. This could not have been easy, especially on those occasions when Chrétien's closest aides publicly expressed their displeasure with us.

For a time I fretted that politicians and pundits would be reluctant to rise early and get themselves to a studio on a Sunday morning. In the West especially, it was brutal sun-up. But the network sent in a wicked smart producer, Jana Juginovic, who created a fresh format with edgy interviews, sharp video, and reports from far-flung correspondents on the scene of breaking news. With a full-time staff of only one and all the others dragooned from other jobs in the bureau, *Question Period* went on to command the highest ratings in its history.

Today, the nation's power brokers sit before our cameras every week, and the program itself often breaks stories that make the front pages of the newspapers on Monday morning. The audience is not a large one, ranging from roughly a hundred and fifty thousand when not much is happening on the Hill to three hundred thousand when major events are unfolding. But its tight focus on parliamentary politics draws a national audience of opinion leaders and politicos. *Question Period* has earned its reputation for setting the news agenda on the Hill for the coming week.

It was inevitable that the *Question Period* team would deal with the communications staff in the Prime Minister's Office on an almost daily basis, yet it seemed my earlier suggestions regarding the importance of respectful relations between the national press corps and political leaders did not go far with Stephen Harper. In the wake of Caroline Stewart Olsen's departure, Harper appointed Sandra Buckler to the more senior position of director of communications. I had never heard of Buckler, but I expected the usual healthy editorial tug-of-war between the chief press aide and our producers, and I was pleased to see a woman finally atop the PMO's communications ladder.

Unfortunately, my first meeting with Buckler did not go well. She kept me cooling my heels for an hour at a local restaurant, and when she arrived she explained that she was very busy, suggesting her time was more important than mine. In the brief conversation we had before she rushed off to her next meeting, it became apparent that she had no experience in serious journalism or in the news business at all. Advertising was her professional milieu, and that explained her approach. Buckler regarded news about the prime minister and the government as a property that she alone owned and had a right to manage as she saw fit. There was no evidence that she acknowledged as part of her job an obligation to be open and transparent with reporters, and through them with Canadians, about what the government was doing. Harper had endlessly promised just such transparency when he was in Opposition and on the hustings.

For her first act, Buckler put herself at the apex of the tightly knit structure, dubbed the "Centre," which directed and controlled communications for every government department. The efforts by *Question Period*'s staff to deal directly with press officers for individual ministers or those who represented individual departments were rebuffed or referred to Buckler's office. Not only was she supreme commander of all government information, she was the self-appointed mistress of all political messaging. I soon became aware that senior bureaucrats and even Cabinet ministers feared speaking without Buckler's approval or coaching. Monte Solberg, a confident and adept minister who had become a friend during his years in Opposition, suddenly would not return calls or agree to interviews. When we met by chance in the halls of Parliament, he would mumble something about the Centre, and then rush off in obvious embarrassment. One of Harper's liveliest ministers, Jason Kenney, told me candidly, "The communications director for the prime minister does not believe in communicating."

Before long the bureaus had received the new ground rules. Buckler decreed that Cabinet ministers should not appear in face-to-face encounters with their Opposition critics. At press conferences with the prime minister, the press officer in attendance would decide who among the press corps would be allowed to ask questions. Harper would answer no question from a reporter who had not first been recognized by the officer. Clearly this was a practice designed to favour reporters with easy or planted questions over those with less friendly or more challenging lines of inquiry, and a number of reporters boycotted the PM's events rather than be subject to such rules of engagement. Eventually a compromise was reached, but it left a bad taste.

In the early months of the government's first mandate, *Question Period* made repeated requests to the Centre for on-air interviews with Cabinet ministers, but with limited success. On occasion a department might agree to produce a minister for us, only to call back shamefacedly to say that for one reason or another, the minister was suddenly unavailable. Buckler's strategy was obvious: If we were able to book only Opposition MPs on a particular issue, she assumed our professional desire for fair and balanced coverage would not allow us to pursue it in the absence of a spokesperson for the government side.

Jane Taber and I and our producers refused to play that game. When the unrepresented government came off second-best, Buckler had no choice but to relent and allow the occasional minister to appear on the show. Invariably they were reliable stalwarts such as Finance Minister Jim Flaherty or Jim Prentice and John Baird, whatever their ministries at the time. Most others were off limits, and when they did come, Buckler wanted questions submitted in advance and an agreement that only those questions would be asked. We would not make that commitment. My first serious run-in with Buckler came when I speculated on air that if Harper could not trust his own ministers to get out front and explain government policy, why should members of the public trust them?

Conservative backbenchers were forbidden to appear under any circumstances, even though it seemed to many of us that there was more talent in the ranks than on the government's front benches. A number of intelligent and appealing figures had not made it to Cabinet and they smarted under the media restrictions. Without exposure for local MPs, their constituents quite rightly wondered what had become of the representatives they'd sent to Ottawa.

Buckler gradually loosened up a little, but that did not end the hostilities. Environment Minister Rona Ambrose was finally allowed to appear on the show, but she was obviously ill prepared to handle tough questions about the government's discredited environmental policy. I pressed her hard, and she was not up to the contest. Buckler exploded, accusing me of harassing an attractive young woman in a hostile and unprofessional manner. Not long after, however, the prime minister pulled Ambrose from the environment post.

I knew the relationship between Buckler and me was beyond recovery when she began to send complaints about my allegedly disrespectful style, first to me and then to bureau chief Robert Fife and to Robert Hurst. But by then I had established a healthy rapport with a number of ministers, among them Jim Flaherty, Peter MacKay, and House Leader Jay Hill, all of whom were bold enough to make their own decisions. They were delighted to tangle with the media and gave as good as they got in almost every round. Buckler's emails were dutifully passed up the line to Toronto, but *Question Period* received no directives one way or the other.

We were nothing if not persistent in our insistence on ministerial accountability. When a serious economic story arose a few months later, we asked for Finance Minister Flaherty. Instead we were told Secretary of State Kenney would fill the slot. Furthermore, Buckler would determine the ministers who were to appear on any given Sunday in future, as she would the topic on which they were to be interviewed. This attempt to dictate the content and lineup of our program took PMO imperiousness to new heights, and I rejected Kenney as being irrelevant to the issue. The following Sunday, the Opposition MPs predictably savaged the government, and I announced that the government had refused to provide us with an appropriate minister.

Buckler responded at once with an email to Hurst: "If you insist on preventing the government's spokespeople from appearing on your show based on your own criteria, which I absolutely do not agree with, I would respectfully request that you be honest and say that you rejected the designated spokesperson put forward by the government." She went on to say that I had misled viewers on the matter of government spokespersons and asked that my comments be corrected in any repeat broadcast of the show. Instead, I went on air and detailed her efforts to control and intimidate us. I explained that this was an issue of who was producing CTV television news programs: the network's reporters and producers or the Prime Minister's Office?

I never heard from Buckler again, but a few days later she announced her resignation. After trying out a few unfortunate replacements, Harper appointed a young Montrealer, Dimitri Soudas, who put the government's press relations on a professional footing.

In January 2005, three Liberal überactivists—lawyers Dan Brock and Alf Apps, along with television producer Ian Davey, son of Keith Davey, the party's famous rainmaker—made a pilgrimage to Boston in search of a messiah. Their objective was to persuade Michael Ignatieff to return home and run for Parliament. They made their pitch over a dinner that lasted until midnight, and when it ended Ignatieff was intrigued but unconvinced. He knew, and so did they, that he was ill acquainted with the country's political terrain after more than three decades abroad.

The three succeeded in winning Ignatieff's agreement to a coming out of sorts as the keynote speaker at the national Liberal Party convention in Ottawa in March of that year, an event that was expected to be a routine affair with few fireworks. Ignatieff was not familiar to most Canadians, but he had enormous credibility with the chattering classes: son of a respected Canadian diplomat, George Ignatieff; nephew of a nationalist icon, philosopher George Grant; award-winning author and broadcaster; and esteemed intellectual. The comparisons to Trudeau were immediate and irresistible. In the event, Ignatieff's speech stole Paul Martin's convention thunder, the neophyte upstaging the prime minister.

Ignatieff's supporters expected him to contest a seat in the next election, spend the requisite time in Cabinet while he built a national reputation, and then run for the leadership when an older Martin stepped down. (Shades of Trudeau and Lester Pearson.) They did not expect Martin's government to collapse in 2006, leaving Ignatieff with his seat in Parliament but contending for the party's leadership well before he was ready for it.

During Ignatieff's inaugural interview on *Question Period*, I decided to make him earn his airtime as a way of judging his temperament. I knew viewers wanted to hear him answer questions about how he could entertain prime ministerial ambitions after three decades of avoiding his country. The comparisons to Trudeau seemed wrong to me, since Trudeau had fought against corruption and separatism in Quebec for years before Pearson recruited him to national politics. I believe I used the word *dilettante*. It was an ambush, plain and simple, but Ignatieff parried every thrust with a cool and cocky demeanour, even inquiring at one point whether someone might have slipped something into my breakfast cereal.

Later, at lunch, I had a chance to make a personal connection with the man. He was open and engaging, not the least annoyed by the rough ride I had given him on television or my recent critical commentaries. As so often happens, it was an odd coincidence that shifted the discussion away from dry policy talk. Ignatieff's wife, Zsuzsanna Zsohar, was contending with vision loss after a botched eye surgery in London. Her condition was serious enough that Ignatieff sometimes read to her at night. She had so far not found a specialist in Canada, and I insisted she see my own doctor at the Eye Institute in Ottawa, an institution at the forefront of Canadian research and surgical practice. She agreed but would not allow herself to go to the head of the line, waiting four months for treatment even though I felt it was unwise to delay.

After our initial encounters, I concluded that Ignatieff was a man with brains and presence but still uncertain of what he stood for. This policy mushiness could be dangerous. Politics is no different than any other job, with success demanding years of

training and experience. Despite his obvious talents, I wondered
if he had the time to acquire the necessary skills.

At that stage, Ignatieff's only obvious rival for the party's
leadership was a man whose apprenticeship was far behind him.
Bob Rae is fond of reminding me that I was the first person
who took him for lunch when he arrived in Ottawa as an NDP
Member of Parliament in 1978, trailing a reputation for intellectual brilliance. He later switched to provincial politics and in 1990
became Ontario's first NDP premier. After six tumultuous years at
Queen's Park, Rae left the field for a decade, returning as a federal
MP in 2008, this time as a member of the Liberal caucus.

Rae had justifiable ambitions to the party's leadership and
the Prime Minister's Office, and he had not been pleased when
Ignatieff announced at a social dinner with the Raes that he
intended to jump into national politics. Rae did not welcome
his old friend to the inevitable competition for the party's top
job. The announcement marked the beginning of the end of a
friendship that dated to their student days at the University of
Toronto, a loss both would regret.

Lloyd Robertson and I were in the broadcast booth in
Montreal in December 2006 when the Liberals gathered to
choose Paul Martin's heir, the individual whose job it would be
to bring down the Harper Conservatives and restore the Liberals
to their accustomed position in power. To almost everyone's
astonishment, the victory went to Stéphane Dion on the fourth
ballot, with Ignatieff running second by fewer than two hundred
votes. Rae bowed out after the third ballot and released his
delegates, but would not declare in favour of any of the others.
He might have handed the prize to his old friend then and there,
had it not been for his pride.

Former Chrétien Cabinet minister Brian Tobin was high above the convention floor with Lloyd and me and noted that half the delegates below were sitting on their hands, refusing to applaud, when the winner, Dion, took to the stage. By the time the convention had ended, the party was suffering from a profound case of buyers' remorse. Everyone knew that the next leadership campaign was already under way.

No other political party in my lifetime has chosen a leader so inept and ill-prepared for the job as Stéphane Dion. In personality he was intensely serious and even sullen. Though intellectually bright—he was an architect of the Clarity Act and his dedication to action on the environmental front was sincere—he was unable to convey his ideas in an easy and informal conversational style in either official language. Once on the campaign trail, he disappointed audiences with flat addresses that were painful to endure and that failed utterly to deliver the necessary partisan attacks on the Harperites.

On October 8, 2008, even the Liberals stayed home and the party was reduced to seventy-seven seats, one of its worst showings in many decades. Within a week, Dion announced he would resign as soon as a new leader could be chosen. By December 10, 2008, Michael Ignatieff had been installed as acting leader until a formal convention vote could make it official the following spring.

In the fall of 2008, Canadians watched the American election campaign, pitting Barack Obama against John McCain, with perhaps as much interest as their own. The pace of those political events, the aggressive tactics used in both arenas, and the increasing influence of new media raised obvious questions. What is truth in news coverage? Who is telling it to us? And where do we go to find it? With so much information blasted at us from so many different sources, the genuine article has never been harder to discern amid the cacophony.

For good or ill, the digital age has given rise to the never-ending news cycle and a need to feed the information machine. We have the gift of instant coverage of any event that can be recorded with a cellphone, and we have the curse of sophisticated campaigns of deception that can go viral in seconds. Anyone with access to the internet can set herself up as a reporter, columnist, or analyst and peddle what may or may not be accurate information via personal blogs, YouTube clips, or online forums. The unsuspecting consumer cannot know if the authors are legitimate journalists, or hired flacks in the pay of political parties or special interests, or simply mischief-makers out to perpetrate a hoax.

It will surprise no one that I believe in the veracity of the mainstream media, by which I mean the professional newsrooms, big and small, which have standards of fairness and balance that the public can trust. Their reporters are sent into the field to witness events for themselves, stories are supported by teams of editors and fact checkers, and the work of all is subject to scrutiny, not just by the bosses but by press councils, ombudsmen and, in the case of broadcasters, the CRTC, not to mention the civil and criminal courts.

But the mainstream media itself has in some ways opened the door to abuses in this brave new news world. In October 1997, CTV brought its twenty-four-hour News Channel to air. (The CBC had preceded us by a few years with its own

CBC Newsworld.) There were no more final editions: We were producing and broadcasting stories around the clock, piling fresh items on top of old with less time for context, analysis, and evaluation. In general, mass media managers were more interested in ratings, hence the demand for colour and drama, if not actual crisis, and a focus on celebrity, crime, and oddball trivia. In some respects, the enemy is us: The explosion of news programming time has created such a need for material that we have debased the coin of what constitutes news itself.

Media minders—the spin doctors, public relations consultants, and communications assistants who now inhabit every government department and minister's office—are delighted to help meet the insatiable appetites of the news channels by creating news events for us. Though billed as public gatherings, these usually involve a "public" of partisan loyalists, summoned to provide the necessary backdrop to a well-staged and professionally produced performance by the minister. Reporters need not even attend and frequently are not permitted. When these events are given airtime, the viewing public is rarely aware that the events have been packaged and produced by a political party.

Unmediated news coverage today is ubiquitous and *caveat emptor* the consumer's only protection. Those of us in the serious-news business can only hope that the public will learn to distinguish between the real thing and the offerings of talk-show barkers, internet snake-oil salesmen, and political hacks.

Stephen Harper won a second term in October 2008 but was denied the majority he coveted. He had promised open, transparent, and accessible government, yet the perception was of an obsessively secretive administration. A few acts, such as the apology to Canada's Aboriginals for the abuses of the residential school system, were universally applauded, while others, like the record number of Senate appointments designed to ensure Conservative control of the upper chamber (including the naming of my former CTV colleague Mike Duffy), inspired only cynicism.

The former initiative, surely one of the most positive and uplifting in the history of the Canadian Parliament, struck a personal chord with me. Speaking on behalf of Canada and with genuine emotion, the prime minister apologized to native Canadians for the policy of assimilation that had done so much harm to their communities and to those students at the residential schools who had suffered cruel mistreatment in those institutions. After my story on the event had appeared on the national news that night, Carole Helin, the widow of my boyhood friend, Art, called to say that for the first time Aboriginal people could feel real self-respect.

But such moments of harmony were all too few. In their first two mandates, the Conservatives endeavoured to govern not like the minority they were, but like a majority. As long as they were able to retain the loyalty of their hard-core base of about 30 percent of the Canadian electorate, they had nothing to fear from the other four parties who split the remainder among them.

Throughout his second term, Harper showed no hesitation in breaking the furniture of the hallowed conventions of the past. Twice the combined Opposition parties threatened his government with defeat, and twice Harper shut down Parliament through prorogation. No other Canadian government had had the audacity to use such heavy-handed tactics so frequently, yet Harper did not flinch.

Another significant innovation of Harper's government was the perpetual election campaign. The Conservatives' election machine and its stokers never shut down between campaigns; fundraising and polling continued apace. Hence the appearance of television attack ads even before the writs were dropped. These messages, paid for by the party and advertised as such, were pure propaganda and sometimes contained outright falsehoods. More than once, the ads had to be withdrawn on grounds of poor taste or objections to gross inaccuracies. The other parties reciprocated with between-election ads of their own, but their spots leaned far less on the personal and more on the issues.

Viewers might claim these ads don't affect them, but surveys indicate that voters go to the polls believing the arguments they have heard in negative advertising. Most people regard themselves as wisely skeptical of any kind of advertising; in fact, they are not. Citizens hardly believe they can be lied to. Radio and TV ads for political ideas are just like those for any other product, and their messages have a way of settling into the public mindset, either by subtly persuading the undecided or reinforcing the biases of the converted.

Much of the government's positive approval rating in its second term was due to the perception that it was a competent and prudent manager of the economy. Faced with the global economic crisis in 2008, the Conservatives' first instinct was to stick with their no-deficit and balanced-budget promises. Only when the Opposition parties threatened to defeat a stand-pat budget did the Conservatives wake up to the political benefits of big spending. Their 2009 stimulus budget outlined a two-year spending program of nearly fifty billion dollars. There was not a city in the country that did not receive a degree of federal largesse, and to the government's credit, the money was disbursed without any financial scandals.

At the height of the international financial crisis in March 2009, the prime minister gave *Question Period* an exclusive interview in advance of a G20 summit in London. In the midst of what appeared to be a global economic meltdown, Harper was cool and on top of every issue facing the summit. Undoubtedly, his steadiness helped to calm the nerves of a jittery nation. Two years later, heading into a third election, Harper told me in one of our private conversations that he believed his unruffled performance during those tense months was responsible for the credibility his government continued to enjoy on the issue of financial management. Harper made clear that if an election came, the economy would be the crux of it, an issue on which he believed he could win. The deficits his government had racked up were not mentioned.

Under Harper, the Conservatives mastered the technique of absolute deniability, the flat assertion of supposed fact about which no doubt could be expressed. Before he became prime minister, Stephen Harper said he would not appoint senators or allow any but balanced budgets. He promised to institute fixed election dates. And he attempted to strike a coalition of opposition parties to defeat Paul Martin's minority government. The reversal of these and other positions was never spoken of or acknowledged by Harper or his ministers. When the media raised inconsistencies or outright hypocrisies, they were simply dismissed.

In his first two years as party leader, Michael Ignatieff endured a steep climb. His critics, including many in his own caucus, worried that he was all resumé and no charisma. The remnants of Dion's team harboured resentment that Ignatieff had played a role in ousting their man, thereby repeating the Liberals' self-destructive practice of tribal warfare between succeeding factions.

Ignatieff pulled together a staff of long-time friends led by Ian Davey, a savvy if politically inexperienced lone wolf who established himself as the sole conduit to the leader. Complaints about access and lack of communication came to a head in mid-2009 at a summer caucus meeting in Sudbury. Ignatieff made a blustery speech in which he boasted, "Your time is up, Mr. Harper." It was an empty and embarrassing display of bravado that utterly failed to rally his parliamentary colleagues.

Ignatieff continued to drift, talking in high-table platitudes while his support in the polls dropped to near-unprecedented lows. The Conservative attack ads that accused him of "just visiting" with no good reason for coming back to Canada took their toll. The central question was why he was in the fray, and he had no answer.

Finally in the fall, Ignatieff gathered the courage to do what leaders must when things are going badly. He fired his old friend Ian, along with an assistant who was Ian's girlfriend and some others. Rocked by the experience, Ignatieff told a visitor to Stornoway at Halloween that "there was blood on the walls" and "he had learned the hard lesson that one should not hire close friends as subordinates." The party's old guard persuaded him to bring in the smoothly Machiavellian Peter Donolo, a veteran of the Chrétien years who wasted no time in putting a sharp edge on the operation.

The Chrétien way was to blindside an opponent into the boards. This was not Ignatieff's style, or at least not yet. In Question Period, he preferred statesmanship over feigned outrage. In policy discussions, he seemed at sea, waffling on his former hawkishness in security and foreign affairs, yet uncomfortable grasping the nettle of left-leaning Liberal social policy. Friends felt Ignatieff had reached a low point by year's end, when he and his wife took a Caribbean vacation and he wondered aloud to a colleague, "Why did I ever take this goddamn job?"

Ignatieff was not the only one asking that question. The old lion Jean Chrétien was restlessly pacing his cage at home in Ottawa. Chrétien murmured darkly to friends that he might have to pull a Trudeau and return to office to save the party. Fearing the Liberals might be headed for a serious collapse, Chrétien encouraged a move to get merger talks underway with the NDP and drew their former leader Ed Broadbent into the plot. The scheme blew up in their faces when some of Chrétien's former Cabinet members who were loyal to Ignatieff leaked it to me and other reporters. After that, Chrétien kept his doubts to himself but never stopped nursing his grievances over the party's failure to choose Bob Rae, the brother of his oldest political friend, John Rae.

Peter Donolo, who had served Chrétien faithfully for years, was embittered by his former boss's machinations, but remained undeterred. His idea for a turnaround was one of the oldest in the political playbook and fitted the moment perfectly. In the spring of 2010, Michael Ignatieff and his wife headed out on a nationwide bus tour. It amounted to a campaign rehearsal and a way of convincing the nervous Nellies in the Liberal caucus that

Ignatieff had the mental and physical stamina to lead them into the next election.

In visiting every corner of the country, Ignatieff discovered a Canada he had not really known, and equally important, he found his voice. As one of his travelling companions noted, the collective voice of the hundreds of Canadians Ignatieff met described the gap between their needs and the Conservative government's policies. The trip provided what Ignatieff had been missing: a way to articulate a clear distinction between Liberal and Conservative visions of the country. Someone who spent a few hours with Ignatieff that Christmas found him very different from the year before. He was serene, prepared to fight, and, if necessary, lose an election on his revivified perception of Canada and the role of its government.

Once he found himself comfortable on the centre left, Ignatieff also found the natural eloquence that had impressed his early admirers. For the first time he spoke with passion about the Canada that was being lost, and he began to sound and look like the leader the Liberals had sought years before. Sadly, however, Ignatieff had come too late to the party.

Everyone in the Conservative Party seems to know someone who was in the room when Harper told his strategy meeting before his first election win in 2006 that he needed three elections to finish off the Liberal Party for a generation. Before I am done, he is reported to have said, the country will be unrecognizable. In truth the Liberal Party's national profile had been shrinking before Harper pledged to destroy it. The old consortium of big business and intellectual and cultural elites tied together by jobs and money and enjoying a docile press may have been fatally weakened even then, but did not recognize its own vulnerability. Harper saw it for what it was: an empty shell.

For the prime minister, however, timing was critical to the achievement of his dream. In late February 2011, Harper met with the NDP leader, Jack Layton, in his office across from Parliament Hill. The topic of conversation was the forthcoming budget, the terms of which could determine the fate of Harper's minority government. Threatened by widening Opposition accusations of dishonesty, the Conservatives did not want an election. Their strategy was to play for time while the economy improved and the parliamentary mood lightened, hoping to face a less combative Commons in the fall.

Harper and the team close to him, including Finance Minister Jim Flaherty, Chief of Staff Nigel Wright, and House Leader John Baird, were convinced that Layton did not want an election either. After all, he was recovering from both prostate cancer and surgery for a fractured hip. The session with Layton was amiable, reinforcing their impression that he was ready to deal, and they hurriedly designed a budget that included the concessions they believed would secure the NDP's support. Those measures, costed out at a billion dollars, embraced enhancements to both the Canada Pension Plan and the Guaranteed Income Supplement, and reintroduced a home renovation tax break. The Canadian Labour Congress urged Layton to take the deal. The Harperites felt confident. Asked whether he expected an election, John Baird surprised me with his certainty that there would be no spring campaign. "Layton really, really doesn't want one," he assured me.

But when Layton saw an advance copy of the budget on March 22, he felt the government had come up short; in his view, the necessary programs were underfunded. It appeared the two men had been talking past one another. Layton announced his decision to defeat the budget, leaving Harper not only surprised but angry. With the Conservatives immersed in a tawdry scandal involving a former close aide to the prime minister, with senior party members facing charges of election fraud, and with his government about to become the first ever to be found in contempt of Parliament, the timing of the election could not be worse.

Ignatieff had been the target of the Conservatives' personal attack ads for two years and at last decided to seize the moment. He took great satisfaction in heading off the budget vote, defeating the government instead with a Liberal non-confidence motion denouncing its treatment of Parliament. Shortly after the government fell, Ignatieff, in a rather unstatesmanlike but feisty remark, observed to a friend, "They really are assholes." Liberal strategists hoped they could turn the character of the Harper government into what pundits term a ballot question. If the election could be fought on the Conservatives' contempt for democracy and all that goes with it—lack of openness, divisive practices, and bullying tactics—the Liberals could move their numbers into minority-government territory at least.

The first weeks of the campaign were listless and largely uneventful, with the media's serious attention focused on Harper and Ignatieff. Layton aroused sympathy for the state of his health; expectations were adjusted accordingly.

Two months before the government's defeat, I'd met with Brad Lavigne, the NDP's national campaign director. He tried to convince me that this time would be different for Layton, claiming that the party's private polls were showing the NDP had captured the allegiance of over 20 percent of voters in Quebec. Indeed, our contacts in Quebec had been reporting voter fatigue with the separatist Bloc Québécois for months. Those voters, said Lavigne, identified with the left-of-centre NDP issues, especially on Afghanistan, the environment, and social issues.

In 2008, the NDP had made the mistake in Quebec of running too hard against Harper. Quebecers wanted to defeat the Conservatives, but they didn't believe the NDP would have the national clout to do it. They turned once again to the Bloc. In 2011, the NDP strategy was to court provincial sentiments by persuading Quebecers that their best hopes for a comfortable berth within federalism lay with the NDP. The party ran a television ad featuring a frantic hamster on a wheel and a voice-over declaration that the separatist party was getting them nowhere in Ottawa. Other ads appealed to soft nationalists and played up Layton's roots in the province.

Layton's own efforts to modernize the party, jettisoning both its lofty intellectual and militant labour images, had started to show results. One staffer recalled asking Layton about a new gizmo he brought into a meeting shortly after becoming leader in 2003; soon they all carried BlackBerry devices. And no matter how often he was told it was a waste of time and money, Layton never neglected Quebec. The crowds in 2011 were modest at first, but there was a noticeable friendliness toward him that organizers could not miss. The party was helped too by a popular champion in the province, Thomas Mulcair, a former cabinet minister in the provincial Liberal government of Jean Charest. Running for the NDP in September 2007, Mulcair won a by-election in the federal riding of Outremont, long a Liberal seat.

My own assignment was the prime minister's campaign tour, which I joined in early May. Members of his travelling press entourage were already grumbling; an incident from the week before especially rankled. Harper's campaign plane had departed for a trip to British Columbia on Easter Sunday, cutting into family plans for the holiday weekend. One of the correspondents asked a press aide if the prime minister could at least come to the back of the aircraft and say hello. He never came. Harper and his handlers were running a campaign that allowed for no unscripted moments with reporters or with the public.

Severe limitations were imposed on reporters' questions so as to avoid any distraction from the party's "economy and stability" message. Harper relied on a teleprompter to keep him resolutely on message, and his events were held before handpicked crowds of party loyalists. Attendees' identities were checked at the door lest ordinary members of the public try to sneak in, a procedure that was modified only slightly after the Mounties expelled two young women and an armed forces veteran under suspicion of having sympathies for other political parties.

The campaign's many facets had been organized as a seamless whole, with the candidate, the message, and the ads all tested and approved by focus groups and market research. The result was deliberately flat and uninspiring, totally devoid of spontaneity and paralyzing in its monotony. Columnists, editorialists, and reporters were almost unanimous in their judgment that the campaign's failure to connect with voters other than hard-core supporters would leave Harper short of his majority.

The Liberal plane, by contrast, offered a lively and

entertaining scene. Ignatieff did his Jerry Springer open mike routine every night to enthusiastic crowds. Shirt sleeves rolled up, mike in hand, he took questions on every conceivable subject for an hour or more. Too many questions, perhaps, and too many answers. By the end of a town hall blitz, reporters did not know what to write as a lead story. The message was mushy.

The Liberal leader was impressive by every standard, and his basic platform was credible; his promises of social programs, education, and pensions were viable and appeared to be fiscally sound. However, if it was such an impressive showing, why was Ignatieff not breaking through with Canadians? In an effort to rouse the voters from their torpor, he took a page from the Obama presidential campaign and its thematic chant, "Yes we can."

"Rise up," Ignatieff exhorted Canadians. His team could not understand why the public failed to respond to the charge that Harper was a threat to democracy. Yet it's hard to make an argument that democracy is at risk during an election campaign, which in itself is what democracy is all about. Nothing could be more democratic.

All the while, Harper was hammering home a single credo. He repeated the need for a "strong, stable majority government" so relentlessly that reporters took to chanting it to each other in unison. Canadians knew instinctively that the outlook for the global economy was murky, and Harper was saying, in effect, trust me because I am the only one offering safe harbour in troubled waters.

By mid-campaign, the Liberals knew their last hope lay in the national televised leaders' debates set for April 12 and 13. Ignatieff had to win them unequivocally. But over-rehearsed and ill-served by memorized ripostes, he simply froze when Layton delivered a barb about his poor Commons attendance. On the national news that night, I judged that Harper had won the English debate by not losing it. He was steely calm, gathered within himself, and he refused to be drawn away from his standard economic speech by his tormentors. Jack Layton, having scored effectively in the English-language contest, was smiling and affable in the French debate the following night. Huge numbers of Quebecers were taken with his confidence, his car-mechanic French, even his personal courage, as many saw it, in campaigning with the support of a cane. The NDP was getting respect—and everyone's attention—at last.

Quebec was the catalyst for the final sprint to the finish. On the Friday night before election Monday, the private polls consulted by Conservative campaign chair Guy Giorno suggested his party was five seats short of a majority. The NDP was enjoying a dizzying surge in Quebec, raising the prospect of a slightly different coalition than the one Conservatives had railed against: an NDP-led minority government supported by a Liberal rump.

On the following afternoon, news crews from nine of the most influential local and network stations in Ontario were positioned in assembly-line style on the shop floor of a steel manufacturing plant in Brampton. Stephen Harper worked his way down the queue from one interviewer to the next, declaring that an NDP government would be a disaster for the economy of the nation's most populous province and rekindling memories of the ill-fated NDP provincial government under Bob Rae.

These interviews, which blanketed the province, were a bold and direct appeal to wavering Liberals. For those in Southern

Ontario who could occasionally wear Conservative colours, including many who were at the throttle of the country's economic engine, an NDP government was anathema. In the hours before the polls closed, these "blue" Liberals threw their support behind the Conservatives in a bid to stop the NDP. Many, such as my former boss Ivan Fecan, will likely stay with the Conservatives if Harper tacks to the centre of the political spectrum in the years ahead.

For the Liberals and for Michael Ignatieff, the campaign was a debacle. In its aftermath, former party president Stephen LeDrew reflected that the losses were not due to the poor generalship of Michael Ignatieff. He did not let the party down, LeDrew observed, but rather "the party failed him." Whatever the verdict, the Liberals face the future without their one-time dream candidate and with Bob Rae as interim leader.

The sweep of Quebec by the New Democrats notwithstanding, the capture of Ontario by the Conservatives may be the most enduringly significant event of the 2011 election. Ontario, with its banking, investment, and entrepreneurial power tied to the commodity and energy resources of the West, had been the source of Liberal hegemony for generations.

The flip side, however, is that Harper has formed the first majority government without significant representation from Quebec. This will be a serious challenge for him when, as most believe, the separatist Parti Québécois wins the provincial election. To prepare "winning conditions" for a referendum on independence, a separatist provincial government will attempt to provoke Ottawa with demands no national government could accept. Since Harper will need the backing of the fifty-nine NDP MPs from Quebec to keep the federalist forces united, he will have to handle his relationship with the NDP carefully.

Fifty years after it was founded, the NDP had been placed in a position where it could realistically expect to form a national government. But the man who put the party there, Jack Layton, would never have the chance to live that dream. His untimely death on August 22, 2011, robbed the party of its best asset and threw our national politics into disarray, leaving Stephen Harper the only full-time national leader in Parliament. The NDP will struggle to find a leader with the prestige and authority to hold together its disparate parts as a historically English-speaking party now dominated by Quebecers. Moreover, that new party chief will have to emerge from the long shadow cast by the individual who, more than anyone since Tommy Douglas, personified what the party stands for. Perhaps the moderate progressive NDP ground Layton staked out can be protected from claim jumpers, but it will not be easy.

Stephen Harper devoutly sought a majority and won it in the end. He will control the Senate and the House of Commons, and by the time his term ends, he will have appointed almost all of the judges serving on the Supreme Court. It is an often-repeated truth that Canadian prime ministers, once handed a majority, are dictators between elections. Now that he is untroubled by the daily walk past the gallows, which is the fate of minority prime ministers, how will Harper govern and use his power? If he can expand his toehold in Quebec and steer for the centre with new moderate MPs in Ontario, he will be well on the way to achieving his objective of replacing the Liberals as Canada's natural governing party.

11

LAST RIVERS

In company with my canoe club colleagues or with other trusted friends, I paddled over thirty Canadian rivers during thirty years of canoe tripping. In the latter years, there were a few missed seasons when an election campaign or some other commitment kept me city-bound. These were sorely missed opportunities that I came to regret as time slipped past and the adventures I did have became all the more precious. Especially memorable were two final expeditions with Pierre Trudeau.

In 1994, the club regulars made plans to tackle the Stikine, a magnificent river that originates in northwestern British Columbia and flows through the Coast Mountain Range before emptying into the Pacific near Wrangell, Alaska. Mom had been terribly ill that summer, suffering fainting spells and disorientation as a result of lung cancer, but at her urging I joined the crew for what proved to be two thrilling weeks.

Trudeau and Ted Johnson naturally formed one of the canoe duos, though their customary roles were reversed in the boat. Johnson, Trudeau's one-time executive assistant and close aide, was the sternsman, responsible for making the critical decisions that Trudeau, his bowman and former boss, was obliged to follow.

We were attempting to run the Beggerly Canyon, a high-risk operation. The river's considerable force and volume is suddenly squeezed into the narrows of the gorge, creating a short, violent passage that leaves no room for error. The rushing water hammers into what appears to be a dead-end wall of volcanic rock, actually a hairpin turn to the left. There the river piles upon itself, forming stacks of surging waves with deep souse holes in the troughs, dangerous in open canoes such as ours.

The Beggerly Canyon is no run for amateurs, but Johnson and Trudeau were an experienced and skillful team who had never dumped. As we usually did, Tim Kotcheff and I went first to try to find the safest route. There wasn't one. We were caught in a powerful upstream eddy and thrown into the wall, cracking the bow gunwales and almost capsizing in the melee. The second boat was swept up by cross-currents, tossed up on top of a wave, and turned around, causing it to finish the route perilously ass-backwards.

Taking in the scene from above, Johnson decided on the prudent approach and told Trudeau simply, "We're not going."

"Of course we are," Trudeau retorted. "The others went for it."

Years as a loyal subordinate took over and Johnson acquiesced. But no sooner had they cast off into the canyon mouth than Johnson realized he had chosen a very bad line. In seconds, he would be irrevocably committed to certain trouble.

"I am heading in to shore," he shouted above the roar.

"No!" his boss yelled back.

The team's indecision was clear to the others waiting on

the bluff. The canoe began to slide sideways. Johnson dug in, an inshore eddy caught the canoe, and the team shot up on the gravel shoreline. Trudeau grabbed his pack and trudged off sullenly down the portage trail. "Intellectually, I know I can lose," he had once said to me, "but I never do." Nor did he like to.

Johnson sat still in the stern of the canoe, collecting his breath. To himself as much as anyone else, he muttered, "Goddamned if I will go down in history as the man who drowned Pierre Elliott Trudeau."

The jungle drums along the Stikine had sent out the word that the former prime minister was on the water. We were more than a mile past an outfitter's camp when a powerboat from the camp came chasing after us. When the boat had reached the last canoe in line, the driver asked whether this was the Trudeau group. If so, would the great man come back for a coffee?

I looked ahead to Pierre who shook his head with a firm *no*. If he accepted, the whole group would have to paddle back against the current on his account. We carried on for another few minutes before the cruiser returned, this time with an attractive young lady, red hair blowing in the breeze, at the wheel. She was the fit and outdoorsy type that so many men find irresistible; certainly Trudeau did. She pulled up alongside Trudeau's canoe to ask if he would change his mind and meet her father, who was a long-time admirer. The bows of our canoes swung back toward the camp, and the young woman had the good sense to tow us in a line astern all the way.

Inside the living room of the outfitter's beautiful post-and-beam log home, Trudeau took a seat on a large sofa and in a voice that was more command than request suggested the young lady come and sit beside him. He was clearly entranced by this vivacious woman. They had such an animated conversation that the rest of us might just as well not have been in the room.

The woman's father expressed his delight and gratitude that the former prime minister had stopped in. He himself was an interesting man, yet his face and demeanour carried a hint of some deep sadness. We learned later that the first thing he saw leaving his home every morning was a scarred clearing on the forested mountainside across the river—the spot where his wife and son had perished in the crash of their floatplane two years before. Trudeau was visibly moved at this news and thankful we had gone back.

The trip over, we made our way to Vancouver by air, stopping overnight at Terrace, British Columbia. Although Trudeau had been gone from the political stage for fifteen years, his presence created a scene at the airport. Eventually a crowd of a hundred or more gathered to request an autograph or simply watch as he made his way from the baggage claim to the taxi stand. That night all of us gathered for a parting dinner at a local restaurant. A big man in his fifties, possibly a logger, approached our table without hesitation and placed himself in front of Trudeau. The table fell into an uncertain silence, but Trudeau sat unflinching and gave the man that famous ice-blue gaze. The giant asked, "Are you Pierre Trudeau?" The reply was affirmative. The fellow held out a hand the size of a baseball glove and said simply, "Thank you for what you did for my country." We were all taken aback, but Trudeau seemed especially surprised and uncharacteristically speechless. I was almost alarmed to see his eyes well up after he and the stranger had shaken hands.

After farewells at the Vancouver airport, I made my way to Mom's apartment. She had been on my mind throughout the trip, and in peaceful moments I could not help but reflect on her own journey. How brief must have been the times when her heart and mind were at peace. Those years long ago when she and Cliff and I had lived together were among the few that had given her a secure sense of home and family. For the rest, she had looked for happiness in work or booze or the approval of others and found only loneliness.

My own experience had taught me that contentment is not to be found in bricks and mortar, however grand or comfortable, but within ourselves. Home is a place in the heart and goes where we go. The other is just shelter.

I found Mom far gone. Her lung cancer had spread to her brain, and her doctor told me that she had willed herself to remain alive for my return. I agreed to the surgery the doctor recommended, which in the end was nothing less than torture for Mom. The decision was made out of love in the hope that the surgery would lengthen Mom's life; too late, I realized I had done the wrong thing for the right reasons. The procedure gave her a few weeks of half-life during which she never stopped smoking. In one of our last conversations, she confessed to me that she and my father had never married. I told her that it did not matter then and did not matter now.

There was a lovely memorial service in a small United Church on the grounds of the University of British Columbia. One of Mom's friends hired a singer to perform her favourite hymn, "Just a Closer Walk with Thee." After the cremation, I took Mom's ashes to scatter in the sea at Jericho Beach. The day was windy and as I crouched down to pour out the ashes carefully, a large wave hit the shore, soaking me from head to toe. Mom had the last laugh.

In the days and weeks afterwards, I received countless messages from friends who had known of Mom's and my sometimes-tortuous relationship. They expressed solace, and I was especially grateful to those who acknowledged Mom's feisty spirit. Jean Chrétien, then prime minister, called me in Vancouver. "I understand how you must feel, he said, "but imagine my grief. You've lost a mother, but I've lost a supporter."

On the day of Mom's funeral, I learned that when our Stikine canoe party had arrived in Terrace, Trudeau had been informed by telephone from Montreal that his brother had died while we were on the river. He had said nothing at the time, though perhaps the loss partially explained his wet eyes at the unexpected encounter over dinner. I wanted to offer condolences to Pierre and perhaps find consolation for our mutual losses, but I demurred. Sharing such intimacies was never his style.

~

Pierre Trudeau's style was to deny any fear, even if he felt it, and to accept any physical challenge. On one expedition our party included an Olympic-level paddler who decided to run a hazardous stretch of rapids solo. The rest of us opted to play safe and portage around it. The man accomplished the passage superbly but in the process unwittingly threw down a red flag to Trudeau, who was determined to make it a competition. Trudeau ran the rapid well, doing it backwards for a short stretch and sideways for another, yet emerging unscathed and confirmed in his ability to read the water well. But the risk was an unnecessary one for him, which it was not for the much better canoeist who preceded him.

For someone with so much pride in his physical courage, growing weaker with age was a bitter pill. Trudeau's declining strength almost cost him his life during our final trip together in 1997 on the Petawawa River in Ontario. He was then seventy-seven and thinner than I had ever seen him. Though we did not know that he had been diagnosed with Parkinson's disease, the ravages were starting to show.

Halfway down the portage trail beside the Rollaway Rapids, a brass cross is embedded in a boulder. It is a memorial erected by the friends of political journalist Blair Fraser, who drowned there in 1968. Trudeau was one of those friends and whenever he passed the spot, he never failed to pause and gaze at it in silent reflection. This time Trudeau lingered a few moments longer than usual before shouldering his pack and continuing down the trail. We camped that night high on one of the bluffs immortalized on canvas by the Group of Seven. Through a break in the clouded sky, a beacon of moonlight poured down directly on our tent spot and made a shining ribbon of the river. "Nature's spotlight," Trudeau called it.

The next day was a tiring one, running rapids and hiking across portages in the late summer heat. We were spent by the time we reached the last rapid of the day. Trudeau and his companion, the experienced canoe guide Wally Schaber, were in the lead. They were backpaddling, stern into shore, sneaking down the edge of a fast stream swollen by recent rains. Trudeau was in the bow, reaching far over the gunnel to draw the canoe out into the current to avoid a rock outcropping. As Trudeau pulled out, the boat was caught for a moment in suspension between powerful cross-currents that he did not have the strength to counteract. The canoe flipped, sending Trudeau headfirst into the rapids.

Behind Trudeau, the rest of us jumped out onto the rocky shoreline, hoping to get a hand on his stern rope, which was afloat on the water. Fortunately Schaber was physically strong, as well as one of the most skillful men in the country in a canoe or kayak. He tossed the canoe aside with one hand and grabbed the back of Trudeau's life jacket with the other. I held on to Schaber to prevent him from being swept downstream with his bowman, who had by now slipped under the waves. With Schaber pulling Trudeau toward him, all made it on to dry land.

Trudeau was quieter than usual around the supper fire, his dignity badly wounded. He had to face the inescapable fact of his own waning stamina, though he referred to it only obliquely. He mentioned that his closest friend, Gérard Pelletier, was dying. "Gérard is very frail," he observed, "but then we are all getting there, I guess."

In 1998, Trudeau suffered the death of his youngest son, Michel, a blow from which he never recovered. He told one friend simply, "I am destroyed," and it did seem to some that he had lost the will to live. When he was urged to treat the prostate cancer he had been diagnosed with more aggressively, Trudeau dismissed the suggestion saying, "I don't care. I have to die of something."

The next year Trudeau was hospitalized in Montreal. The family issued a statement saying he was suffering from pneumonia, leaving the impression that his condition was not too serious. In fact, Trudeau was deathly ill and spent several days drifting in and out of consciousness. In the same wing of the hospital, one of his long-time friends woke up following cancer surgery to find Trudeau grasping his hand in support.

In August 2000, I was in Saskatoon covering Stockwell Day when I received a call from the Trudeau residence. I was informed that Trudeau was in grave condition. His sons and close friends had gathered, and the family intended to call in a priest. I put the phone down and burst into tears. Since I was told that the family would issue a news release, I went on CTV News Channel and made just one broadcast, which is all I had the composure to do. With as much dignity as I could muster, I reported that Pierre Trudeau was dying.

National Post columnist Paul Wells wrote that Ottawa journalists took one look at my ashen countenance and headed for Montreal. There, a ring of television trucks and milling reporters surrounded the Trudeau home, giving the family no rest day or night. When some family members were disturbed by what seemed an insensitive death watch, I reminded them that the reporters were there because the country cared and they were its eyes and ears. Though the family knew the end was near, they issued a carefully worded statement that made it appear Pierre might have some time left yet to live. The reporters decamped and left Trudeau to die in peace. The end came at 2:40 in the afternoon of September 28.

In a telephone conversation some time before, Trudeau had urged me to come down to Montreal and have dinner. Although two people could hardly have been more dissimilar, we invariably enjoyed each other's company. But I was busy and postponed the dinner, believing there would always be time, since Trudeau seemed somehow immortal to me. When the seriousness of his illness became apparent, I booked a meeting but, to my everlasting regret, I was too late.

Those of us who were Trudeau's canoe companions were deeply moved by the closing words of a tribute that appeared in *La Presse*: "He has gone to paddle the river Styx in search of his beloved son Michel." I was honoured to receive an invitation to Trudeau's funeral service, but I had one last duty to perform on his behalf. Of a lifetime of television reports, the one of which I am proudest is the Trudeau funeral service in Montreal, which I covered with Lloyd Robertson and Trudeau's old friend Senator Michael Kirby. We wore red roses in our lapels, and only with great difficulty did we fight off tears to finish the broadcast.

In June 2001, Ted Johnson and I met at Peter Stollery's Senate office to nail down the final details of that summer's planned trip to the Horton River in the western Arctic. Most of the old gang had committed themselves to come, but more than a whiff of hesitation permeated our conversations. John Macfarlane caught the general mood. He was coming, he insisted, but only because everyone else was and he couldn't bear to be left behind. No one wanted to be the first to admit, or try to deny, that we were growing too old for these annual expeditions.

Almost all of us were now in our sixties, and spouses and friends were beginning to object. We had never had to think seriously about heart attacks or the consequences of a long swim down a frigid northern river. My eyesight was worrisome and Tim Kotcheff's hearing was no better, plus he was feeling the pangs of arthritis. Goldenberg had undergone three surgeries on his leg following a serious break. Denis Harvey's knees were simply gone, and Allan Rock had fought prostate cancer the previous winter. Then too there was the issue of money for all of us who were no longer the free and easy bachelors we had been at the start. Fuel prices were sky-high. The flight to Inuvik and then private charter into the headwaters would make our children's private schools seem cheap.

The three of us looked at one another glumly. Our planning meeting turned into a disassembly session as we set about pulling down the arrangements we had made during the previous months. "Maybe next year," we agreed, though it was not to be. The club's next trip to the Far North remains a dream.

In the meantime, I will hang on to memories of that bitter-sweet moment when passengers and gear have been unloaded and the Twin Otter barrels across the tundra and disappears over the horizon, the drone of its engines echoing back and around until it is gone and silence falls into the space left behind. Its departure always left me with feelings of keen loneliness and wonderful peace. There follow the sounds of a wilderness campsite, metal zippers announcing every coming and going, tent flies flapping in wind and rain, and mosquitoes assaulting the netting, crazed by the smell of blood. Nowhere else can I hear the hollow thud of muskox butting heads in the distance or the champagne-like pop of glacial ice in my rum daiquiri. I will remember falling asleep to the unremitting roar of rapids and waterfalls. Above all, I will try to retain the sound of the cut-loose laughter of my companions who, for this brief time, had not a care in the world beyond what faced them downriver.

Those who go to the wilderness to discover themselves or

God would do better to visit a therapist or a priest. I found no answers to the great perplexities of life in my years of wilderness adventuring, but rather the joy of personal achievement. I was reminded countless times of the power of the mind and will to overcome obstacles and that the darkest, most miserable times give way to bright days for those who persevere. Certainly too, there were life lessons.

In the voyage down the rivers and meandering tributaries of our lives, we cannot hope to change the end, yet we can control the journey.

Never speak of opposing or conquering or defeating a river. Think instead of seducing a river. You do not run a rapid; you negotiate it, just as life itself is a series of negotiations. Chart your own course and trust the compass, but heed the counsel of those who have done this trip before you.

Foolish bravado or rash decisions can end a trip too soon. If circumstances land you in a bad spot, you must try to think rationally and stay cool. Whenever possible, avoid confrontation with powerful natural forces that can undo you. Join the mainstream and shape its power to your own ends. Point the prow gently into the strong current. Edge it out by degrees, delicately absorbing the impact of the surge against the gunwale. Then, as far as you can, go cheerfully with the flow.

But don't commit yourself unequivocally to the direction of the current, for it may lead into a fool's bay or to disaster over a ledge. And, if your river courses down to the ocean, take the flood tide or else be left in the unhappy shallows of a backwater. Coming troubles always announce themselves noisily. Be prepared to slow your forward progress momentarily, to backpaddle, to ferry back and forth, dodging the silent sweepers or deadly logjams that await the careless. Practise flexibility at all times, not rigidity.

Become part of the river; harness its force to control your speed and direction. In the worst of rapids, look sharp for openings to thread your fragile craft between granite and undertow and the large curling waves that can swamp you. Then, seeing the safe line, throw caution to the winds and dig hard for your objective. The calm, still pool on the other side will be your well-earned lasting reward.

12

EYE OF THE BEHOLDER

I have written this book in a race against inevitable blindness. Over the past fifteen years, my regularly scheduled eye examinations showed a slight but greater loss of visual acuity with every visit. Afterwards, I would return to the computer to enlarge the screen's type size once again.

My eyes had always been weak, but the progressive damage was less obvious to me as a younger man. One of the first hints of a serious condition came on a canoe trip down the Pelly River in 1975. In an early morning mist that hung about three feet above the slow-flowing river, I spied a moose grazing along the bank. I asked Tim Kotcheff to grab his camera. He did so with a curious smile. We approached as quietly as possible, barely paddling. Despite that, I was surprised the animal did not start as we drew near. When we were almost alongside, I saw that my moose was a Hereford cow. Some Yukon entrepreneur was trying to make a go of what was certainly the most northerly cattle ranch on the continent. "Have you thought about getting your eyes checked?" Tim asked. Would that it had been so simple.

Back in Ottawa, I visited an ophthalmologist who surprised me with the news that I was suffering from glaucoma. The disease is painless, which is why so many people, especially children, do not discover it until it is far advanced. I was stunned by the diagnosis and by this first evidence of decrepitude. I had assumed glaucoma was an old person's affliction, but I was thirty-seven at the time.

The doctor prescribed eye drops to reduce the buildup of pressure in the eyeball, pressure that would gradually cut off the blood supply to the optic nerve. I thought of it in television terms: Something was pinching the video cable that sends pictures to the brain. The ailment was unstoppable and would worsen as I grew older, although with careful management its progress could be slowed. I had a brief period of self-pity, which my friend Peter Stollery quickly dismissed. "You can't do anything to avoid it, so you'd better learn to deal with it," was his blunt advice.

The house lights dimmed in stages and the incremental nature of the changes allowed me time to adjust. In my mid-forties, night vision and peripheral sight declined to the point that, though I still had a valid driver's licence, I allowed it to lapse. Blind spots were starting to develop in my central field of vision, and occasionally I missed a stop sign or failed to recognize traffic lights in time to react. Without wheels, I changed my priorities when it came to dating. No longer was physical attractiveness paramount. On meeting a potential girlfriend, I quickly determined whether or not she owned a car. Imagine my delight when I found out that Anne-Marie was uncomfortable with the loss of control when others drove and was glad to take over as my Seeing Eye driver.

In my fifties, I began to experience what can only be described as fog rolling in. Early on the mist seemed distant across a thin horizon, but with time it grew closer and denser. Then the fog gave way to tiny spots of emptiness here and there, spots that eventually connected and grew larger. The progress of the disease would plateau for a time, then speed up with sudden strength. Once I woke with a start from a nap and, before I was fully awake, thought the house must be on fire. The room seemed full of smoke, but with none of the acrid odour that a burning building produces. The glaucoma was making a comeback after a few months of relative dormancy. How curious and odd to know that a finger on a hand held in front of my face must be there but was invisible. I could measure my worsening condition by counting the disappearing fingers until the entire hand was obscure.

The science of ophthalmology has made enormous progress in combatting glaucoma and other eye diseases. At every stage, I found that new and improved eye drops were coming on the market just as I seemed to need them. I had laser surgery twice, which helped to maintain adequate vision for a time, and I was impressed with the talent and dedication of most of the eye doctors I came to know. I learned too the importance of being one's own advocate as much as possible. While under the care of one specialist, I lost the central vision in my left eye. I felt the eye was worsening, but the specialist would not treat it aggressively, a course of action that might have delayed its deterioration.

The moment I hit my sixties, there was another precipitous drop: The right eye went into a rapid decline, as if competing with the left to be the first to shut down completely. Cold-steel surgery, performed by surgeons at the Eye Institute in Ottawa, helped slow the process. This delicate procedure involved cutting a kind of trap door in the eyeball and allowing fluid to escape, thus relieving the pressure on the optic nerve. Unfortunately, it left me with much lower visual acuity. Even the big *E* on the eye chart became hard to distinguish.

That had been a risk I fully understood and was prepared to take, but the results pitched me full-blown into the world of the visually handicapped. I was promoted to the status of so-called "legal blindness" and joined the ranks of those in similar circumstances at the Canadian National Institute for the Blind. (The designation "legally blind" sounds like a permit one might apply for at city hall, but it simply indicates a specific level of reduced vision, as attested by a physician. It allows one certain tax breaks and discounts on any special equipment that may be required.) As I sat at home recovering from the surgery, one eye patched and the other not much use, I decided to accept what fate had handed me with whatever equanimity could be mustered and, following Stollery's recommendation, to deal with it as best I could.

In the past I had never experienced more than fleeting moments of depression, the expected short-term downers at the deaths of friends or relatives. The loss of such an important sense as sight might have brought on some serious black dogs, but that did not happen. When anything akin to depression started to close in, my brain seemed to release some chemical as an antidote, and the cloud lifted almost as quickly as it came. Occasionally, I wondered if I was denying reality or suppressing painful emotions, but I chose instead to focus on the positives that shone through. Thousands of visually impaired people are much worse off, many of them young people or adults who have been blind from childhood. I could not spend a moment feeling sorry for myself.

As with any change in life, embracing blindness was far preferable to resisting it. For me the biggest adjustment was accepting the loss of independence. To ask others for help has not been easy, but it has been liberating. There is a certain freedom in finally admitting that I can't do it all myself. In fact I never could, and I am content to put false pride and vanity in my pocket at last.

Like all sightless people, I owe a great debt to my family for their endless patience. Most people who misplace their keys or glasses will usually find them for themselves; I rarely can. At least half the time, my underwear, T-shirts, or pullover sweaters are put on backwards or inside out. Sometimes I cannot apply toothpaste to the right side of the brush. I once made tea with two teabag-sized hand warmers. Living with these realities is a daily confirmation that those close to us must love us. They otherwise could not stand the frustration.

Obviously, there are things I will never be able to do or enjoy to the same degree again, but they are really very few. I regret not being able to see the face of my daughter, Annie Claire, or that of my wife, who is by everyone's account a lovely woman. And I miss being able to see my own face in the mirror. I have lost the pleasure of viewing a well-shot television clip or a good film, nor is art appreciation what it used to be.

The inability to read print is a genuine nuisance. Nothing I bring back from the grocery store is the right item. After my experience in shops, I could identify with a man in a drugstore whom I overheard asking for assistance, explaining that he was wearing the wrong glasses. I know that old trick. Beyond that,

I am forced to reveal to my wife the secrets of stock market losses now that she reads my mail from banks and brokers. But technology has been my saviour in other realms. A computer program reads emails to me as well as any newspapers I may care to browse. Most books are available digitally and are therefore accessible to my audio reader.

Perhaps the loss I feel most acutely is the ability to recognize individuals. I can see the fuzzy big picture—doors and windows, sidewalks and buildings—but people are just shadows to me. For those of us in front of the television cameras, being easily recognized means that people we don't know are always saying hello and greeting us by name. A flattering and well-meant courtesy, it is a problem for me. Until I have nailed down the voice, I can't tell whether the person and I know each other or not. I am forever responding to strangers as if they were long-lost friends or initiating pointed conversations with the wrong individuals. However, I have picked up a few techniques: If I think I know the people in question but not overly well, I open with a question like, "What are you up to these days?" Of course, I am sunk if they remind me of something we did together the day before.

Equally embarrassing are the times when I respond to greetings not intended for me at all, for fear of offending someone who is a friendly viewer. This habit leaves people wondering if I am desperate to be recognized. On other occasions, I will sail by people I would be eager to talk to if I knew they were there. This is not an issue for acquaintances, who know me well enough to shout out as I pass; they understand I appreciate their making themselves known. But sometimes I hear second-hand that I missed seeing a friend who was in clear view and dismayed that I appeared to ignore him or her.

At the 1995 funeral for slain CTV sportscaster Brian Smith, I introduced myself to the man sitting next to me in the dimly lit church. To this day I am sure that Peter Mansbridge, whom I have known since we were young reporters in Winnipeg, thinks I was putting on airs. Another time I ran into the late CBC broadcaster Barbara Frum on a street in Toronto. I responded to her warm greeting with the formality normally accorded a stranger. Then, realizing my mistake, I apologized, offering the excuse of poor vision from glaucoma, which she could not have known. That magnificent and sharp-minded woman was skeptical. "Show me your eye drops," she demanded. I whipped the bottles out of my pocket and that satisfied her.

Serious risks are more numerous than social missteps. Traffic is tricky, and bicycles more dangerous than cars. Automobiles and other powered vehicles give themselves away with sound. Headlights are visible to many of the visually impaired and one can usually judge where motorized vehicles are going, their pathways being predictable. Bikes on the other hand come from all directions and often out of the blue.

In Washington one sunny day, I crossed a street on a yellow light after a cursory glance to be sure the intersection was free of automobiles. I was startled by a sickening screech of brakes. A female biker hit the pedals so hard she swerved, crashing sideways and skidding across the pavement to avoid me. "You must be blind," she shouted angrily. I hurried away from the scene in embarrassment, but I am thankful to that anonymous cyclist. I realized for the first time that my weakening eyesight could be a fatal flaw. Unlike that cyclist, too many think nothing of running red lights and stop signs, unaware that when moving at speed, bikes are too narrow to be easily seen or avoided.

Consequently, I have become like one of those timid Ottawa bureaucrats Allan Fotheringham always poked fun at: I never cross the street against the light. Even then, I usually wait for someone else to come along and then fall into step with these individuals who will be unaware they are performing a helpful service by running interference for me.

A sturdy sense of humour makes this particular handicap easier to endure. Let's face it—Mr. Magoo is funny. An incident from the eighties comes to mind: A girlfriend and I were driving through the Eastern Townships of Quebec, trying to find the road to a ski hill. Light snow was falling, and I suggested to my girlfriend that she pull over so I could ask directions of a kid in a red parka standing by the road up ahead. When the lad greeted my question in English with dead silence, I turned to my companion and said, "That's what's wrong with this country. He won't answer me because I am speaking to him in English." She explained that the real problem was the inability of the fire hydrant to speak either official language.

As well, when I address a question to an empty chair at the office, I join in the laughter of others, feeling not at all demeaned. Hanging a lantern on the problem spares others discomfort and the worry of giving offence. It also allows everyone to deal frankly with the issues and cope with the special needs that arise. I have been blessed with an understanding employer in Bell Media and wonderfully helpful producers and reporters who have created a supportive working environment for me. Colleagues read aloud any especially important news wire stories, and at public events they point me in the direction of the people I need to speak with.

It has been many years since I have been able to read a teleprompter. Fortunately, I never aspired to be a news anchor.

Whenever a broadcast requires words read to the camera with exact timing, I memorize the script. Working on-camera as a reporter or commentator, I ad lib, developing ideas that I have mentally sketched out beforehand. Thanks to a sympathetic technical crew, a strong portable light affixed to the camera tells me where to look when I am addressing the viewer. When I have to present a voice report over visuals, I dictate it first and the producer records and edits it if necessary. Then it is played back to me in the sound booth over my earphones and I deliver it in turn onto the tape.

To keep track of countless documents, letters, and invitations in my professional and private lives, I have devised a filing system that relies on my own drawings of symbolic images. Two or three together serve as the building blocks of a whole thought. A stick drawing of a girl represents my daughter; when combined with a rudimentary schoolhouse, that image serves as a label for anything that has to do with my daughter's education. I understand now how written language originated among the ancients.

With effort, one can grasp at some advantages. For example, my friends no longer age. Their faces do not bear the insults of advancing decades, nor do telltale lines of worry or hardship betray the women I have known and loved over the years. To me these women remain as young and beautiful as I ever knew them. My world is a wrinkle-free shirt, and minor clutter doesn't register. I still go horseback riding almost every summer with Lloyd Robertson in the foothills near Bragg Creek, Alberta. My regular sure-footed horse knows my limitations as well as any close friend. Together we allow the other riders to get well ahead of us on the trail, and then wait for them to signal an all-clear.

Once released, we break into a full cantor, heading gleefully in the direction of the other riders' voices.

If we are fortunate, the past comes more clearly into focus as we age, and in my case, facing the loss of my vision along with my youth has helped me view the world from a different perspective. Perhaps this is what Canadian poet Margaret Avison called the "optic heart": We perceive and appreciate others more deeply, beyond their surface appearance.

Waning eyesight sometimes isolates its sufferers, causing them to turn inward. That impulse is all the stronger for those in my profession. We are outsiders by nature, preferring a position on the fringes where we take no risks but are happy to shoot barbs at those who do. I discovered that the better solution for me was to reach out and embrace my handicap. Doing so demanded that I trust others, even with my physical safety and when all my childhood instincts warned me otherwise. I felt I had become a grown-up at last.

Occasionally I am asked to give a fundraising speech for the Canadian National Institute for the Blind and I am happy to do so, assisting an organization that is shaking off its former grey image and plunging into new technologies for the benefit of the blind across Canada. I felt indebted to Ottawa's Eye Institute as well for its exciting research initiatives and the extraordinary care it extends to its patients. As I approached my seventieth birthday in 2008, I suggested the idea of a fundraising event for the institute in support of education in the field of ophthalmology. No one knew if a single ticket would be sold, but we set to work on our respective Rolodexes.

Early on I personally asked Prime Minister Harper if he would attend. He declined, saying he was not at ease at big public gatherings—a peculiar admission for a politician, as he himself conceded. I respected it, however, and was prepared to welcome the stand-in he promised. Happily, all of the other party leaders confirmed their attendance.

On an evening in early December 2008, the ballroom of the Fairmont Chateau Laurier was packed with hundreds of well-wishers, among them at least two generations of political warriors from four political parties and a large contingent from the press gallery. Most younger Members of Parliament had never experienced such an event—a gathering of politicos that was, for once, free of poisonous partisan bickering.

To the delight of the organizers, just hours before the event word came that the prime minister would attend after all. He gave a witty, well-timed speech that perfectly suited the roast-the-host theme as he recalled my reportage of man's discovery of fire and Champlain's landing at Quebec. The audience was charmed and amazed by this uncharacteristically hilarious perform- ance and wondered why we did not see this side of Harper more often. Jean Chrétien and Lloyd Robertson also spoke to good effect, while everyone tried on the googlie-eyed joke glasses found in their gift bags. We raised a hundred and fifty thousand dollars that night for the W. Bruce Jackson Endowment for Fellowships in Ophthalmology at the University of Ottawa.

When people ask what the world looks like through my eyes, I refer them to French Impressionism and to one of the greatest painters of the nineteenth century, Claude Monet, who suffered from cataracts. In his youth, Monet led a busy life of travel across all of Europe, immortalizing what he saw in oils on canvas. As he grew old and infirm and his vision faded, Monet turned to his own garden for the inspiration of some of his greatest work. He found fulfillment in what was closest. The scenes he painted resemble the world I see every day, a pastiche of shapes and shadows and swirls of colour with no crisp outlines or sharp details. The other senses are no less sharp, however; the parade of life is no less exhilarating. I have to say it's not a bad view.

ACKNOWLEDGMENTS

For more than half a century politics has been the theatre of my life, and it has presented an engrossing stage show.

I have been the eager critic, dashing out of my comfortable seat when the curtain falls to report, assess, and judge the work. The actors tell the story, not me; everything hangs on the script and the performance. When the house lights come up, I have not had to care how the play ends and so I have remained uninvolved, or as some critics of the critics would observe, I have avoided the responsibility yet savoured the power. While courageous men and women have contended with one national crisis after another, I have judged from a safe distance. Whatever fleeting notoriety I have achieved owes everything to those players.

Almost without exception, I have genuinely liked and admired the politicians I have covered. I make no apologies for knowing many of them well backstage. Media managers expect their senior staff to be well acquainted with the powerful in all parties: Senior staff need access for reasons of accuracy, fairness, and competitiveness. And politicians need to get their message out. The Parliament Hill precinct is a village of fewer than a thousand men and women. Journalists, bureaucrats, and pols bump elbows at the same bars, attend the same charity and cultural events, and play golf and squash together. Inevitably, friendships develop.

That closeness is as common today as it was decades ago, although some rules of engagement have changed. No politician can expect to be protected from exposure of serious wrongdoing. When their opponents fling mud at them, politicians can hope at least for a fair hearing from the media, but at some point the responsibilities of the journalist's job may trump the friendship. As for gossip about the private lives of the public people we cover day and night, my own belief is that these details become news only when they seriously affect the performance of the politician's elected duty. Otherwise, there is nothing to be gained by ruining the lives of public officials who display the same frailties and foibles as the rest of us.

I hope the members of our band of canoeing adventurers will feel that I have reflected our collective triumphs and mishaps fairly. To my bowman, Tim Kotcheff, and my trail-riding companion, Lloyd Robertson, thank you both for a lifetime of loyal friendship.

I must offer my deep appreciation to the staff of the CTV Ottawa bureau for creating such a supportive environment.

My thanks to Diane Turbide of Penguin Canada who was the first to read a few lines of this work many years ago and encouraged me in the fanciful thought that I might have a book in me. I'm grateful too to my agent, John Pearce, who placed the manuscript in the capable hands of my publisher, and to my copy editor, Sharon Kirsch, who gave it a final polish. I cannot write *thirty* to this project without acknowledging my own editor, Jan Walter, for her unerring good judgment and skill.

A reporter's life can take a tremendous toll on those closest to him. I am thankful that my wife, Anne-Marie Bergeron, worked in the same business and could roll with the unpredictability of a newshound's calling. Too many nights my daughter, Annie Claire, kissed goodnight to my image on the television screen. The experience cannot have been completely off-putting, since she will shortly begin studies at the Columbia Journalism School in New York City. My greatest hope is that she will find a career as rewarding, challenging, and satisfying as her old dad did.

INDEX